DOU

MW01679825

Deanna L. Rowley

Molly,

Let's get dirty!

Deanna L. Rowley

Copyright © 2022 Deanna L Rowley All rights reserved. No part of this book may be reproduced in any form or by any electronic or mechanical means, including information storage and retrieval systems, without permission in writing from the publisher, except by reviewers, who may quote brief passages in a review. This is a work of fiction. Names, characters, places, and incidents are products of the author's imagination or fictitiously used. References to real people, events, TV shows, organizations, establishments, or locations are intended to provide a sense of authenticity and are used fictitiously. Any resemblance to actual events, locales, organizations, or persons living or dead is entirely coincidental. The author acknowledges the copyrighted or trademarked status and trademark owners of the products mentioned in this work.

I'd like to thank my editor, Ann Attwood, for the beautiful job she does on my books.

CHAPTER ONE

Kameron Kilbourne looked up from the engine he was working on, when he heard a golf cart come up beside him, and blow it's horn several times.

"Kilbourne!"

"What?" Kam frowned as he straightened, and grabbed a rag to start wiping the grease from his hands.

"Party at your RV tonight? Or did we already miss it, and it was last night?"

"Um, no, why would you say that?"

"Not to be rude, but your RV smells like at least fifty French whores are in there all wearing a different kind of perfume." Pete, one of his brother's mechanics laughed. "Where's Kurt and Kev?"

Kam gave a whistle, and everyone who had been gathered around watched as three tall, handsome, well-built men appeared. Kam looked at them, then at Pete. "There's Dad, Kurt, and Kev. I don't know what you're talking about."

"What's going on?" Ken Kilbourne, the father to the three men, asked as he came forward, wiping his own hands on a greasy rag.

"Pete says my RV smells like a bunch of French whores are in there."

"Hey, where's Ky?" Kevin asked, and the four men looked at each other in shock, and it was Kurtis who rushed over to actually pull Pete from the golf cart. The Kilbournes jumped in, and as they rushed away, the men who were left stood around watching them and listening began to laugh. As they approached Kameron's RV, all of them swore.

"What the hell?" Kam bellowed, and jumped from the cart before it even stopped. He whipped open the door, and didn't wait for the steps to be lowered, just jumped in, and stopped dead in his tracks as he started to gag on the smell permeating the air.

"Holy fuck, son. What the hell is that stench?" Ken asked as he joined his son. They were soon joined by Kurtis and Kevin.

"Damn, it smells like all of our aftershaves and shaving cream put together. All mussed up," Kurtis, Kameron's identical twin said.

"It does," Ken said, and his three oldest sons glared at him, but he grinned and held up his hands, laughing and shaking his head at them. "Hey, it's your RV."

"But, he's your son," Kameron said, and glared when the bathroom door opened. They watched as their ten-year-old brother, Kyle, came literally dancing out of the bathroom with a towel wrapped around his small, bony, non-existent hips. Kam frowned at the sight of his brother's small arms and chest, and looked at his twin on one side of him, then their nineteen-year-old other brother on his other side. He whispered to his twin. "Damn, were we ever that puny looking?"

"Yep," Ken, their father said from the other side of Kevin, the nineteen-year-old. They watched as Kyle danced to whatever tune was going on in his own head, and everyone followed Kam when he stood tall, crossed his huge, muscled arms across his chest, and glared. Kyle was several feet into the living room when he looked up, and stopped so suddenly that he started to lose his towel, and he grabbed that, then grinned.

"Hi. Get your plugs changed?"

"Almost," Kam said. "Whatcha' doing?"

"Taking a shower."

"I smell that. Did you save me any water for later?"

Kurtis had to turn his head and cover his snort, when Kyle shrugged. "I might have. I don't remember. I only turned off the water when the hot ran out."

Kam groaned and elbowed both his brothers when they snickered and snorted a laugh. It wasn't funny. Each of them had their own car to drive at the races, each of them had their own RV, the twins, Kam and Kurtis being twenty-six, then Kevin was nineteen, and Kyle being the baby at ten, he was the one that would sneak into the other's RVs, and take a shower, using up all the water. This was the first time it'd happened to Kam.

Kam sat on the small couch and indicated with his finger that Ky was to come forward. When he was standing before his oldest brother, he frowned. "What's wrong?"

"Why does it stink in here? Pete was driving by and he said it smelled like fifty French whores were in here. And like Kevin said, it smells like you used all of our aftershave at once."

"I did." Ky grinned, not bothering to lie.

"Why?" all four older men asked. Kurt joined Kam on the small couch, while Ken and Kevin sat at the kitchen chairs. They had hurried around and opened all the windows, and Ken had sent a text to his wife to stop at the store on her way to the track to pick up several bottles of Febreze.

"Because, she might be here tonight," Ky said, and grinned.

"She?" Kam frowned.

"Yeah, it's the first race of the season, and I have to look good for her. She comes to this track. I wanted to make sure I smell good for her."

"So, you have a girlfriend," Ken asked, and the twins smirked at each other and then grinned at their father. When Kyle turned to their father, the others leaned back and watched to see what Ken would say.

"Well, she's a girl and she's my friend, but she's not my girlfriend. Not like that. Girls are yucky," Kyle said, and frowned at his older brothers when they burst out laughing.

"But, you had to have a shower, and what did you do? Go into Kurt and Kev's RVs and take their aftershave to mix with Kam's?"

"Don't forget yours, Dad. I didn't know which one smelled better, or what one she would like, so I mixed them all together."

"So, what does this girlfriend that's not a girlfriend look like?" Kurtis grinned. Kyle's brothers stared in shock when their brother practically melted into the floor as he described his girl.

"She's beautiful." When he didn't continue, his brothers prompted him.

"Hair?"

"Yes, she has hair." Kyle smirked at Kurtis. He stared at the little scamp in shock, then grabbed him and started to tickle him. Ky squealed, and begged him to stop when he started to lose his towel.

"What color is her hair?"

"Different. Depends on the sun. Sometimes it looks really blonde, other times it looks red."

"What color are her eyes?"

"Same as her hair, sometimes blue sometimes green, but she wears these dark-rimmed glasses, so it's hard to say, and she smells like fresh strawberries." Ky rolled his eyes, and actually rubbed his stomach, which caused his brothers to grin and their father to groan.

"What else can you tell us about her, son?" Ken asked.

"She's got boobs," he said, and grinned as he actually held his hands at least two feet away from his own scrawny chest.

"What do you know about boobs?" Kevin frowned.

"I saw them in that magazine you keep under your mattress at home, Kev. *Duh*."

"What magazine?" Kam grinned when Kevin turned beet red.

"Jugs, Jugs, Jugs." Ky provided the name of the magazine proudly, much to his one brother's embarrassment and his other's amusement.

"Son, do you know about the birds and the bees?" Ken asked, and Kam jumped to his feet.

"And that's my cue to leave." He looked at his younger brother sternly. "Before you leave here, I want you to clean up the mess you left in the bathroom, and take this bit of advice from your oldest brother. Mixing different aftershaves doesn't work. Stick with one and leave it alone, because know that I'm telling you this, because I love you with all my heart. You stink. I think you need to take another shower, then decide on one fragrance, and only one."

"But, I just took a shower."

"And you stink. And don't forget to wash that aftershave out of your hair. And..." He paused when Ky crossed his arms, and sighed. "Return everyone else's aftershave. Dad sent a text to Mom to bring some Febreze. When she gets here, I want you to spray down my RV, I don't want to smell this shit when I'm ready to crash after the race tonight. Understood?"

"Yes, Kam."

"And don't let Mom do it. You're old enough to know that you need to start cleaning up after yourself. You've said over the winter that you wanted to start staying with one of us in our RVs this year. You're only ten and I said you could stay with me, but it's only been a few hours, and you're not living up to your promise."

"I'm sorry, Kameron," Kyle said, and hung his head in shame, but Kameron reached down and lifted his brother's chin, and looked him in the eye.

"Don't be sorry, just learn from your mistake, and don't do it again. Ask any one of us, even Dad. We've all done something stupid over a girl at one time or another. Hell, I think every man on the face of the earth has done something stupid over a girl. Thankfully, yours is an easy fix. Just re-shower, pick one fragrance, and maybe if you don't like any of ours, we can pick out one of your own when we get home. Don't forget to spray the Febreze, and don't forget to close the windows. I don't want all that dirt in here." He grinned when the others snorted.

"Thank you, Kameron," Kyle said, and hugged his oldest brother. Kameron hugged him back, then watched as Kurtis and Kevin gave him their own piece of advice, and as Kam left his own RV, he heard his father repeat his question about the birds and the bees.

"Damn," Kurt said as they slowly drove back to the pits that they had left in a hurry.

"What?" Kevin asked.

"I think Kam and I were at least thirteen before Dad gave us the talk."

"Almost thirteen," Kam said from his side, and grinned. "How about you, Kev?"

"I was thirteen, and I had a girl that was a girlfriend." He grinned when they laughed.

"So did we, but god, to think Ky's only ten and he's getting the talk. I hope Dad doesn't scare him. He even showed us how to use a condom using a banana."

"Mine was a cucumber." Kevin laughed. "I didn't have the heart to tell him that Missy Johnson, my girlfriend at the time, had already showed me." He grinned when his older brothers laughed.

"Everything okay?" Pete asked as they returned to the pits and their race cars.

"Yeah, Kyle was getting cleaned up for his girlfriend that's not a girlfriend. He stole all our aftershave and mixed it," Kameron said. "Thanks for giving us the heads up."

"Not a problem. Hopefully you told him to shower that shit off. I about gagged when I drove by there."

"I know, but yeah, I told him to re-shower and clean up his mess. Mom's going to bring some Febreze, and he's to use it to clean up."

"Where is he?"

"Dad's giving him the talk." Kurt laughed when they stared at him in shock.

"No way, he's only what, eight?"

"Ten, but when he described his friend that's a girl, he mentioned she had boobs." Kam grinned.

"Oh, lord," Larry, Kameron's pit chief groaned. "What is this world coming to? I was at least thirteen, and my son's eight. What the hell, I thought I had years yet before I had to have the talk with him." The bunch of men, averaging in age from nineteen to sixty started talking then about their first girlfriend, and when their own fathers had talked to them about the birds and the bees.

*****

Kali Kilpatrick sighed as she saw her father's phone number flash up on her caller ID. "Hi, Dad, what's up?"

"Thought I'd come down and mow your lawn, then maybe take you out to dinner."

"Sorry, I'm busy tonight, and before you say anything, I'm also busy tomorrow night."

"But, you're always busy on Friday and Saturday nights. What are you doing that you're not telling us about? Are you dating someone, and don't want us to meet him? Are you embarrassed of your parents?"

"Dad, stop it." Kali laughed, then sighed. "Tell you what, why don't I meet you at your house for Sunday brunch? I can be there at ten."

"Make it eleven. We get out of church at ten."

"Okay. I'll see you then. But, I really have to go. I don't want to be late." They said their goodbyes and Kali finished getting her things together, then made sure she had money, and grabbed a bottle of water before she walked out of her house. Tonight was the first night of the new race season, and she wasn't about to miss it. She'd been going for the last four years. This was her fifth year going. On her way to her SUV, she did a little happy dance, and grinned when not ten minutes later she was standing at the front of the line, waiting for the admission stand to open. Living only two miles away from this track was a dream. However, the other two tracks she went to were an hour and a half to three hours away, respectively.

"Welcome back," the ticket taker said as she opened her window, and Kali paid her fee and went to hand in her ticket, get her hand stamped, and after picking up her bag she always carried to the races, she made her way to the stands, and walked up to the seat she sat in at all three tracks. First section, at the fourth turn slash start line, top row, in the last seat. She arrived and saw she was the first one there, so she set up her cushion, made sure her sweatshirt was beside her, because it was late-March, and it got cold after the sun went down. She made sure she had her gloves, then sat down, pulled a book out to read, and waited.

Kali knew it was ridiculous being the first one there, but she couldn't help it. For years she'd been shy in crowds. She found that if she was first, then she could get her seat and get settled, before the bulk of everyone came, and she wouldn't be stared at when she walked up the steps. Sometimes she was so shy that she even packed a sandwich, chips, cookies, and a bottle of water to eat as her supper during intermission. She was glancing around, when she heard a piercing whistle, and looked down to the walkway at the bottom of the seats, and grinned as she waved to the little boy who she'd been waving to ever since her first day. When he grinned this time and pointed to his mouth, she laughed and nodded. Last September, he'd grinned, and she'd seen that he'd lost his two front teeth, and now they were back. She gave him a thumbs up sign, and watched as he followed an older woman, whom Kali assumed was his mother, and watched as they went all the way to the far end, and halfway up to their seats.

Fifteen minutes later, she saw that same boy come running up the steps in her section, and he sat two rows down from her. "Hi. Mom said I can come over and say hi."

"Hi."

"I'm Kyle."

"I'm Kali." They shook and when he frowned, she immediately hugged herself and buried her hands into her sides, but sighed in relief when he didn't say anything. She looked at his shirt, and asked, "You like number eighteen?"

"Yes. They're my favorite."

"Don't tell anybody, because I don't like to get anyone mad, but I have three favorite drivers."

"Really? Who are they?"

"I don't know their names, but I know their cars."

"Can you tell them to me? I know all the cars."

"Well, they all have the number eighteen. Like your shirt, but they drive in different classes. The e-mods, crate, and late model."

"Wow, I know those drivers." Kyle grinned as he pointed to his shirt. They shared a laugh, and he grinned again. "It was nice meeting you Kali, but I have to go now."

"Nice meeting you too, Kyle. Are you going to be at McKay tomorrow?"

"I am. You?"

"I am."

"Then, I'll see you there," he said, and before Kali could say anything he was up, down the stairs, and over to his mother in seconds. Kali continued to watch as the regulars began pouring into the stands. She felt the wind as the sun began to go down, and decided to put her gloves and sweatshirt on now. If she became colder, she had a heavy coat with her, so she should be fine, but this year she'd put a warm blanket in her bag. At six on the dot, she heard the cars begin to start in the distance, causing her to do a little happy dance in her seat. She loved the sound of their engines. According to the announcer, the first group up for hot laps were the super late models and she did a happy dance again. During this, only two cars went out on the track at the same time, and they only did three laps. Personally, Kali thought it was to smooth out the track, but what did she know.

When the wind shifted just as her favorite driver, number eighteen entered the track, she grabbed her face mask, put that on, and grinned when the dust just rolled over her, but she could still see. She saw the people sitting around her turn their heads to avoid the dust rolling over them. Suddenly, several people were asking her where she bought her face shield, and she laughed when she gave them the simple answer. For the last four years she'd heard the laughs and snickers around her when she wore it, but now they wanted one for themselves.

She'd been so busy answering their questions that she'd missed seeing number eighteen on the track. She swore silently, but then realized she'd have several more times to see him race that night, and again the next night at a different track. She was surprised that during intermission as she ate her supper, Kyle joined her, and because she wore her face shield like a welder's mask, he frowned at her. They were both filthy from the dust.

"Where'd you get that? And does it work?"

Kali actually took it off and had him try it on. "Oh my god, this is so cool, you can still see, and I bet it keeps the dust out."

"And the wind. Just tuck your chin and the bottom blocks the dust and wind from going down your front." He did and grinned.

"Are they expensive?"

Kali decided to play with him. "What do you consider expensive?"

"Ten dollars."

"What would you say if I told you that I saw an ad for them, and they're on sale for only two dollars?"

"No offense, but I'd call you a liar." He grinned to soften the blow, but she laughed and told him where he could get one. She ended up writing the name of the store down for him.

"And guess what?"

"What?"

"There's one of those stores on the way to McKay if you go down route sixteen."

"Cool, and I have five dollars, I'll have my driver stop." He grinned.

"Your driver?"

"My brother." They shared a laugh, and Kyle left again just as quickly as he had earlier. She continued watching the rest of the race, and several times she was on her feet yelling at the flagman and safety crew when they didn't see an accident in time before others plowed into them. At one point, several of her neighbors were yelling at them right along with her.

"God," she said as she slumped down. "Are these guys freaking blind, or what? If they'd been paying attention those last three cars wouldn't have wrecked."

"I know," the woman in front of her said. "Thank god, each track has their own officials, flagman, safety crew, and tow truck drivers, and McKay's the best in the circuit. You going tomorrow?"

"I am. I only go here at Dusty Hill, McKay, and State. I'd like to go further or to the two or three day events, but I don't have a camper, and it's only me."

"You don't have a boyfriend or husband as a driver? Someone in the pits you're rooting for?"

"No, it's just me. When I moved into my house one night, I heard this noise and I investigated." Kali grinned. "I've been hooked ever since."

"So you live close?"

"Two miles down the hill." They laughed and settled back to watch the rest of the race, and Kali jumped to her feet when car number eighteen passed the leader, and crossed first right at the finish line. That was the end of the race, and she waited a few minutes and had to remove her outer coat, shake that off, then her sweatshirt and shook that. She put the sweatshirt back on, and slowly packed everything, and just as slowly made her way to her SUV. She ended up sitting in it for a good half an hour, before traffic cleared out enough, and she was home and in the shower fifteen minutes later.

The next morning, she did her weekly housework, laundry, and even went grocery shopping, making sure what she called her race bag was packed and loaded in the back of the SUV. Tonight's race was at McKay, which was just over the Pennsylvania border, and it took a leisurely hour and a half to get there. Oh, don't get her wrong, she'd made it in an hour, but she hated to be rushed. So, she left two hours before the admission gates opened, and sighed when she was again the first one in line. That night was the same as the night before, but this time she grinned when Kyle whistled to her, and she saw he had a face shield pushed up on his forehead, but he didn't join her that night.

CHAPTER TWO

Standing in her parents' kitchen, Kali looked up from chopping vegetables for the salad, and frowned when her father sat at the table in the breakfast nook, laid his head on it, sighing deeply.

"What's his problem?" she whispered to her mother, but she only shook her head, rolled her eyes, and gave her own sigh.

"Ask him."

"Dad, is everything okay?"

"No," he sighed, and with his arms at his sides he rolled his head back and forth. If Kali didn't know better, she'd say he looked and acted like her older brother, Kelsey when he was a teenager.

"What's wrong?"

"I'm bored," he sighed, and Kali snorted out a laugh.

"What happened to that garden you were going to put in when you retired?"

"Your mother won't help me. She said I had to do everything." He lifted his head, and his puppy-dog look was so sweet, she giggled. "I have to till the ground, plant the seeds, weed it, harvest it, and then can or cook it. You know I don't cook, except to grill," he actually whined.

"So, help Mom out around the house, do the dishes, vacuum, do the laundry." She frowned when her mother actually snorted.

"Look at his jeans," Kathy snorted as she pointed at her husband's attire. "That was the first load he did without instructions."

Kali frowned and looked at the black jeans her father wore, and burst out laughing when he stood and one whole leg from the butt to the ankle was white. "Didn't you know you're not supposed to pour bleach directly onto dark colors?"

"I do now."

"So, why don't you go see Kelsey? Or Karen?"

"Because, Kelsey lives in San Diego with his husband and their two kids. Karen lives in Houston with her husband and their three kids. They're too busy for an old man like me."

"Hell, you're not old, and you have to give this retirement time. It's been what? Three, four months? You used to tell us growing up that if we didn't like something, we had to try it for at least six months before we could give up. Now, suck it up and go start the grill." She grinned when he dragged himself out of the back door, and to the grill on the patio.

"Thank you," Kathy sighed. "When he wanted to retire at age fifty, I didn't think anything about it. You know how hard he's worked all his life, ever since I met him when he was fifteen, he worked. When we married, he made a vow that we'd be maybe not filthy rich, but extremely comfortable, and he was going to retire at fifty, but I can't see myself retiring yet. I love my nursery and the work I do. He's just going to have to find something else to do to get his mind off his boredom."

"He's always been in construction right? That was his business he sold when he retired?"

"Yes, he loves playing in the dirt, that's why I'm surprised he has such a black thumb when it comes to plants." They shared a laugh, and Kali lost herself in her own thoughts, until they were settled at the table and started eating. Halfway through the meal, she paused and looked at her mother.

"Can you take off anytime you want?"

"I can. I don't do it very often, but since I'm the boss and owner, I can. Why?"

"Because, I think I may have a solution to Dad's boredom." They talked like mother and daughter, totally ignoring the man in the room, who perked up, sat straighter, and leaned forward.

"Really, and you think it'd get him out of his funk?"

"It may, but he'd have to keep an open mind."

"Hey, I'm sitting right here, young lady. What do you have in mind?"

Kali grinned and laughed at his excited expression. "I want it to be a surprise. I don't want to tell you, and have you research it on the internet, and form an opinion from that before you even have a chance to see what I'm talking about. I want you to experience it firsthand."

"So, what do we have to do, Kal?" Kathy asked as she passed the veggies to her husband.

"Be at my house no later than four thirty this coming Friday, and plan on packing a bag. You're more than welcome to spend the night, and you know I have the room. Dad called last Friday and wanted to come mow my lawn, but I had to be someplace. I've been going to the same place every Friday and Saturday for the last four years. I'm ready to share that with you two, but you have to keep an open mind."

"We can do that. Anything else?" Keith asked excitedly.

"Yes, don't wear anything good, but you'll be outside until almost midnight, so bring warm clothes. I'll have everything else you need, and bring a hat."

"What do you mean by don't wear anything good?"

"You can wear your normal everyday work clothes, but not like I dress for work. I have to change into jeans, sneakers and layers when I get home from work. But, trust me, it'll be worth it if you keep an open mind."

"And you say no later than four thirty. What time do you get home from work?"

"Four twenty, and I leave at four thirty. If you're not there, I won't wait."

"And we won't know what you have in mind for us." Kathy giggled. "I like it. So, we live here in Norton, and you live down in Devil's Nose. Exactly, how long does it take from here to there?"

"Leisurely, an hour and a half."

"So, I can get out of work at noon, come home, shower and we can be on the road no later than one thirty."

"That'll give you plenty of time, and you have a key to my house. So, go in and make yourself at home."

"Do we drive separately or together?" Keith frowned then, when his daughter just stared at him, he sighed. "If you drive?"

"We can go together. I'll drive. It's not that far. And I'd like you to think about something."

"What's that?"

"If you like what I'm going to show you, you'd be Jonesing to go again sometime, maybe taking the camper and letting me sleeping in it with you."

"Something to look into." Keith nodded. "Do we need the camper this weekend?"

"No, because we'll be going to two different locations. One Friday and one Saturday."

"God, you've got my mind working. I think that's the first time since I retired, but it's all good." Keith grinned and rubbed his hands together. "You've been doing this for the last four years?"

"I have." Kali grinned and looked at her mother who mouthed 'thank you' to her daughter. Later as Keith was in the kitchen loading the dishwasher, Kali looked at her mother and grinned. "Don't thank me yet, you guys might hate it. And that's okay, I just thought it'd get Dad out of the house."

"Time will tell."

*****

Kali grinned when she pulled onto her street, and saw that her mother was weeding her flower garden, and her father had gotten out her lawn mower, and had mowed her lawn. She had been promising herself she'd get to it this weekend, but now she didn't have to, and since it was the first mowing of the year, it was going to be thick. She noticed that there were several piles of the thick stuff that had been raked. She parked and stepped out of her SUV, and grinned.

"Hey. Give me ten minutes and I'll be ready to go."

"Okay." Her mother waved and hooked up a cart behind the mower, and followed her father and together they picked up the piles of mown grass. Kali ran into her house and to her room, stripping as she went. In her bedroom she pulled on a long-sleeved shirt, a tee, and a flannel, then a pair of thick jeans, heavy socks, her sneakers, and grabbed an extra blanket she'd gotten out during the week. In the kitchen her parents were washing their hands, and she quickly made a sandwich, put some chips and cookies in baggies, and grabbed a water.

"There's food where we're going if you want to eat there, but I always pack mine, so you can do that or buy what you want there."

"What do they have?"

"Hot dogs, hamburgers, chicken fingers, French fries, chili, nachos, coffee, pop and water, and one stand has pizza slices, popcorn, and candy." She watched as they exchanged looks. "I think there might be Italian sausage, too. I think I smell it sometimes."

"We'll buy."

"Okay. You ready?"

"Yep, I decided not to go into work today, so we've been here since eleven. We're going to spend the night. We've also decided that if we like what we see tonight, we'll go tomorrow also."

"Cool." Kali laughed. They settled in and Kali pulled out of her driveway, and at the stop sign she took a right and went up the hill. She took another right, then slowed down and pulled into a very, very bumpy road. She drove on the side, mostly in the grass and grinned. "Hang on." She parked and hopped out.

"We're here?" Keith frowned when she opened the back, and began pulling things out, but he hurried over and took the bag, and one chair. Kathy took the other one and Kali grabbed the last one.

"Yep. I'll pay your entrance fee, but I don't go to the pits. I'm sorry, but if you want to go to the pits, you'll have to pay the extra price."

"I'll pay for all of us," Keith said. "And I have absolutely no idea what you just said, but you piqued my curiosity," he said, and they waited in line behind Kali. Keith looked around as cars started entering the field they'd parked in, and was confused as to why they were standing in line to pay. They were in the middle of a hayfield, for criminy sake. When the window opened, he stepped up and asked for two pit passes and one regular pass.

They took their tickets, got their hands stamped, and Kali said, "Follow me." She went to her normal seat and set everything up, then she turned and spread her arm out wide. She saw the shock on her parents' faces.

"What is this?" Kathy frowned.

"Dirt track racing. This track is called Dusty Hill. Tomorrow's race is down at McKay Family Raceway in Smith, PA. It's not open yet, but I also go to State, that's south of Jamestown, and they only run when Dusty Hill doesn't."

"And this pit pass?" Keith asked as he held up the ticket in his hand, and waved it to her.

"Okay, I sit here in this spot at all three tracks I go to. If you look..." She pointed down behind her, and they looked over the backrest to the stands. "Restrooms, pizza and popcorn stand. Beer. Then, over there is the regular food. To the left of that building is the pit entrance. With that pass you can go in to where the cars and drivers are." She pointed and grinned. "Cars like that." It just happened to be the three number eighteens that were driving in, and she saw there was a truck hauling a camper coming in with them.

"What type of cars?"

"Street stock, crate, e-mods, super late model, young guns, tonight is also the sprint and mini sprint cars."

"What are they?"

"They have the wings on them."

"Oh," Keith frowned and actually scratched his head. "So, when do they go out onto the track?" He turned and watched as the equipment was still getting the track ready. "Looks like they have a lot of work to do yet."

"Pits open at four, gates at five, and hot laps start at six. So, you have an hour before anything on the track starts."

"Okay, we'll be back," Keith said, and he and Kathy made their way slowly down the rickety steps, and disappeared around the corner.

An hour later, Kali looked up and saw her parents walking up the steps, and before she could say anything after they sat down, she looked up at the loud whistle, and waved to Kyle, who pointed to his shirt, and she gave him two thumbs up when she saw it was a number eighteen, but he didn't come up to talk to her.

"Who was that?"

"Kyle. We've been doing that since my first race. It wasn't until last week he came up and introduced himself. He pointed to his tee, because there are three different classes that have the same number, and they're my favorite drivers."

"Number eighteen?" Keith asked. "I saw their cars and they look pretty snazzy." He jerked when the cars started up far behind them, then she reached in her bag and handed her parents each a set of earplugs. She put her face shield on, but left it up and her father only shook his head at her.

"So, let me tell you a little about what goes on. There are the tow trucks coming in, to take the cars off if they wreck, or stall out. The guys on the four wheelers are the safety crew, and then you have the flagman on the other side of the track. But, the guy up there is the main flagman. And each and every one of them are blind fucking idiots."

"Kali," Kathy looked at her in shock.

"Trust me, Mom. After you see them in action, you'll think the same way. Tomorrow at McKay, you'll understand what I mean. That track has the best crew around."

"Aren't they the same at every track?" Keith asked.

"Excuse me." The woman ahead of them turned, and she pointed to her own head, and she and Kali laughed at the face shield she had on. "I'm Sally, and I've sat during these races for the last ten years."

"Kali," They shook, and when she frowned like Kyle did, Kali hugged herself and didn't dare look at her parents, but she saw the tightening in her father's expression. "These are my parents, Keith and Kathy. This is their first ever race."

"If you have any questions, I'd be glad to help Kali answer them, but she's right, this is the worse track for flagmen and officials, but I heard a rumor this past week."

"What's that?" Kali leaned forward.

"I heard the track's for sale."

"This one? Dusty Hill?" Keith asked.

"Yes. Years ago, it was a great track, I mean the best in the circuit. Kind of like McKay is now. But, the owner, who at that time owned it for almost forty years, became sick and died. His daughter tried to keep it going, but she had four small children, a husband, a job, and then her mother became sick, and she took care of her, so she sold the track, but not before closing it for a year. The new owners never got it back up to snuff, and then they only had it for two years before selling it to the current owner, who's only had it for three years. I heard he is going through a nasty divorce, and needs the money from the sale of this track to pay for his lawyer."

"Damn," Kali sighed, then she laughed. "Hell, Dad, you're so bored with retirement, why don't you buy it?"

"Because, your mother has her business in Lock, and we'd have to sell that, sell the house, and move here. If I ever did something like that, I'd want to make it a family business. I know Kelsey and Karen would never come home, and your mother loves her business, and you're happy with your job, so it isn't an option."

"I was only joking," Kali said, not really paying attention to her parents. What she missed was her mother looking at her father with a raised brow, and he only gave her a sheepish grin and shrugged. Because, he had heard the same thing in the pits that seemed to be the buzz of the day, that the track was for sale and they had discussed it briefly, but their ultimate decision was to watch a race, and see if they liked what they saw, then they could compare this track to the one they'd be at the next day.

CHAPTER THREE

Sunday morning Kali stumbled into her kitchen, and grinned when she saw her father sitting there with a cup of coffee before him. "Morning, where's Mom?"

"Still sleeping," he mumbled, and watched as his daughter poured her own coffee, then joined him at the table.

"How are you? Never thought the race would run that late. I've never seen it go that long."

"It was good though," he grinned. "Never thought there could be so many cautions in one race. Hell, in one lap. But, you were right about the safety crew. Comparing Friday to Saturday, Friday royally sucked."

Kali snorted a laugh and nodded. She grinned as her mother stumbled in drying her hair on a towel. "I wore a hat, I took a shower when we got home, but I had to take another one, because I felt so dirty."

"So, you're a dirty girl?" Kali laughed.

"Yeah, and I'm surprised, because I own a nursery, and I play in the dirt all day, every day, so I should be used to being as you say, a dirty girl." She laughed when her husband grabbed her around the waist, and settled her on his lap.

"You can be my dirty girl anytime, babe."

"Dad," Kali said, and shook her head at her parents. She was used to it and she was twenty-four, so she shouldn't be embarrassed. They laughed and Kathy sat in a chair and drank her coffee. After several minutes of silence as they let the coffee kick in, Kali finally turned to them, and asked. "So, what did you think?"

"It was fun." Kathy grinned. "I can see why you like to go, and I can see the difference in the two tracks. I heard the announcer say Friday that they won't be racing next week?"

"No, but I'll be going to State. I'll be leaving directly from work. I'm getting out at two and I'll have all my things with me, and if you heard, McKay won't be running either. It's State's opening race and they race for two days. Friday and Saturday, and on Saturday afternoon, the younger kids, like my friend Kyle, race go carts."

"Does Dusty Hill have go cart races?"

"I don't know. You'll have to look them up online or talk to a driver."

"Why don't you go to the pits?"

"Dad," Kali said, and only stared at him.

"Come on, it can't be that bad after all this time."

"You saw Sally's reaction. Kyle did the same thing the night before."

"And is that why you pack your own supper, and don't leave your seat once you're there?" Kathy asked. "Show me." She held her hand out palm up, and when her daughter didn't do anything, she only wiggled her fingers, and grinned at Keith when Kali sighed. Kali took her right hand and laid it into her mother's, the back of it to her mother's palm. She closed her eyes when both her parents leaned forward and inspected her hand. They moved it this way and that, and leaned in and studied the scar between her ring finger and pinky.

"Do you wear the braces we had made for you?" Keith asked.

"Sometimes. It helps a little, especially if I'm shaking hands, but it's a pain in the ass when I have two stiff fingers that don't move when I'm trying to work."

"Let's see the rest," Kathy said as she and Keith stood, and walked behind Kali after she removed her sweatshirt. They took an arm each and studied the scars radiating out from her elbows, up the back of her arm, and down the back of the forearm. To look at her from the front, she had completely smooth skin, but to look at her from behind in short sleeves, her arms looked like she'd gone through a meat grinder.

"Do they hurt?"

"Not anymore, and I still put the Vitamin E on them every night."

"Do you want us to contact a doctor about your fingers?" Keith asked.

"No, I'm okay. I've lived with it for over twenty years, and I'm alive, so a couple crippled fingers aren't bad. I can live with it."

"Okay, it's your decision, but as you said, it's been over twenty years, a lot of new techniques have come along in that time."

"I'm fine. It hasn't slowed me down yet. Maybe if it does, then I'll look into it."

"Okay, but let us know," Keith said, and hugged his daughter from behind.

"At least I have one thing going for me." Kali grinned after Kathy filled their coffee cups again.

"What's that?"

"I'm so damn pale that you can't really see the scars at a quick glance. Unlike the two of you and Kels and Karen, who go in the sun and become ten shades darker in all of five minutes."

"I wouldn't say it's five minutes," Keith said as he removed his watch, and grinned at the tan line. "Maybe ten." They shared a laugh, and decided to go out to breakfast, instead of cooking anything. They drove separately, because after breakfast Keith and Kathy were going to head home, and they discussed the plans for the next weekend. Because Kali couldn't ride in a vehicle without freaking out, unless she was driving, and she was coming directly from work, they decided that she would meet them there and they would have their camper, and she could stay with them.

*****

Almost two weeks later, Kali was at work, still on a high from the two days she had camped with her parents and watched some great races, when her phone on her desk rang, and she sighed as she picked it up. She only had to get through today, and she was off for the four-day weekend, being Easter and all. Normally, there wouldn't be any races, but Dusty Hill was having a three-day race starting tonight. She didn't know if she'd make tonight's, but she'd definitely be there for Friday and Saturday.

"Kilpatrick," she said briskly as she answered her phone.

"Mr. Wright called a meeting in the big conference room."

"I'll be there." She hung up, grabbed a pad of paper and a pen, and headed to the big conference room. She saw that several others were walking toward it, and they all went in and grabbed the first seats available. Kali sat where she always sat at these meetings, and a fellow co-worker, Matt, sat to her right. They were talking quietly when she felt someone staring down at her.

"Can I help you?" She frowned at the girl she'd never seen before.

"That's my seat," the girl said snidely, and actually used her knee to try to push Kali from the chair.

"Hey, Suzie Q." Matt mocked her. "You're only an unpaid intern here, Kal's been here the longest, so she's the most senior ad executive here. I think you better stand in the back with the rest of the interns."

"But, I always sit in that chair."

"For how long? I've never seen you, and I work sixty hours a week here," Kali said. She waved her left hand like she was swatting a gnat, and turned away, ignoring her. She didn't see the death look the young intern gave her, but Matt did. He leaned forward and whispered.

"Oh, you pissed someone off."

"Who the hell is she anyway?"

"I only know her as Suzie the intern, but rumor is she's Tony Wright's niece, but I wouldn't worry about it. You've brought in the highest accounts in the last five years, and if this is something new, I want to be on your team." He grinned when Kali laughed. They quieted down when Tony Wright himself came in, and slapped four folders on the table.

"I'll get right to the point, since we're all off for the next four days, and it's almost lunch time. We have a possibility of a new account. The client wants a fresh perspective on an old business. That's all I'm going to say. We're going to break up into four teams," he said, and smiled when six people huddled as close as they could around Kali.

"Ah, not going to be that easy, folks. Kilpatrick."

"Sir," Kali said, and caught the file he literally shoved at her. "That's the information. You're on your own."

"Excuse me?"

"That's right. A team of one. And don't worry, you can see for yourself, but all the folders have the same information as yours."

Not that she didn't trust him, but she stood and went and compared them, and when she was satisfied she nodded. "So you want me to work this account all on my own? No video? No audio?"

"Nope. You're on your own, and Matt is on his own." He grinned when Matt stared in shock.

"I don't know everything yet."

"Learn. The other two teams." He looked up and pointed. "You on this side, you on that side. Those are your teams. On the left, Suzie, you're in charge of the team and account. Heather, you're in charge of your team." He saw the shock and then grinned evilly. "That's all."

"Wait," Kali called out. "Do we present to you or the client?"

"Client."

"All on the same day?"

"Yes, and he'll pick the one he wants that day, and same as before, you don't get your commission until he signs on the dotted line."

"How long?"

"One month from today," he said and walked out, leaving twelve people staring at each other in shock. Kali grinned and hurried out, and ignored the calls of the people from behind. By the time they caught up with her, the file was in her purse, and she was headed to the door.

"Where are you going?" Matt literally ran to get in front of her, trying to stop her to see what she'd be doing for the campaign.

"Lunch." She grinned when the others stopped in their tracks and didn't follow her. She hurried four blocks away, ordered a sandwich, a bag of chips, and a water. Once she ate half of it at a nearby park, she pulled the file and a pen. The only information was a man's name and phone number, and under what he wanted, it said, 'New ideas.' She grinned and pulled her cell, and dialed.

"Dillard."

"Hello, is this Max Dillard?"

"It is, who's this?"

"You don't know me, but my name is Kali Kilpatrick, and I work for The Wright Group, the advertising agency in downtown Buffalo."

"Yes, I talked to them this last week, what's up?"

"Mr. Wright is making your account into a contest. We were given your information only twenty minutes ago. There are four teams working toward your presentation in one month."

"Okay, you've piqued my interest." Max laughed. "What can I do for you?"

"The only information we were given was your name, phone number, and in the section for what you're looking for it only says new ideas. Can you answer some questions for me?"

*****

Max Dillard pulled the phone from his ear and frowned, then jumped to his feet and closed his door, flipping the sign that said not to disturb as he sat back down. "What do you want to know?"

"What do you do?"

"Wright didn't tell you?"

"No, as I said, it only says new ideas. That's why I'm calling. Tell me what your business is."

"Auto parts."

"Like Napa?"

"Yes, we've been in business for the last thirty years, but it's all been from the west of the Rockies. We've been here in the Buffalo area for only a few months. We just closed on a location for our office and factory."

"If you sell auto parts, why do you need a factory?"

"Because our specialty is motors. We build them."

"What is the name of the business out west?"

"Dillard's. It's our last name."

"Okay, and do you want to keep that name?"

"I don't mean to toot my own horn, but it is a well-known name. At least out west it is. We want to establish ourselves here, hence the vague new ideas."

"Where are you located?"

"Arcade."

"Really, I know that area well, I live in Devil's Nose."

"Small world. So you know where the Napa store was across from Tops?"

"Yes."

"We bought that and are using that as the retail store, and we just closed last month on the factory next door."

"The fabrication place?"

"Yes. You do know the area."

"I do." Kali laughed and settled back. "So what type of motors do you build?"

"All types. Out west we specialized in racing motors. I'd love to find some local racers and sponsor them. That's what I was looking for when I said new ideas."

"Really. So what if I could turn you on to some dirt track drivers? I heard they were losing their sponsors at the end of July, not the end of the season."

"I'd say that I'd give you whatever you wanted."

"Could I maybe interview and film your workers, asking them what it means to work for Dillard's?"

"Absolutely. And we can get together next week, in person and talk."

"Okay. Now bear with me, I'm only a fan, and I don't know all the answers, but I've been going the three local dirt racing tracks for the last four years. I personally have three favorite drivers, but I don't know their names."

"Do you know what class and what their number is?"

"Yes, got paper and pencil?"

"Yes, go ahead."

"E-mods, number eighteen. Black and purple. Crate, number eighteen, black and orange. Super late model."

"Let me guess, number eighteen?" Max laughed.

"Yep, And he's black and green."

"And all three of these cars are looking for sponsors?"

"I heard they were. I have a friend that goes into the pits, and he's the one that mentioned all three of them were looking for sponsors. His name is Kyle, that's all I can say."

"Thank you Ms. Kilpatrick."

"Kali please. I think we'll be working closely together in the next few weeks, but I'd really like to interview your workers."

"Call me next week and we'll sit down and talk. Now, can you tell me where I can find these three cars?"

"Oh," Kali laughed. "Ever hear of Dusty Hill race track?"

"No, I have to admit I've only been in the area for a month. If you give me directions I'm sure I can find it."

"Okay, I'll try. Where are you right this minute?"

"I'm sitting in the office of the old Napa store across from Tops."

"In Arcade?"

"Yes."

"Okay, Dusty Hill has a three-day race this weekend. Pits open at noon today. You are literally fifteen minutes away from it."

"Where," Max demanded, and waved his father over when he tried to open the door.

"Do you happen to know how to get to Devil's Nose from where you are?"

"Yes, I just came back from the DMV there when you called."

"Great. Go back there and to the left of the plaza with the DMV you'll see a road named Devil's Nose Road."

"I saw that, it's at an angle?"

"Correct. Go to the first stop sign. That's Church Street. Turn left. You'll go over a set of railroad tracks and then start going uphill. Keep going. At the top of the hill is a T, turn right, less than a half mile away you'll see a sign that says 'pit entrance' a quarter mile after that is where the general public enter."

"Great, you're right, literally fifteen minutes away, but what side of the road is the pit entrance on?"

"Oh," Kali laughed. "It'll be on your right."

"Thanks, Kali. I'll let you know how things work out. How do I get ahold of you?"

"I called you on my personal cell. But, don't be surprised if others from Wright Group will be calling you, because we're working as competition to get your account."

"Well, I can honestly say you're the only one who's called so far. But, I'm going to let you go, because it's going on two and the pits are open. Maybe I can get some people to sponsor before the weekend's out."

"Great, talk to you later." Kali hung up and grinned as she sat back and finished her lunch. She'd noticed she'd taken a lot of notes, and after cleaning up she went back to work, and was able to sneak into her office without being seen, and got to work.

*****

Max Dillard hung up the phone, grabbed the directions, and grinned as he whipped open the door. "Dad, what are you doing here?"

"Came to see how you're doing, and don't give me any shit, I ain't dead yet."

"I know. Want to go for a ride?"

"Where?"

"Someplace we might be able to sponsor some people. I just got a lead... A very good lead." He looked at the paper in his hand, then back up at his father. "At least, I hope it's a very good lead."

"Sure, don't have anything else to do," Maxwell said, and turned slowly and shuffled his way to his eldest son's truck. It took some time, but he finally settled in and adjusted his oxygen tank.

"God, I hate this sucker."

"I know, I hate seeing you using it, but if it helps you live longer, we'll both have to live with it," he said, and stopped as his two brothers, Paul and Andy pulled in.

"What's up? Hey, Dad," Paul said.

"Got a line on possibility of people to sponsor. Dad and I are going to go check it out."

"Where? The most ideal place would be a race track, but there's nothing around here."

"Damn right it would," Maxwell said. "That's what Dillards cut their teeth on."

Max only grinned and said. "Follow me."

"What? You found a track?" Paul and Maxwell asked at the same time, but Max only put his truck in gear and was out of the parking lot as Paul turned, and must have caught the yellow light or turned on red, because he was directly behind him.

"Son?" Maxwell asked. "Are you joking with an old man?"

"First, you're not old, second, I have information that someone driving an e-mod, a crate, and a super late model, is losing their sponsor at the end of July."

"Holy shit. Hey, we just came from here. Isn't that the DMV we went to?" Maxwell Dillard asked as he pointed to the plaza they were driving by.

"Yes. I was told to take the left road that angled here."

"Okay, and at the stop sign?"

"Take a left, go over tracks and go up the hill." They did that and Maxwell grinned. "Now this is a hill. Now what?" he asked, when he saw the T up ahead.

"Turn right, and less than half a mile away is a sign on the right that says pit entrances," he said, and he slowed as he approached the stop sign, then looked at his father and grinned. "What if we follow those guys?" He pointed and watched as Maxwell leaned and looked to the left.

"Holy shit. They going the same way we are?"

"No clue, but my source says there is a three-day race starting today, tomorrow and Saturday. And that the pits opened at noon today."

"Well, it's after two. And that's the tenth rig that just passed us." Maxwell grinned and looked back at his other sons in the truck behind them. "I think Paul and Andy are excited."

Max looked in his rearview mirror, and saw his brothers giving each other a high five and looked toward him and gave him four thumbs up. Once the rigs drove by, Max eased into the right turn, and had to go slow as those rigs pulled into a driveway only half a mile away, and sure enough he saw the sign that said pit entrance.

CHAPTER FOUR

Kameron Kilbourne was the leader of the racing rigs, and pulled into the pits at Dusty Hill first and went slowly. He nodded as he saw the people behind him slow to a crawl, letting him get to his spot. Once he was parked, his brother Kurtis pulled in next. After he was parked, several others drove by and then across the way, his father pulled in with his truck and fifth wheel camper. Finally, at the end of the line Kevin pulled in.

The first thing Kameron did was leave the driver's seat to go to the back of his RV. He stopped short and stared down at his youngest brother, Kyle. He shook his head as he gently lifted the boy's legs off the floor, and laid him out on the couch. He must have either rolled off or was bounced off. Kam loved racing at Dusty Hill, but the road to get to the pits was horrendous. Satisfied he hadn't damaged his baby brother, he disembarked and quickly went to the back of his rig, and began unlocking his trailer. He saw that Kurtis and Kevin were doing the same thing.

They were at the same point and then they stepped away, and while looking at each other they did rock, paper, scissors, and Kameron grinned when his two brothers groaned, and started toward him. Normally, they had a crew each, but some of them were still at work, and they helped each other. They unloaded Kameron's super late model car first, then Kurtis and Kevin did the rock, paper, scissors, and the three of them went to Kevin's rig and helped unload his e-mod, then over to Kurt's to unload his crate model car.

They looked up when they heard a whistle, and hurried across the road and helped their father lift out Kyle's go cart. Then, Kam took it over, so it was between his and Kurt's rig. They saw their father had the fifth wheel hooked up, then they moved their rigs over so the family was in a square with the doors to their RV's facing the center.

"Who's that?" Kurtis asked as they saw two trucks drive by for the third time, and saw an elderly man point to their cars, and the first driver slammed on his brakes and whipped his truck into park, then so did the truck behind him. The four Kilbournes stood before Kameron's truck with their arms crossed over their chests, and let the men come to them. There were four of them. Three looked to be about ten years older than the three of them, and the eldest was about twenty years older than their own father, and they frowned when they saw he used a portable oxygen tank.

"Help you?" Kameron asked.

"Actually, I hope so. I'm probably not going to make any sense, but I was told you were looking for new sponsors by the end of July."

"What the fuck?" Kameron demanded. "We only found out last week, who the hell are you, and how did you find out?"

"Um, a friend of Kyle's told me?"

"Dad? What the hell's going on?"

"No clue? Where's Ky?"

"In my rig. He's sleeping on the couch," Kameron said, and started back across the road, but Ken held him off. Ken went to the rig in question, and when he opened the door he didn't see his son. He finally found him on the back side of Kurt's rig, and only shook his head.

"You done?"

"Not yet," Kyle said as he continued to pee into the weeds. Standing behind him Ken shook his head and sighed.

"Can I ask you a question?"

"As long as you don't mind my dick hanging out while we're talking."

"Kyle, who taught you to talk like that?"

"Kam and Kurt." He grinned over his shoulder, then as he finished, he zipped up and turned to his father. "What's up?"

"Did you tell anyone that we're looking for sponsors at the end of July?"

"I might have?" he answered in the form of a question. "Why? What does it matter?"

"Because, someone is here saying that a friend of yours told these guys we're looking for sponsors. Do you have any idea who that might be?"

"My girl friend that's not my girlfriend. Her name is Kali, and Dad," he whispered and leaned in.

"What?"

"She's old. Too old for me."

Ken smirked and whispered back. "Is she as old as your mother?"

"DAD! Bite your tongue, Mom's not old."

"Oh. So how old is she?" Ken asked, thinking about fifteen or sixteen, since his son was only ten.

"Older than Kevin, but not as old as Kam and Kurt. I think I heard her say she was twenty-four. And that's *waaaay* too old for me."

"Yep. It is." Ken grinned. "So, do you think she'd go out with Kam or Kurt?"

"I don't know, but she is beautiful. So, who are these guys?"

"No clue. I came to get you," Ken said, and watched as his youngest squared his shoulders, and walked across the road where everyone was at a standoff.

"Hi, I'm Kyle, who's looking for me?"

"I am," the tallest of the four said. "A mutual friend of ours says you know some people looking for sponsors. She said they were cars with the number eighteen on them." He looked at the paper and grinned as he read it off. "E-mod, black and purple, crate, black and orange, super late, black and green."

"Yep, that's these. And they belong to my brothers. I'll introduce them in the order you said the cars. Kevin, Kurtis and Kameron. All with Ks and that's our dad, Ken, and our last name is Kilbourne. Now, who are you?"

"You've probably never heard of me, but I'm Max Dillard, this is my father Maxwell, and my brothers Paul and Andy."

"No fucking way," Kyle said. Three men behind him, said sternly, "Kyle, where did you learn to talk like that?"

"Kam and Kurt." He threw his oldest brothers under the bus, and Ken glared at them when he saw his twins' cheeks turn red.

"We'll talk later, boys."

"Yes, sir."

"But, holy freaking cow? Are you the Dillard that makes engines? Especially race car engines? You specialize in crate motors. The motors that help you get across the finish line. Those Dillards?"

"Yes."

"Holy fucking shit," Kam said, and stepped forward. "And you want to sponsor us? Why? Aren't you located on the West coast? What made you look us up?"

"So, you've heard of us?" Maxwell asked.

"Yes, all four of us have a Dillard engine in our car," Kurt said, and pointed to them.

"Four? I only see three." Max frowned.

"My go cart."

"Damn, sounds like a Dillard is a family that races together," Paul said, and looked at the crate model. "How's the tranny holding up in that crate?"

"Like shit. You guys don't happen to do trannies do you?"

"We're working on it. What seems to be the problem?"

"It's shearing bolts," Kurt said, and he and Kam removed the hood, and Kam was surprised when all four Dillards looked under the hood, and the oldest one began moving things.

After fifteen minutes he looked at two of his sons, and said, "Go down to the shop and load up a six thirty. That's the only engine that'll prevent the shearing with this type of tranny."

"Wait. What are you talking about?" Kurtis demanded. "I don't know if you know this, but I have to have a special motor for this car, it's not like Kam's and Kev's."

"It has to be in a crate, right?"

"Yes."

"That's what I thought. What are you two waiting for?" He barked at his sons, who literally ran to their truck.

"You got the receipt for this engine?"

"I have it," Ken said, and went to the camper and came back five minutes later.

"Okay, as I'm sure you know, Dillard's has a money-back guarantee. Let me ask you this, when you bought this motor, what did you buy first, the motor or the tranny?"

"Motor," Kurtis frowned. "And I got the tranny, because they said it was compatible with this motor."

"They lied," Maxwell said bluntly. "I have a lawsuit going against them. I've replaced several motors because of this problem, and my lawsuit is that it's not the engine, but the tranny. But, we've made a new and improved engine that will go with this tranny. What time do you take the track tonight?"

"About six thirty."

"You got a crew?"

"Not until after five thirty, they have day jobs."

"Max call in our crew," Maxwell barked out. He stood away from the car, and said, "I know you have questions, so I'll give you the rundown. I'm Maxwell, I started the company thirty years ago in LA, that's Los Angeles, but as the town grew, so did we and we moved over to the Nevada border, and found dirt track racers there. We were only in business six months, when we started talking to them, and developed the crate engine. Once we sold one to a driver out there, and he won every race in his season, word got around and our business skyrocketed.

"Six months ago, my father-in-law had a stroke, and my wife wanted to come home. My brother started the business with me. My boys, Max, Paul, and Andy came home with us. My brother's in charge of Dillard's West, I guess you could call it.

"We've only been here six weeks, we just closed on two buildings, and we're going to start Dillard's East."

"Where?"

"Arcade."

"Where?"

"Our retail store will be the old Napa store that went out of business three months ago, and we bought the fabrication plant next door. That's where we're going to be making the engines," Max said. "Andy and Paul just went to get an engine we've made in our garage over the last six months. No one has seen it yet."

"And you're giving it to me?"

"Yeah, but you'll have to pay the difference from that engine to this one."

"What if I want to keep this one?"

"For what? It won't fit any tranny without shearing off the bolts, and we're still a couple years away from making a tranny."

"Oh," Kurtis said. "Dad? Kam?"

"Max, you excuse us please?" Kevin asked the Dillards.

"Sure, but do you have any records of your wins?"

"In the back of our trailers."

"I'll show them," Kyle said, and headed over to Kevin's first.

"What do you think, Dad?" Kurt asked.

"I don't know. It sounds too good to be true."

"And what's with this sponsor shit?" Kam rubbed his face, and watched as three more rigs pulled in and behind them were four pickup trucks, and they saw they were loaded with men and tools.

The thing that sealed their minds was when one of the men in the back stood and let out a howl, and yelled, "Thank god! Racing! Mama answered my prayers. As long as there's racing, I can live with the fucking snow."

"Yes," Kam looked at his brother and grinned. "But the final decision is yours."

"I think I'll do it," he said, and walked forward and introduced himself, and it wasn't long before the old engine was out and in the back of a truck, and a new engine was in. By the time Kurt's crew arrived, the new engine was getting the fluids put in, and Kurt climbed in and turned the key. After another twenty minutes of tweaking, he was happy with it and everyone except for the drivers were standing around and drinking a beer.

When it came time for the cars to hit the track, every car had been gone over and tweaked by, not only the owners, but the builders of the engines. And by the time the end of the night came around, the four Kilbourne brothers had new sponsors. They only had to give the Dillards their hood for the advertising, because that was where their current sponsor was. Everyone was happy, and Kam and Kurt were extra happy when they both won their feature races. So, when it came time for Kevin to run his, everyone was standing on the small hill at the pit stands, and at one point Kam heard a woman yelling for Kevin to go faster, and he looked over and up and saw a beautiful redhead with a face shield, like the one Kyle made him stop and buy for him.

"What's up?" Kurt asked, or he would have if it wasn't so loud. Kam used his hand signals and pointed the woman out to Kurt, and they exchanged looks. Just then, Kevin went over the finish line first, and the woman went wild. Kam grabbed Kyle by the shoulder as he jumped up and down, and leaned down and pointed to the woman.

Kyle grinned. "My girl/friend, that's not my girlfriend. Watch." He put his pinkies in his mouth and let out a piercing whistle, and Kam and Kurtis watched as she looked around, and when Ky did it again, she looked over, and when he pointed to his shirt, she gave him two thumbs up and a mock high five. Then they lost track of her as the crowd rose.

"What was that about?"

"Her favorite drivers are the number eighteens." Kyle grinned at their shock.

"Us?"

"Yep, but I didn't tell her I was your brother. I just said I knew those drivers."

"Good idea," Kam said, and was dragged by his father out onto the track to take pictures with his brother. The entire time he was thinking how he could get closer to the woman, but first he had to talk to Kyle, and ask him why he didn't tell them the woman was his age.

CHAPTER FIVE

Kali sighed and buried her face in her hands and groaned. She was at a standstill with the Dillard account, and she was becoming paranoid. Earlier this week, she had stepped out of her office, and on her way back she'd seen Suzie coming out, and when Kali saw how messy her desk was, she realized Suzie was trying to steal ideas from her. She knew she was being paranoid, but there was no other reason for her to be in Kali's office. Luckily, she'd been working on a joke to get her creative juices going, and the biggest joke of all was that the mockup of the joke was missing. She sighed and looked at her watch.

"The hell with it," she said, and gathered up her papers and packed them away, she slipped into her private bath and changed into jeans and sneakers. When she came out she caught Suzie reaching for her black portfolio where the papers were. She waited until Suzie had it halfway open, then demanded angrily.

"What are you doing, Suzie?"

The woman screamed like she was being attacked, and jumped back, falling on her ass and twisting her ankle in the five inch heels she wore.

"You scared me."

"What's going on?" Matt asked from the doorway.

"I only asked Suzie what she was doing."

"What was she doing?"

"Opening my portfolio where the Dillard account is."

"Ah, she's stealing ideas from you too? I caught her in my office a couple hours ago."

"I don't need to steal. I'm the best there is here."

"Sure you are," Matt said. "Can't wait to see your presentation. I hear she went so far as to invent a new product in addition to new ideas."

"Really? What's that?" Kali said, and leaned against her desk beside Matt.

Matt grinned and wiggled his brow. "We'll have to wait and find out, won't we?"

"I guess we will," she said, and watched as Suzie limped out without saying a word. When they heard a door slam, Matt looked at her, and grinned.

"Blinker fluid, Kal? What the hell?"

"So, she did steal it from me?"

"Yep. But once I found out about it I made up a mockup, and left it on my desk before lunch. Was gone when I got back."

"Oh, we're bad."

"Speaking of bad. Why are you dressed in jeans and sneakers?"

"Because, I'm leaving for the weekend. If I leave now I can make it with only being late by twenty minutes."

"Where are you going?"

"I'm going to go get dirty." She grinned, grabbed her purse and portfolio, and laughed at his expression. She turned off the lights and kept going. She hurried out to her SUV and nodded. She'd been working a lot of overtime, and hadn't been to the track in three weeks. Thank god they'd been told that the account was extended by two weeks. Now, if she only knew how to approach the people she needed to, she'd have it in the bag. She headed out, and just before she arrived at McKay Family Raceway, the inspiration she needed struck, and with a happy smile and pep in her step, she grabbed her things and after she paid her entrance fee, she headed up the ramp that led to the stands.

It was a blind corner and she should have had her head in what she was doing, so she wasn't surprised when she rounded the corner at the same time two huge, sexy-looking men did at the same time. She was entering and they were exiting.

"Oomph," the three of them said, and Kali actually felt herself being lifted and walked backward. It was several seconds before she realized they were moving her out of the way, because several people had crowded up behind both of them.

"You okay?" Kam asked the woman who he'd practically run over. If it hadn't been for his quick reflexes, he and Kurt would have plowed right over her. "I'm sorry for almost knocking you down.

"I'm fine, I should be apologizing to you. I wasn't paying attention. I'm so sorry."

"Don't be," Kurtis said from her side. "We were in a hurry."

Kali should have felt trapped, because she had a fence at her back, a soda machine to her right, a huge, sexy man at her left, and one in front of her, but she felt anything but. For the first time in years, she felt safe. She looked up and up, and then did a double take, and frowned when they grinned.

"Yep, we're twins."

"Oh, I guess you were, but I wasn't looking at that. You look like my friend." She laughed, then sighed. "But, then again how many black-haired, blue-eyed people are there in the world?"

"In our family?" The man still holding her by her upper arms grinned. "Six."

"Oh, wow."

"Who's your friend?" the man to her left asked, and touched her forearm and ran his finger down her arm. Luckily it wasn't the back of her hand, so she didn't struggle to get away.

"I don't know his last name, but his first one is Kyle." She frowned when the men exchanged looks, then there was a whistle, and all three of them turned, and Kam sighed. She turned back and sighed. She didn't recognize the man, only the whistle.

"Sorry, but we gotta go. Enjoy your night."

"I will, I hope you win."

"How do you know we're drivers?"

"Your suits. Isn't that what drivers wear?"

"Yep," they said, then shocked the hell out of her as they leaned down and each kissed a cheek, stood up, and grinned at each other. "Strawberries." They smiled as they rubbed their stomachs, and mimicked Kyle from weeks ago. The man let her down gently, and they both steadied her, then when she was okay they gave her a mock salute, a bow, then turned and hurried away. Still stunned, Kali stayed there for a couple minutes, then made her way up to her normal seat. She was shocked when she saw her mother sitting there.

"Mom?"

"Kali! I didn't know you were coming. I thought you were working late again."

"I couldn't handle it, I had to get out of there."

"Want to talk about it?"

"Not really."

"Okay, just know I'm here when you need me."

"Thanks, Mom. But, it's been a week from hell, all I want to do is lose myself in the noise and dirt, and let my mind clear. Is Dad here?"

"He is, he's in the pits, and we brought the camper if you want to stay."

"No, I'll probably go home. I have a lot of work to do at home."

"Okay, but the offer's still there."

"Thanks," she said, and sighed when cars entered the track, and she lost herself in the track, and after it was done she was glad her drivers each won.

*****

In the pits, Ken was waiting for Kameron as he climbed out of his car. "What the hell was that? Both you and Kurtis?"

"What was what?"

"You start sixteenth out of twenty-four, and by the fifth lap of thirty you're in the lead and lap other drivers? I'm not complaining. It's the first win in three weeks, but damn, son. I'm proud of you."

"Thanks, Dad." He grinned and looked at Kurt as he came out of the RV, all showered and changed.

"You win?"

"Yep. You?"

"Yep." Kevin shook his head. Even after twenty-seven years he still never understood the twin thing. Kam went into his RV, and in his back bedroom he stripped and immediately went into the shower, and left the door open.

"You think she have anything to do with it?" Kurtis asked as he leaned on his shoulder, and talked to his brother while he cleaned up.

"I don't know. Maybe. Kyle said she hasn't been around for the last three weeks. We've both lost for the last three weeks, and we literally ran into her tonight, and we both won."

"Yeah, I think it was her. When you finish up here, I have something I'd like to talk to you about."

"Okay," he said, and ducked his head under the shower and used extra shampoo to get the dirt out. Even though he was in a car, with a helmet on, the dirt still got everywhere. He wondered how the fans did it, especially if they had to drive for any distance before they got home. And that brought to mind where their mystery woman lived. He finished his shower, grabbed a towel and stepped out, not caring that his brother was sitting on the end of his bed. He dried off and slipped on a pair of jeans, commando, then a tee. He slipped his bare feet into a pair of sloppy sneakers, and went out to the living room. In the kitchen he opened his refrigerator, and sighed.

"Mom, got any food?" He grinned as he said that, and his door opened and in walked his mother with a dish of lasagna. "I love you." He grinned, grabbed the dish, and cut it in half. He then cut that in half, giving himself and Kurt those pieces. Kerri only shook her head, and sighed.

"You talk to him yet?"

"No. He just got out of the shower."

"What's up?"

"Do you and Ky talk when he sleeps in here, or rides with you?"

"Some? But, he sleeps when we drive, so not much talking there. Why? What's up?"

"I'm starting to get worried about him," Kerri said, and went around the kitchen and poured drinks and got out napkins, and then settled in a seat at the island.

"What's he doing?"

"Hanging out with a man I don't know. Never met him."

"Really? This man give you the creeps?"

"No, but I've never met him, and when I ask Ky about him, he says it's a secret."

"There's a red flag." Kam paused with the fork halfway to his mouth, and exchanged looks with his brother. "You know about this?"

"No, first time I'm hearing it. I only wanted to tell you that Mom wanted to talk to us."

"Where's Ky now?"

"Over in the fan section talking to that man."

"We'll be back," Kam said, and dropped his fork, stood and walked out.

"Don't do anything stupid, Kam." Kerri called after her oldest.

"Don't clean up my food. I'll be back." He knew Kurt was with him. He didn't see him, but he felt him. They took the short cut, keeping to the shadows, and paused and listened. When they heard Ky's laugh, they made their way forward. There was no way to sneak up on them, so together the twins slowly walked forward, and paused across from the guy talking to his brother.

"Ky?"

"Kam." Kyle jerked, and looked guilty and then when he saw Kurtis, he hung his head and sighed. "It's not what you think. Mr. Kilpatrick isn't doing anything bad. He's a grandfather for Christ's sake."

"Language," the three adults said at once.

"So what's going on?" Kam asked, and took the seat this Mr. Kilpatrick offered him. He made sure he was on one side of Kyle, and Kurtis on the other.

"It's a secret."

"Wrong answer," Kam said. "I know you don't understand, but that's a huge red flag to Mom, that's why she told us."

"And that's why you're here?"

"Yes. Out with it."

"Kyle, it's okay. I thought you would have told your brothers."

"No, you said it was a secret."

"I should have clarified. It's supposed to be a secret from my daughter."

"What's going on?" Kam demanded.

"My name is Keith Kilpatrick. I'm fifty years old, and sold my business last fall and retired at the end of last year. And, forgive my language, but I'm bored out of my goddamn mind. My wife owns her own business and is only forty-eight, I can't ask her to quit what she loves to travel with me, and I hate to travel to begin with. We have three children.

"Kelsey, our oldest lives in San Diego with his husband and their two children. Karen my oldest daughter lives in Houston with her husband and their three kids. And then, my baby, Kali lives in Devil's Nose and works all the time. At the beginning of this season, Kal invited us to a race. We've never been, ever. Never even heard of it."

"Where do you live?"

"My wife, Kathy and I live in Norton, and Kathy's business is in Lock."

"What does she do?"

"She owns Kilpatrick Nursery."

"Mom's favorite flower place." Kyle grinned when they glared at him. "Hey, you don't live at home, and I have to ride that way to pick up the stuff."

Kam covered his grin, then looked at Keith. "So, what's the secret?"

Kam and Kurt frowned when Keith looked over both his shoulders, then leaned in and motioned them forward. They leaned in and was shocked by what he had to say. "Dusty Hill is for sale. I've been talking to Kyle about it. He's befriended my daughter Kali, and I've listened to him talk to her, and I realized he'd be the perfect person to talk to."

"How?"

"Because, how many times do adults have conversations and don't pay attention to the kids around them, and they absorb anything the adults talk about."

"Damn, and you've been telling Mr. Kilpatrick all the track gossip?"

"Yes, and how the flagmen, officials and tow-truck drivers are hired and the safety crew."

"I've listened to my daughter, my shy, introverted daughter, scream profanities at Dusty Hill at the first race we ever went to, and she told us to wait until we went to a real track and saw how they should act. Let me tell you, the next night, we came here and holy hell, what a difference."

"We know." Kam sighed. "So, what else do you need or want to know?"

"I'd like to find out who has owned the track for the first forty years or so. But I can't find anything on the internet, and I've been kind of skulking in the background, listening to everyone. It's not public knowledge that the track is for sale, and once I do some research and talk to my wife, I'm going to offer a private bid before it's even listed."

"Hence the secret." Kam nodded. He looked at Kurt and they stared at each other, and when the hand signals started, Kam grinned when Kyle looked at Keith and sighed.

"They do that all the time, and nobody can understand them, but when they're done, they get bossy."

They finished and Kam looked at Keith. "You going home soon?"

"No, as a matter of fact, my wife's in the stands. She likes to listen to the fans, and hear what they have to say." He grinned. "Another spy."

Kam looked at Kyle, and said, "Go get Mom, Dad, and Kev. Tell Mom to bring our supper, tell Dad to bring the Dusty Hill file, and tell Kev to bring chairs."

"Why me?"

"Because, you scared the hell out of Mom, and this way you can tell her that if she comes, she can find out the secret."

"Oh," Kyle said, and jumped to his feet and ran away.

"Are you sure you're not his father?" Keith asked.

"Nope, just his oldest brother. Kurt's next, and then Kevin," Kam said, then held out his hand. "Kameron Kilbourne."

"Kurtis Kilbourne." Hands were shaken, and the three of them sat back and enjoyed the fire. Keith put more wood on, and from behind Kurt, Kam saw his family approach. He jumped to his feet and grinned as he hurried forward, and took the covered plate from his mother.

"It's all good, Mom. Nothing sinister," he whispered, and kissed her cheek and saw the relief in her face. They settled in and Kam made the introductions.

"Ky, I think you should start."

"Mom, the secret I've been keeping is that Mr. Kilpatrick asked me to help him. Dusty Hill is for sale, and he wants to know everything he can before he buys it."

"Say what?" Kevin asked in shock. "Where did you hear that?"

"A fan from the stands about two months ago, and then I talked to the guy who grades the track at Dusty Hill, and he said the same thing."

"God, I hope you know something about racing, because that track is horrible," Kam said as he shoveled a forkful of lasagna in. He grinned as he chewed. "Sorry, but I'm starving."

"I don't know anything about racing, but I know dirt."

"How so?"

"I owned and operated a heavy equipment company for thirty years. I sold it last year for a huge chunk of change, and retired, but I'm only fifty and bored out of my mind. I walked the track, and I'd like to bring in some clay, dig it up, add the clay and let it sit for the winter. Then I'd like to grade the driveways going in and marry them to the road."

"What about the stands?"

"I have my eye on new ones, where I can get dirt cheap. The only thing I don't know about is that damn scoreboard that doesn't work."

Kevin was the one that snorted. "The wiring is underground, and rumor is that it's broken or pulled apart."

"So, that means the track will have to be dug up to get to it?"

"Actually, no." Ken grinned. He opened the file Kam asked for, and passed over a paper. "According to this blueprint, someplace in the middle of the grassy spot in the center of the track is a metal cover, and it's basically a crawl space from the announcer's stand to the sign. You'd have to have someone Ky's size to access it."

"I'll do it." Ky grinned.

"We'll look into it," Ken said, and frowned when his youngest son's face lit up like it was Christmas, Thanksgiving, his birthday, and him winning the title for go carts in his class all in one. Oh, and a snow day and summer vacation. He jumped to his feet and actually yelled as he ran forward.

"You're here!" Ken turned in time to see confusion on the rest of his family's faces, and saw his son practically tackle a woman.

"I am." Kali said. She hugged the little boy, and held him out by the shoulders. "What are you doing here?"

"Talking to my friend and family. What are you doing here?" Kyle asked in confusion, as Mr. Kilpatrick stood and rushed forward. He grabbed his friend by the shoulders, and hugged her tightly.

"I didn't know you were coming."

"Last minute. I had to get the hell out of the office. Mom convinced me to spend the night." She looked around. "But, if you have company."

"No, no. Stay." He put his arm around her, and grinned as he turned. "Kathy and Kali, my wife and daughter. These are the Kilbournes, Kyle's family."

Kyle took his cue, and pointed. "My Dad, Ken, my mom, Kerri, my brother's Kevin, Kurtis, and Kameron." He grinned, and said, "I said that backward. Kam's the oldest, then Kurtis, then Kevin, and guess what?"

"What?" Kali frowned as she recognized the men who'd run into her when she'd arrived. She watched as Kyle walked behind his brothers, and put his hand on each shoulder proudly.

"Number eighteen, e-mods. Number eighteen crate. And number eighteen super late model."

"You little scamp," Kali said, and actually grabbed him and started tickling him. She looked up and saw everyone looking at her. "When he asked me if I had a favorite driver, I told him it was number eighteen for those three classes, but

I didn't know their names. He only said that he'd heard of them."

Everyone laughed and Kam stood. "So, you've only heard of us, huh?"

"Kam, I didn't mean anything by it. Please, don't tickle me, I have to pee already." Everyone laughed and Kam stopped.

"Introduce us to your friend, and then go shake it."

"Kameron," Kerri said firmly.

"Oops," he said, and grinned at his Mom.

"Everyone this is my not girlfriend Kali."

"What does that mean?"

"I told them I had a friend and she was a girl. They kept asking if you were my girlfriend. But, I didn't know how to explain you were a girl and my friend, but not my girlfriend."

"I actually followed that." Kali laughed. "How about we stick to just the label of friend?"

"Sounds good," he said, and ran away. While he was gone, Kam stepped forward and held out his hand. He saw her swallow hard and hesitate, but reluctantly took his hand and shook it.

"Kameron Kilbourne."

"Kali Kilpatrick," she said, and sighed when he didn't react to her deformed finger. But, there was some severe tingling going on, and she felt her nipples harden beneath her sweatshirt, and her girly parts wake up. The next man who offered his hand, said his name was Kurtis and the same thing happened when they shook hands. Same reaction and her girly parts woke further, but when Kevin shook her hand she felt nothing, and he did give a reaction. It was slight, but his eyes and nostrils flared.

Next, she was introduced to the parents, and afterward she excused herself and went into the camper. She took a quick shower and bundled into some clothes she'd left behind the last time she'd been in the camper.

"Hey, Mom," Kali asked, when she joined them, and laughed when two women sitting side by side answered her. "Do you have anything to eat? I'm starving. Haven't had anything since noon."

"I have some lasagna here," Kerri said, and jumped to her feet and took the dish out of Kam's hands.

"No, I don't want to take food away from him."

"Don't worry, he and Kurt's already eaten most of it. It was full when they found it."

"If you're sure?" she said, and went in for a fork. She sat down and was surprised the only empty chair was between Kameron and Kurtis. "Oh god, this is so good."

"Thank you," Kerri said, and everyone went back to their talk.

"Where's Kyle?"

"He said he had to go over to the RV," Kam said, then laid his head back and groaned. He looked across her at his twin, and they made hand motions and Kali frowned. It was a form of silent communication. Right in the middle of this they paused, then looked over their shoulder. Kali wrinkled her nose and stared at the men on either side of her. Suddenly, they leaned forward and closed in on her.

"Please, go along with it," Kam said, then leaned back. He nodded toward his other side, and Kali watched as Kyle came sauntering back into the circle around the fire, and sat down without saying anything, but she also noted that he kept edging his chair closer to her, but Kam was in his way. Kali studied him, and saw his hair was slicked back, and when she felt someone grip her hand, she jerked and looked down, then she grinned when she saw the napkin that Kurtis had given her, and she subtly wiped her eyes, because Kyle had put on some aftershave, and by the looks and smell of him, he had doused himself in it. She nodded to each man beside her and finished eating, and for Kyle's sake she was glad no one had said anything.

CHAPTER SIX

Early the next morning, Kali slipped out of her parents' camper as quietly as she could. She'd left a note propped up on the coffee pot, so they wouldn't worry about her, and she looked around in the early morning dawn, and frowned when she didn't see her SUV. Then, she grinned when she realized she'd arrived late the night before, and headed to where she thought she'd parked. Grinning she opened her door and started it up. She slowly left and was on the main road heading home as the sun broke over the horizon behind her.

During the drive to the track yesterday, she'd had an "aha" moment, and after getting to sleep after two this morning, she woke at her normal time of five, and a whole slew of new ideas for the Dillard case were running through her mind. She didn't normally stop at a fast-food place to eat, but decided to treat herself today, so she pulled in, ordered a breakfast sandwich, juice and coffee, and was back on the road in under five minutes. When she arrived home almost two hours later, she hurried in, made a pot of coffee and immediately went to her office, where she buckled down to get her ideas down on paper. Several hours later, while hugging a cup of coffee to herself, she walked slowly past the wall she used as a storyboard, then stepped back and did a happy dance.

The idea that had been eluding her was now all down on paper, just a couple more bugs to work out, and she was ready to rock her presentation at the end of the following week. Not bothering to check the time, she picked up her phone and made the first call.

"Dillard."

"Max? This is Kali Kilpatrick."

"Who?"

"Kali Kilpatrick, the woman working on your ad for The Wright Group."

"Oh no." Came the laugh. "The woman who has all the golden connections. I never did get back to you, so we could meet up, but I have to tell you this first. Thank you. I was able to sign all four Kilbourne brothers."

"Four? I thought there were only three?"

"Did I tell you we also make go-cart engines?"

"Oh my," Kali said, and laughed. She looked at her board and started moving things around, and grinned. "I'll get right to the point, I called because I'm at the stage that I need to start filming, or at the very least taking stills. I was wondering if we could meet up, so I could talk and interview your employees, and maybe talk to some of the customers."

"Why?"

"Because, I want to see what their opinion of working for Dillard's is. I have this idea, and I think if I talk to them, I'll be able to get what you're looking for on this ad."

"The thing is, I'm in California right now."

"Oh. I hope everything is alright?"

"It will be. See the wildfires going through Northern California took out one of our stores. I'm here assessing the damage, And will be for a few more days. Tell you what, I'll call my father and tell him what you want, and see if he can walk around with you. Is it alright if I give him your number."

"Absolutely, after all, he started this business thirty years ago. No offense to you, but I think your father will be a great help. What's his name?"

"Maxwell." Max laughed. "I gotta go, but I'll call him and tell him to call you no later than tomorrow."

"Thanks, Max." She hung up and did a happy dance, then looked at her board and did some more adjusting. She pulled out her list of people to call, and after the fifteenth call she actually put her hands in her hair, and screamed in frustration.

"That's one way to keep the burglars away," came a voice from the doorway of her office, and she screamed and picked up her stapler, and threw it before looking. When the tall, lanky man dodged the "bullet" and laughed when Kali screamed again, then jumped to her feet and reached him in only two steps. She tackled him to the ground, hugging, and kissing him.

"*KELSEY*! What are you doing here? How did you get my address? Where's Lyle and Jordan? Can you stay long? Do Mom and Dad know you're here?"

"Looks like he found her." Keith laughed as he stood at the end of the hallway, and watched as his oldest and youngest child reacquainted themselves after almost six years apart.

"Dad," Kali said as she sat up, and ended up sitting on her brother's stomach, like she'd always done when they were younger. "Why didn't you tell me Kelsey was coming?"

"Because, they didn't know until this morning." Kelsey grinned as he lifted her off him, then jumped to his feet and helped her up. With his arm around her shoulders, he grinned. "I had business in the area and have a couple days free. I went to Mom and Dad's, but they weren't home and when I called, they gave me your address and gave me directions. They said they'd be here later this afternoon."

"So, Lyle and Jordan aren't with you?"

"Not this trip, but hopefully soon." He grinned at his parents. "If you don't mind, I've been cooped up in a plane and car, so I'm going to steal Kal and have her walk me around the neighborhood, get the kinks worked out."

"Sure," Kathy said. "I'll just raid Kali's refrigerator, and put the stuff with what I have in the camper, and fix something for a light lunch."

"And I'm going to mow her lawn." Their father grinned as he reached up, and grabbed the keys to the garage and quickly left. Kali shook her head and slipped her feet into the shoes she'd kicked off earlier, and led her brother out of the back door, and around to the front.

"What do you own?" Kelsey frowned as he looked around her yard. He didn't flinch when she took his hand and walked down to the end of the land. "From this creek," she said, and moved her arm out straight. "All the way to that road, then up to the railroad tracks. Follow the tracks to that line of pine trees, then follow that back to the creek."

"Christ, how many acres?"

"It averages to be about six and a half."

"And how much did you pay for it?" When she told him he stumbled, and she frowned as she caught him.

"What's wrong?"

"For that price you can't even own a cardboard box in an alley where I live. And you have all this space. What are the schools like?"

"You really want to go for a walk?"

"Yes."

"Then, let's go this way," she said as she walked down her huge empty lawn, across the road and down a side road. They were silent as he looked all around the area. Halfway down the side road, she turned left onto another road, and then she stopped at the stop sign at the end of that short road.

"Why did we stop?"

"That's the elementary school." She pointed and looked at his shock. "The middle school and high schools are over in Arcade, but this is for pre-K through third. That's the public library, and the building there is the back side of a doctor's office, the post office, a bank, and the DMV office."

"All right here? All within walking distance?"

"Yes, come this way," she said, and linked her arm through his and turned left. At the end of that road she took another left, and pointed to the front of the building with all those businesses, and then they crossed another street and then crossed it again. Only a little way away she stopped on the sidewalk, and pointed. "There's the public park. The fire hall, the town hall."

"Holy shit." Kelsey turned in a circle and frowned. "So, where are we exactly? What's the name of this town?"

"Devil's Nose. If you go that way, South, you'll run into Machias, Farmersville, Franklinville and then into Olean. Go north and you'll run into Yorkshire, Wales, Holland, and eventually Buffalo. Then, some of the surrounding towns are Arcade, Springville, Strykersville, and Sandusky."

"I've heard of some of those towns when we grew up where Mom and Dad live, but what's the tax rate here?"

"Since we're in Cat County, it's eight percent. And before you ask, I work in downtown Buffalo, and on a bad traffic day it takes an hour and ten minutes to get home, but it's pretty much expressway all the way." They started walking back toward her house, and when he stopped suddenly, she looked at him. "What?"

"That's your house."

"Yes. Kel, what's wrong?"

"Keep a secret?"

"Of course."

"I told Mom and Dad I had a couple days free from an appointment, which is true, absolutely true, so that's not the secret. But, as we speak, Lyle's at his own appointment and he's going to pick Jordan and Missy up at his parents' house and come here. We are ninety-five-percent sure that we will get the jobs we interviewed for, and move back here. We've been talking about it, and didn't want to move close to our parents. We want the kids to be able to run and grow."

"Wait! Who's Missy? What do you mean kids, plural?" Before he could answer, a strange car came slowly up the road, and Kelsey ran to it and started pointing. Kali saw her father in the back yard, and waved to get his attention. Once the mower was shut off, she bellowed, *"MOM!"*

"What in the world?" Kathy asked as she and Keith came around the corner of the house. "What are you bellowing about?"

Kali only pointed and the three of them turned and watched as Kelsey's husband, Lyle, exited out the back of the car with their adopted son, Jordan, and Kelsey backed out holding a baby not much older than six months, and her parents rushed forward in shock. Kali arrived just in time to hear her brother say, "It's a girl." The excitement went on for several minutes, and when it calmed down, Jordan spoke.

"Daddy, what's that?" And he pointed to the ground.

"What's what?" Lyle asked his four-year-old son.

"That. On the ground?"

"Show me." Lyle put him down, and everyone watched as they saw the little boy reach down and touch the grass and giggled.

"It tickles, what is it?"

"You mean the grass?" Lyle asked in shock. He joined his son, and it wasn't long before Kelsey was with them, and they walked around and told him what everything was. At one point Keith took over, and Kali told her brother to take his husband for a walk. The three of them took care of the kids. By the time they were back, the kids had been fed, baby Missy was sleeping, and Jordan had just fallen asleep.

Lyle, always one to get right to the point, walked up to Kali, and after he hugged her and kissed her cheek, he said, "Not that I don't believe Kel, but do you have proof for how much you paid for this place?"

Kali laughed and dragged him to her office, and pulled the file and showed him. "Holy shit. We live in a one-bedroom loft and our rent alone is three times of your monthly mortgage payment, and that's not including utilities or insurance."

"So, what are you saying?" Kelsey asked.

"I got the job." Lyle grinned. "I say we move. As much as I love both sets of our parents, I don't want to live in the city. When our son doesn't know what grass is, it's time to give them space to run. Hell, what's an hour's commute compared to what we're used to?" He looked at Kali and grinned. "A good commute is three hours, one way."

"Holy shit."

"Son?" Kathy asked from the doorway. "What's Lyle talking about?"

"Looks like we're moving home, Mom," he said, and Kathy squealed and hugged them both. They spent the rest of the afternoon talking about plans, and it was decided that Keith would leave the camper at Kali's, and for the next two days Kelsey, Kyle, and the kids would stay there, but they had complete use of Kali's house while she was at work.

CHAPTER SEVEN

On Monday when Kali returned home from work, she was shocked when she saw a little boy running and laughing through her lawn, and remembered her family was staying with her. She parked and waved to Lyle as she got out of the truck, and slowly made her way into her house, and stopped and grinned. Her brother, Kelsey, was at the stove and he was stirring several pots and pans. What surprised her was that there wasn't a huge mess.

"Hey," he said as he saw her, and adjusted the flame under the pans. "I didn't know what time you'd be home, but we always eat around six, so I thought I'd just plan on that for here. You don't mind do you?"

"Not at all. Let me go change," she said, and paused long enough to kiss his cheek, then went to change. Ten minutes later she was walking back down the hall, and paused when Kelsey called out to her.

"What's this?" He pointed to the ad she'd been working on. He stood in her office, looking at her wall.

"An advertisement that I have to present next week, but I'm having trouble with it."

"Looks good to me, what's the trouble?"

She went on to explain how she was in the contest, her concept and then the problem she'd run into. During the telling of it, Lyle had joined them, and she was happy with the intelligent questions they asked.

"So, let me get this straight," Lyle said. "This is your ad." He waved his hands around the boards on the wall. "And you need to make this into a commercial, so you need someone with video equipment and experience, but they can't work for The Wright Group?"

"Correct. See Matt and I always work together, he's the tech guy. I do this, we put it to film, then he tweaks the bugs out, but for this campaign, he has to work on his own, and I have to work on my own. I've been at the Dillard factory today, and took some stills, but it's not the same."

"If you had a tech person, could they use this work as part of their portfolio?"

"I don't know. I'd have to look into that." Kali frowned. "Why do you ask?"

"Remember my brother, Brian?" At her frown, he grinned. "He was the youngest that stood up at the wedding."

"Oh, yeah. He's what, sixteen, seventeen?"

"No, he's actually twenty-two, but he's taking AV and all the tech stuff at UB. I could call him to see if he wants to help. He mentioned he needed a huge project before the end of the semester, and was clueless as to what he was going to do."

"Yes." Kali grinned. Lyle stepped out and Kali helped Kelsey finish cooking the meal and set the table. They were almost done when someone pounded on her front door, and when Kali jerked in shock, both men jumped to their feet and told her to stay there. When they came back, Kali looked in shock. "Brian?"

"Hey," He grinned. They exchanged hugs and everyone laughed when he helped himself to the leftovers, and mumbled between mouthfuls. "Broke college student."

When he was done, Lyle cleaned up while Kelsey started getting Jordan ready for bed, and Kali took Brian to her office.

"Before I tell you what I'm looking for, tell me what you're looking for? Lyle said you had a major project for the end of the year?"

"Yeah, and the bitch of it is, that's three weeks away. I had a project going with someone I was dating, but we broke up and she took all the work with her. That was last week, and we were almost done. Just had to do the final tweaking."

"Damn. So what was it on?"

"We were able to pick our teams of workers, but we had to draw from a hat the subject matter. And of all things, we pulled automotive."

"Really?"

"Yes, all subjects were in the broad spectrum, and it was our project to narrow it down to one aspect and roll with it. She picked car sales, she was the one that came up with the concept, I just let it shine on film."

"And what did you have to make?"

"Oh, a three minute commercial."

Kali leaned against her desk, and grinned. "What would you say if I admit that I'm about to rock your world?"

"I'd have to say eew, only because you're my brother-in-law's sister. You're family."

"I am. And family has to stick together. I was given a case that's due at the end of next week, and this is for a paying client. All the information I had been given was they wanted new ideas."

"So, it's basically an open slate."

"Yes. I have the concept, I almost have all the story, but my boss assigned us to groups, he's making it a competition, and the tech guy I always use is a team of his own, like I am. The other two teams have five members each."

"That's not fair."

"I know. Would you like to see my concept?"

"Yes." Brian rubbed his hands together, and stood where Kali positioned him, then she reached up and started taking the white sheet down that she'd covered her board with. She stepped back and looked over her shoulder when Kelsey and Lyle joined her. Brian took his time as he walked each board then stepped back and formed his hands into a square, then looked, and it was a good thirty minutes before he said anything.

"Two questions."

"Yes?"

"One, who and what is Dillard's, and two, where are you going to get actors and race cars?"

"Leave the race cars to me. They're only a phone call away. As for Dillard's, they're an auto parts store on the west coast."

"Think a store in every town in California," Lyle said. "But, also in Oregon, Washington, Idaho, Nevada, Utah, Arizona. Almost every major big city west of the Rockies. We're talking multi-billionaire, and yes, that's with a B."

"And if I help you, can I use this for my college presentation?"

"I'll make sure you can."

"But, if they're multi-billionaires out west, why are they here?"

"They had some family issues and came home. The owner that started Dillard's with his brother thirty years ago, moved his family and came home, as his wife's family is here. While the brother and his family stayed in Cali to run Dillard's West. Well, that's what I call them to keep them apart, Dillard's West, and Dillard's East. The only question now, is when are you available? I can work on this during regular working hours, so I don't have to punch a clock."

"I don't have classes on Tuesday and Wednesday. Then I'm booked until about two Friday afternoon. And I'll be free for the weekend."

"Perfect. If you're available tomorrow, then can you be at The Wright Group at nine?"

"I can, that's downtown, right?"

"Correct," Kali said, and hugged him. "Don't worry, after tomorrow I'll be strictly professional, but since we're family I had to hug you. We're going to rock this and you'll have access to the school's equipment to do the final cut?"

"Yes, and when I go into class on Thursday, I'll sign up for night time, after five for the equipment, then you can come over after work, if we need to reshoot anything, we'd have the next day."

"Excellent." They talked for a few more hours, and everyone was happy after Brian left. When she was locking up, she frowned when she saw someone sitting out on her deck. She let herself out quietly and listened. She approached, and her brother looked up and grinned.

"She couldn't sleep, so I'm showing her the stars. We don't see these where we are."

"Never thought you'd survive in the city as long as you did, but it's wonderful that you're coming home."

"That's what we missed the most there, being with family."

"Well, we're here for you. I'm going to turn in, I'll leave the back door open for you if you need it."

"Do you normally lock it at night?"

"No."

"Damn, I grew up where we never locked our doors, and remember how many times Karen couldn't find her keys?"

Kali giggled. "Because, she left them in the ignition overnight. I still do that here. I don't lock my doors unless I'm going to be gone overnight, I've been known to leave my keys in the truck, and even in the lawnmower. Dad's the only one that hangs them. Hell, I've even left the key to the garage in the lock for weeks on end."

"So, you're happy here?"

"I am. And I'm not going to beg you to move to this area, I'll support you wherever you and Lyle move to. I'm just happy you're coming home, and I get to see my niece and nephew more."

"I know," he said, and put Missy on his shoulder and began rubbing her back, and they smiled when she sighed and began to fall asleep. Kelsey then took the opportunity to reach out and take his sister's hand in his. She started to jerk her hand from his when he began massaging her two dead fingers.

"And you? Are you happy? Are you dating anyone?"

She shrugged, and when he gave her a look, she sighed. "I have my work and my house. It's hard to get out there."

She held up her hands to indicate that both her ring fingers and pinkies were permanently bent. "I was trying for a while, but seeing the subtle to not-so-subtle reactions, I gave up, and decided to concentrate on my home and career. I'm only twenty-four, Kel, I've got plenty of time to look for someone, but I want it to be special from the beginning."

"I understand. But, I want you to know that I'll be here for you."

"I know, but I can handle it, and I know what happens when you're there for me, especially when you and Karen are there together." She grinned when he scowled and reached up and rubbed the side of his head.

"I swear you gave us each a concussion when you knocked our heads together. You need to find that girl again, then you'll be unstoppable. Do you know Dad's calling you the shy, introverted one?"

"I am I guess, especially in new situations. I'll get there. It just takes time."

"Twenty-one years Kal? It's been that long."

"I know." She sighed and stood and kissed the top of her brother's head. "I love you, Kelsey, and I know you want to protect me, but no matter how much you try, there's always going to be some asshole out there that's going to freak the fuck out, and start calling me a cripple. It's happened before and I appreciate you beating them up for me, but there comes a time when a girl's got to grow her own thick skin. I'm not there yet, but I'm working on it. I believe with my whole heart that there's a man out there that won't even notice my problem. That's the man I'm looking for."

"Good luck, and I won't push."

"Thank you." She kissed him again, and slowly turned and went into her house.

"That went well," Lyle said as he joined his husband, and looked at him holding their daughter.

"It did. I was surprised. Five years ago, she would have jerked her hands away, and wrapped her arms around her middle, and cowered in a corner. That's the first time in years she's let me touch her."

"Maybe you should listen to her that she's thickening her skin, but she's doing it on her time. Do you think she's remembered?"

"I don't know. Mom or Dad hasn't said anything. Maybe I'll talk to Dad about it tomorrow."

"Maybe you should, but I came to tell you that I heard back from California."

"And?"

"And we both can stay for another full week."

"Thank god," he said, and he stood and together they slowly made their way down to the camper, and as they settled in bed, they quietly discussed the houses in the area they wanted to go look at.

CHAPTER EIGHT

"That went well." Brian grinned as he and Kali loaded everything in the back of her SUV, and climbed in.

"It did, and I knew Max and Maxwell would help you with your school project."

"It was great that they gave me permission to use whatever we did, and from your point of view, I'm liking this more and more every day. I'm glad the first part is done, now we'll just have to work on the second."

"Let me get that. If my plan pans out, we can do it this weekend."

"Really? That fast?"

"Yes, what's the earliest you can be at my house on Friday?"

"Noon? It's the class for this project, so I can tell my professor I'm working on it."

"Perfect, I'll see you then, and bring your cameras. I don't know what you're going to need, but definitely stills and video."

"I'll have it," he said, and they rode in silence back to her office, where Brian took everything with him. Kali wasn't about to give Suzie another opportunity to steal from her. She went into her office and answered her e-mails and voicemails. When she looked up and realized it was already going on six, she quickly called her brother and said she was working late, then when she saw she was the last one in the office, she decided to make a very important phone call.

"Hello."

"Dad, its Kali."

"Hey, what's up?"

"Question for you."

"Shoot."

"Do you happen to have any of the Kilbournes' phone numbers?" When there was nothing but silence on the other end of the line, she frowned. "Dad? Hello?"

"Oh, sorry. I thought you said you wanted the Kilbournes' phone numbers."

"I do. Or if you don't have them, you seemed pretty chummy with them this past weekend. Do you know when they'll be at Dusty Hill again?"

"Friday."

"That's what I thought. Do the pits open at four?"

"No, noon. And when I talked to Ken last, he said the boys would be there around one."

"Perfect."

"Can I ask what this is about?"

"I'm working on that commercial for Dillard's and the Kilbournes figure into it. I've got most of it filmed and I need to talk to them about it. I'll need their permission and then when I show them what I want, get their input."

"Okay. Your mother and I are planning on being at your place at noon on Friday. Thought I'd run up and see them. Want me to tag along? Break the ice?"

"Sure, that would be great. I'll see you then. Oh, and Dad?"

"Yes?"

"Do you remember Brian? Lyle's youngest brother?"

"Sixteen, seventeen now? He was the youngest groomsman in the wedding?"

"Yes, but he's twenty-two and a senior at U of B. He's my tech guy, taking pictures and video, so he'll be with us."

"That's fine," Keith said, and began to grin. "So, we'll see you Friday, and you'll have the plans or whatever you call them with you?"

"I will. Thanks, Dad, I know I should suck it up and pull up my big girl panties, but..."

"You don't have to explain anything to me, Kal. But don't be surprised if Kelsey doesn't tag along. He doesn't know what we do on the weekends. I've never told him."

"Neither have I." Kali laughed. "You think he and Lyle would like it?"

"I don't know, but your mother and I ordered child headphones for them, and had them rushed overnight. They arrived today."

"For their ears, and I'm sure we can adjust the face shields."

"That's what I thought," Keith said. "Maybe if they go with us to talk to the Kilbournes, with us walking around and seeing it, they'll want to go, but I won't push them."

"Neither will I. If you remember, I only said I'd introduce you to what I liked, and you could take it from there."

"And I did. Okay, I'll let you go, so you can get back to work."

"Naw, I'm going home now, it's almost six thirty, and I've put in a long, hard day, I was out filming most of the morning, but I'm ready to go home. Hopefully, Kelsey will have a meal waiting for me." She laughed when her father said he was on his own, because his wife was off to some garden meeting.

*****

At exactly noon on Friday, both her parents and Brian pulled into her driveway, and it was Keith who decided to park in the side yard. He came up and joined them and took his grandson from his son. "I parked down there, because it'll be easier to get out."

"You're right." She grinned and went to get her stuff. Brian followed her and watched and when he realized what she was doing, he helped her.

After helping her load everything into her truck, he asked, "So, what next?"

"Next, we go talk to the people for the second part of the commercial, and explain what we want, why we want it, and when we want it. Then, we ask if they'll do it."

"Damn, and you know someone who could help you or us?"

"Watch and learn, grasshopper," Kali said, and Brian stared at her, then burst out laughing. She looked up and saw her mother showing Jordan the different flowers they were going to weed, and Kelsey and Lyle opted to ride with Keith, and Brian rode with Kali as they headed to the track.

"How long has this been here?" Brian asked in confusion as they followed Keith into the 'pit entrance' driveway.

"Fifty, fifty-five years. I'm not sure."

"Damn." He looked around like a kid in a toy store, and he jumped out as soon as they parked, then grabbed a camera and began snapping pictures. No one saw the expression on Keith's face.

"Where to?" Kali asked her father, and tightened her grip on her portfolio, and was grateful none of the men offered to carry it for her.

"They park over here," he said, and then held his arm out and pointed. They waited as several rigs with cars enclosed or out in the open on trailers drove by. After crossing the road, they slowly walked forward, with Keith and Kali in the lead, Kelsey and Lyle behind them, and Brian flitting around snapping pictures.

"There." Keith pointed, and Kali stopped and studied the people she'd come to see. Everyone waited for her, and after she drew in a deep breath and let it out slowly, she nodded to some inner statement, then said, "I'm ready."

They approached and stopped while still several feet away, and Kali covered her mouth and giggled. "Oh my. I wonder what he did." They watched as Kyle came running out of a camper with Kevin hot on his heels. Ky didn't get very far before he was lifted literally by the seat of his pants, and Kevin started yelling at him.

"You little brat. Wait until Dad gets here, he's going to make you clean it up."

"But, I was hungry. Kam doesn't have any food in his RV. Kev, I'm just a growing boy." Kali heard Kyle whine to his brother.

"That's because you ate all my damn food," came a voice from further away and then a huge sigh. "Better put him down, Kev. Don't want the poor starving boy to waste away to nothing. But little does he know, Dad told me that he's got to clean all the RVs before he can go over to the track tonight." Kameron grinned at the shock on his youngest brother's face, then turned and began working on the engine of the car with the hood up.

Kali saw all the cars, but she only focused on Kameron, Kevin and Kyle. She stepped forward only a few steps when she stopped and covered her mouth. She looked at her father and pointed. Kyle was sneaking up behind Kameron and he bent down and picked up a stone, then actually pulled a slingshot from his back pocket. Kali and her family crept forward and were only about four feet away when Kyle let the stone go, then suddenly there was this ungodly scream, Kameron jerked to a standing position, hitting his head on the hood latch, and whipped around and glared at his brother.

"You son of a bitch," he yelled, and put his hand on his head, and scowled when he pulled it away and everyone saw the blood.

"Mom's not a bitch, you moron. Wait until I tell her you called her that," Kyle said, and stuck out his tongue at him and whipped around, and stopped when he saw Kali and the others.

"Oh." He had such a guilty look on his face that Kali giggled, then frowned when she saw and heard Kurtis.

"What the fuck, Kam! What the fuck did you do, I've got this ungodly pain on the top of my head," he said from the back of his trailer, and stalked toward his brother.

"Twins?" Kelsey asked from behind them.

"Yep," Keith said, and looked at Kali and saw her expression. He looked back and saw that Kurtis had removed Kam's hand from his head, and he was bleeding so badly the blood was running down his face and though his fingers. Suddenly beside him, Kali let out a bloodcurdling scream and fainted. It was so sudden that the men with her didn't catch her in time.

Believe it or not, it was Kameron who ran over, picked her up and said, "My RV." He carried Kali up the steps, right in and laid her on the couch. As soon as he stood, some man he'd never seen before rushed to her side, and his brother and Keith rushed to his. Keith began barking orders, and Kameron was surprised they were followed, even by him.

"I said sit your ass down, Kilbourne," Keith said sternly, and pushed him into a chair. He inspected the cut and breathed a sigh of relief. He quickly washed and bandaged it, then pointed to the sink, and demanded he wash his hands and face.

"What's going on here?" Ken asked as he rushed in, and saw how crowded the RV was. When no one said anything, he finished entering, put his fisted hands on his hips and glared. He only had to say one word before the guilty party caved.

"Boys."

"It was Kam's fault. He didn't have any food in his RV, so I made a sandwich at Kev's. He told me I had to clean all the RVs before going to the stands tonight, and I hit him in his fat ass with a stone from my slingshot. It's not my fault he hit his hard head. If he would have bought some food, it wouldn't have happened," Kyle said all this in one breath.

Ken closed his eyes, and sighed. "So you hit Kameron in the ass with a slingshot, and he hit his head and is bleeding, all because you were told to do something around the house."

"But, Dad, it's not a house, it's an RV."

"So, who screamed like a bloody girl?" Ken glared at Kameron while asking this.

"She did," Kyle said, and everyone looked to where he pointed. Ken saw Keith, and Kali, who happened to be passed out on the couch. Then, he saw three other men he'd never seen before.

"Do you know what's going on?"

"We only arrived a few minutes before the slingshot deal, but it's a long story as to why Kali passed out." He looked down and saw her coming to, and when she sat up she swayed and looked at Kameron, and slammed her hand over her mouth.

"That way," Kameron pointed to the bathroom, and everyone watched as she bolted down the hall, and as they heard her empty her stomach, everyone left to give her privacy.

Outside, a man Kameron had never met handed him a wet rag, and said, "It's the blood on the hand and face." He watched as Kam scrubbed his face and turned it this way and that, and Kurt made sure it was all gone. "I'm Kelsey Kilpatrick, by the way, Kali's brother, and this is my husband, Lyle, and his brother Brian, who happens to be a work colleague of Kali's."

"So, you guys aren't dating her?" Kyle spoke up.

"Kyle," Four men said in exasperation, and sighed.

"No we're not." Kelsey grinned. "We're her family."

"Oh. So, why's she puking?"

"That's it," Kameron said, and rushed into his RV, and everyone heard rustling and doors or drawers slamming, then he came out and no one said a word when he handed Kyle a solid black card about three inches wide by six inches tall. Kali was watching out the bathroom window, and saw all of the Kilbournes stare at Kyle, while her family had confused expressions. She finished up and went out and stood in the doorway to watch what was going on.

"Kyle," Ken said sternly, and everyone watched as the cocky young man turned into a sullen little boy as he reached for the card.

Before he took it, he looked at Kameron with soulful eyes, and his bottom lip quivered, when he asked quietly, "How long?"

"Thirty minutes," Kameron said firmly, and watched when the boy took the card, put it in his pocket and turned and walked away. As he passed Kurtis, he reached down and took the slingshot from Kyle's other back pocket, and received such an evil glare that Kali had to use both hands to stifle her giggle. No one said a word as they watched Kyle climb the steps to Kevin's RV, and shut the door behind him.

"Thanks a lot, Kam," Kevin said, and sighed. "God, that was hard to watch."

"I know," Kam said, and put his hands on his knees and breathed deeply.

"Can I ask what that was about?" Kali asked, and everyone whipped around and stared at her. It was Kam who reached her first. He helped her down the steps and lifted her chin to look into her eyes.

"You look better."

"I'm fine. I'm sorry I made a scene, how are you?"

"I'll survive." He shrugged, then sighed. "How long have you been coming to the tracks?"

"This is my fifth year."

"So, you know what it means when a driver gets a black flag?"

"Yes," she said, and looked at the three that didn't know about racing. "A black flag for the driver means they're being kicked off the track for the rest of the race, for mostly unsportsmanlike conduct."

"And in a drivers' meeting, if a driver gets one of those cards, that means they're kicked out of the whole circuit, never to return, but we use the black card for a time-out process. That's why he asked for how long. It'll give him time to reflect on why he received it, and time for us to get a break from him. Don't get me wrong, I love him with all my heart, but it's been a trying few days, and it's going to get worse."

"Why?"

"Because, he's almost out of school for the summer, and he's going to be cooped up in the RVs and traveling with us. Track to track to track. He won't be able to run and play with his friends."

"Oh."

"So, if you're okay, can I ask why you're here?"

"Oh," she said, and stepped away from him and looked around, and smiled when Brian held out a huge black zippered thin case. "If you have the time, I'd like to talk to all of you," she said, and pointed around at the Kilbournes.

"How much time?" Kurtis frowned.

Kali looked at Brian with raised brows. "Thirty minutes?"

"Yeah, that'll work."

Then, she grinned and turned back. "Thirty minutes, but I need a space everyone can see."

"My RV worked earlier, let's go there," Kameron said, and they went in and he passed out bottles of water, and Kevin swore.

"That little shit."

"What?" Kam frowned.

"You have plenty of food in your refrigerator. He said it was empty."

"It is of what he eats, but I don't eat pies, and cakes, and junk. I have plenty of lunch meat, fresh veggies and fruit."

"Oh," Kevin said, and everyone saw him blush.

"You'll learn." Kam grinned, then turned to Kali and did some fancy hand signals to Kurtis, and suddenly the lights came on.

"Must be a twin thing." Kali shook her head. "Okay, may I use this island?"

"Yes. Where do you want us?"

"Sitting in front there will do fine." She waited until everyone was situated, then drew in a deep breath, and began, "As you know I'm Kali Kilpatrick. I work for a company called The Wright Group, and I'm an ad executive, which means a client comes to us wanting an advertisement made up about their product, and it's my job to talk to them and get an idea of what they want, and present it to them. If they like it they hire us."

"Okay, I understand," Kameron said. He seemed to be running the show. "Anyone have any questions so far?" When no one did, he nodded to her.

"Almost five weeks ago, my boss called all us ad execs, and techies together and passed out an assignment."

"Techie?" Kam frowned.

"The guy who takes pictures and video." Brian spoke. "And, in this case, it would be me."

"What Mr. Wright did that day was very unusual. I've worked for them for seven years, and not once in all that time has he done what he has with this case."

"Which is?"

"Normally he assigns the cases to an ad exec, and they have their own team to work with, but on this case he called us together, and divided us into four teams to compete for this account. However, if a techie isn't on your team, you can't use them or the office equipment. There are two teams of five, and two teams of one. I am a team of one, and my techie I always work with is also a team of one. We're lost. Because, he doesn't do what I do, and I don't do what he does, but my brother-in-law told me about his brother and I hired Brian to help with this."

"You're going to pay me?" He looked at her in excited shock.

"I was, but since you're doing this for a school project too..." She let that die out, and laughed at his disappointment. "Anyway, we were all given the same information and six weeks to do what we do. The six weeks are up next Friday. I've contacted the client and have his permission to do some things at his factory. This is going to be a two part commercial for national television and I'd like your help for the second half."

"Ours as in how?" Kameron frowned.

"Show them, Kal," Brian said, and she jerked, then grinned. She opened the portfolio and began laying things out, and stopped cold when Kameron told her to.

"Your client is Max Dillard? Oh my god. It was you."

"Excuse me?"

"Max showed up here a few weeks ago, and it just happened to be a few days after we found out we were losing our sponsor. He not only signed on as all of our sponsors, but he even gave Kurt a new motor. He said a friend of Ky's told him about us. That was you, wasn't it?"

"It might have been," she hedged, then as he looked at her, she sighed. "Yes, it was me. I thought that maybe we could help each other out. I tell him who needed or wanted sponsors, I do his ad, he hires me, and you get your sponsors, and maybe help me sometime."

"For what you did," Ken said. "I personally have no problem helping you, but what type of help are we talking about?" Kali began going over her commercial, and ended up taping the papers to the doors and refrigerator, so they could see the whole concept and then at the end she had to discuss several times what she wanted them to do.

"The only problem I see right now, if you agree, we have the drivers and the cars, but where would we find a track?"

"Why not use Dusty Hill?" Ken asked. "I know the owner, I can ask him for permission to use it. It's not like we'll be running a race."

"I agree, it might take a few takes to get it the way I want it, and then I'll have the cue cards for you to read. Should only take a couple hours, and I don't know how you feel about this, but I was thinking that when you drive on the track we'll start with Kameron, then Kurtis, then Kevin, leaving Kyle for last. But, when you drive off, I want you to leave, youngest to oldest. And I don't know how it works, but as one leaves the track, I'd like it dark, as in nighttime, but with the all the track lights on. Then, have one set of lights turn off, then another as another drives off, so that the screen goes black after Kameron drives off, then in the commercial the Dillard logo from Max comes on the black screen, and I'll have a voice saying the tag line."

"Damn, and they pay you to do this?" Kurtis asked in shock.

"Who do you think makes the commercials? Not a Hollywood crew, it's people like me and Brian that are in the trenches doing this for a living."

"Are you any good?" came a voice from behind them, and they turned to see Kyle standing there. "I mean, have you done any commercials we might have seen?"

"Ever see the Buffalo Bills commercials? Or how about the commercial for Red Solo Cups?" Kelsey asked the younger man.

"Of course."

"Kali did those. She even won awards for her commercials."

"Oh," he said and with his hands behind his back he walked the boards and everyone watched him with a smirk. He turned, and said, "I'll do it, but you have to change this."

"What?" Kali asked, and walked over to him.

"If you have Kam, then Kurt drive up and get out, have them stand almost shoulder to shoulder," he said, and went to his brothers, then had them stand the way he described. "Then, have Kevin drive up and he stands here. I'll drive up, and sit on the two cars here." He sat on a chair before them. "What are the Dillards saying?"

"From our family to yours."

"Then, if we're last have us say, 'And from ours, you can always trust Dillard's to get you down and dirty to get to the finish line.'"

"Oh my god, perfect," Kali said, and began hunting through drawers and it was Kam that directed her where to find paper and pen.

They wrote it down, and then Brian said, "I've been thinking about this. Why not have their parents off to the side. They don't have to be in the shot, but because the dirt will be flying, and if they use the cars out there, then the Dillard logo will be front and center, but what if their mom calls out something about it's getting late, and they've played in the dirt long enough for one day. They look at each other, and say..."

He paused, and without prompting the four Kilbournes looked at each other, grinned and said, "Aw, Mom."

"That, exactly like that," Brian said, from behind his camera as he snapped pictures. "Then, Kyle can start going off the track, then whatever order, they follow each other and the lights go out, but just as Kameron, right, the last one leaving?"

"Yes."

"Just before Kameron goes off and it's like a setting sun, their father could say something along the lines that at least with a Dillard motor, they can trust their family will be safe."

"I like that," Kam and Ken said.

"And then Kam goes off the track, the last set of lights go off and the screen goes black?" Kurtis asked as he came around and pointed to some papers.

"Yes, then the Dillard logo will appear, and I can have a voice say what Ken says. "Trust in Dillard to keep you and your family safe."

"I like it," Keith said into the silence. "I know I don't have a say, but I pictured it. What was the beginning of the commercial?"

"It's statements with the workers over in the Arcade factory. I've asked them to describe working with Dillard's in five words, and that's where Brian will do his thing and piece them together."

"Have you done that already?"

"Yes. And some of the statements they've made have been, family, honest, safe, and trustworthy."

"So, that ties into what you want us to do," Kam said, and sat back down.

"Yes. But, I have to warn you."

"About?"

"At my presentation, mind you, there are three other teams, but if my presentation is picked, then this commercial will be national, not just local, but I can guarantee when it goes local, the attendance at the tracks you race will rise almost by fifty percent."

"How can you say that?"

"Because this." She waved her hand in front of the four of them, and laughed. "What you have going on here. You are four hot, sexy men, and I guarantee that fifty percent of that rise in attendance will be single women wanting to get to know you." She laughed as they stared at her in shock, but then someone outside called to them and they all exited the trailer, except for Kameron and Kurtis who helped her take the papers down that she'd taped up, and before they were completed, Kali found herself boxed in the corner at the kitchen sink.

"So, you think we're all that, huh?" Kam whispered, and he lowered his head to her.

"You think we're hot and sexy?" Kurtis whispered from her other side, and she swallowed hard.

"Yes."

"Good, because we think you're hot and sexy too," they said, then stepped back and put the papers on top of the others. "Shut the door on your way out." Kam grinned at her and they left. Outside the twins looked at each other, and high fived and went back over to their cars. They didn't see the grins Ken and Keith exchanged, after having seen what they'd done.

"So, Sunday night?" Keith asked Ken.

"I think so. If Kali's coming to the races tonight, then I'll find her after intermission, and tell her I talked to the owner, and he said Sunday will be fine."

"Works for me, just don't talk to her during any of the boys' races, or she'll literally slap you down. I tried to ask her questions when I first started coming here. I still have a freaking bruise on my shoulder." They laughed as Keith went to his family and Ken went to his.

CHAPTER NINE

Kali stepped out of the shower Sunday morning, and after drying off she didn't bother with her blow dryer, and only ripped a brush through her hair, letting it dry naturally. With a towel wrapped around her, she went into her bedroom, and sighed as she looked into her closet. Because it was only ten in the morning, and it was almost eighty degrees, she decided to get out shorts. She normally only wore them around her family, and since that was all who was there, she nodded and threw on a tank. And because it was only family and too freaking hot, she didn't worry about the scars on her arms.

She went into the kitchen and poured herself a cup of coffee, and went to her office. Yes, her brother and his family and her parents were there, but she had last-minute work to do before she had to film the Kilbournes that evening. She frowned when the sound of a rumble finally penetrated, and she got up to go investigate. She didn't see anything until she saw Kelsey and Lyle holding the kids, and staring out over her empty yard. She joined them and frowned.

"What's going on?"

"No clue," Kelsey said. "You expecting company?" He pointed and she looked down on the street where her father was directing traffic, and one, two, and then three rigs backed smoothly into her yard, all lined up against the street, then just as slick a huge fifth wheeler backed in.

"What the hell's going on?" Kali frowned and watched as the Kilbournes exited their RVs and joined her father, and once they were all together they started up the hill, but she also noticed that the three oldest boys all carried a cooler.

"Morning," Kameron said as he paused beside her. "Where do you want this?"

"What's this? What's going on?"

"You live here right? That's your property down there?"

"Yes."

"Your Dad said we could park there until we're needed tonight. It's closer than us driving home, then coming back. At home we're scattered. Here, we're together."

"And where is home?"

"Sandusky."

"So, you live over the other hill?"

"Yep. Howdy neighbor." He grinned and saw her mother, and started forward when she called to him. Kali continued to stare in shock as everyone walked by her. Once the last Kilbourne passed, Kelsey put Jordan down and he ran after them, and it wasn't long before he had Kyle chasing him. An hour later Kali found herself again sitting between Kameron and Kurtis, and for the life of her she had no clue how that had happened.

"So, how much do you own?" Kameron asked her, and she explained, and when she turned and pointed to the pines, she whipped back around and looked at him in shock.

Kam whipped around and jumped to his feet, and called out, "Kyle what the hell are you doing?"

"Can't you see I got my dick in my hand, you dickhead. I'm taking a piss, what does it look like? If you had a dick maybe you'd know the concept."

"I'm going to kick his ass into next week," Kameron said "I swear to god." He glared down at Kali when she giggled. "This isn't funny. He's gone too far this time. Kurt, you go that way and I'll go this. He's hemmed in by the tracks and creek. I'll hang him by his ankles from that oak tree when we get him." He pointed and started forward.

"STAND DOWN!" came a deep, deep voice that was so authoritive that everyone in the back lawn, even six-month-old Missy, froze. They all turned and watched as a man standing tall at six foot four, dressed in military fatigues, stepped out of the shadows, and stood there. With one look, Kali knew he was active military.

"Kent!" Kerri was the first to react as she screamed the guy's name, jumped to her feet, and literally jumped into his arms, and it was seconds later they were locked in a lip lock. That spurred the others into action, and Ken was the second one who reached him, but he only slapped the man on the back, hugged him, then stood on the other side of Kerri.

"Dad," Kameron and Kurt said at the same time, and hurried forward and hugged him, then shook his hand, first Kam, then Kurt, and finally Kevin. When the man named Kent looked around and frowned, he shook his head and whistled. Everyone turned to see Kyle as he was climbing a tree, and when he saw who'd whistled at him, he jumped several feet and screamed. *"DAD!"* Then, ran full tilt to the man, and jumped up and flew through the air when he was still several feet away.

The Kilpatricks sat and stared in shock. Slowly the Kilbournes retook their seats, and Kali noticed Keith got the chair for Kent. He settled down on the other side of Kerri, so she was sandwiched between them, like she was between Kam and Kurt. She scowled at Kam, but he only grinned at her.

"How did you find us?" Kameron was the first one to speak.

"Just because you can't know where I am, doesn't mean I don't know where you are at all times," Kent said sternly, but then broke the sternness with a grin. "Naw, I pinged your phones. Saw they were all in the same location that wasn't a track, so I decided to investigate. Plane landed two hours ago."

"Why didn't you tell us you were coming home? We would have met you."

"I know that, but I wanted to surprise you. I've got something to say."

"Actually, so do I," Keith spoke. Before anyone could say anything, everyone looked up when they heard several car doors slam.

"Now, who the hell is here?" Kali asked in frustration. She jumped to her feet and started forward and stopped, then yelled, running forward again.

Kam looked at Kurt and they both frowned, then looked at Kent, and at his hand motions they both nodded, then he grinned and stared at the woman who'd been sitting between them.

"Karen!" Kali had yelled, and rushed forward, followed by Karen's husband Chuck and their three children, eight-year-old Charles, six-year-old Megan and four-year-old Jessica.

"Karen!" Kelsey said, and gently moved Kali aside, and hugged his middle sister. Next came their parents. After hugs and drinks were passed around, Kali was the only one left standing and she looked utterly confused.

"Kali?" Kam sat forward, and asked gently, "Are you okay?"

"I don't know." She looked at him in confusion. "I've lived here for four years, and this is the first time I've ever had visitors. And I don't even know everyone that's here." Kam stood and went over, and hugged her in front of everyone, and with his arm wrapped around her they stood before everyone.

"Why don't you start the introductions, because I have a feeling when we do ours, there's going to be a lot of questions." Kali sighed and did just that, then Kam introduced his family, and left Kent and Ken for last.

"And this is Ken and Kent Kilbourne, our father." When everyone frowned, he looked at them, and said, "Your turn."

It was Ken that stood, and explained, "I know I'm probably going to shock all of you, but this is something our family's done for generations. As far back as we can trace it. But, it doesn't happen to everyone, but it never skips a generation."

"What my brother is trying to tell you is that we are both married to Kerri. We are both her husband, and yes, we both sleep with her."

Beside Kam, Kali started to giggle, and Kam looked at her in horror. "You think this is a laughing matter?"

"No, not at all," she said, and continued to giggle.

"Then what's the problem?" Kurt demanded as he came up to her other side, boxing her in.

She only looked at Kerri, and asked, "You understand, don't you?"

"Absolutely. I say it almost every day."

"What the hell you talking about, woman?" Kent demanded, and that caused Kali to laugh harder. She ended up sitting down, and Kam had to put her head between her legs.

When she waved her hand, he let her up, she looked at the older Kilbournes, and asked, "And you don't care who the father of the kids are?"

"Doesn't matter as long as they're healthy." Kent glared at her and then his sons who still stood behind her. "What's that got to do with anything?"

"I've only known your family since racing season started this year, but I've known Kyle the longest for five years. It's only in the last two days that I realized that Kameron and Kyle are practically alike in temperament, that's why I think they argue all the time, but it's fun arguing, and that's why Kyle can push Kam the most, and then you stand up and blurt out the facts, and only the facts, and you sound so much like the two of them when they argue. I know you don't care and it's none of my business, but I'd bet money that you're Kam and Ky's father, and Ken is Kurt and Kevin's."

"Kali, I know you're supposed to be smart." Karen frowned at her. "But, from where I'm sitting, it looks like those two are twins."

"So, what's that got to do with anything? You can't have sex with two guys and get pregnant with both, but I'd bet my left nut that Kent and Ken are twins."

"But, you don't have a left nut," Kelsey said.

"Figure of speech," she said, and saw that Kent was looking at her funny. "Am I right? Are the two of you twins?"

"Yes."

"Holy fuck!" Both Kam and Kyle said at the same time, and everyone laughed. "Since when?" Kyle asked.

"Since we were born." Kent frowned and then realized what Kali had said, and shook his head. "Fine, you got me there, but enough about this. I have an announcement to make, and I think this gentleman said so too." Kent had pointed to Keith.

"Ooh, I have something to say." Karen grinned.

"And me," Kelsey said, and they stood there arguing with each other as to who was going to give their announcement first, and nobody could get them apart, not even their husbands.

It was Chuck, Karen's husband, who said in exasperation, "For god's sake, Kal, do your thing."

Kali grinned and walked over to her siblings, reached up and grabbed their outer ears, and literally banged their heads together. To the shock of everyone, and Kent looked at the shock on Kam and Kurt's faces, and grinned when they stared at him and swallowed hard.

"Listen up, you two. This is my house, so no arguing. You understand me?" When they stared at her, she said again, "I said, do you understand me?"

"Yes."

"Then, sit down and we'll do this my way," Kali said, and put her arms behind her back, and said, "I'm thinking of a number between—"

"No!" Kelsey and Karen said at the same time, and held their arms out. "You do that all the time. It's not fair, because you can only hold up six fingers. No fair, Kal."

Kali grinned, then sighed. "Fine. Can you say what you have to say in five words or less?"

She watched as they looked at each other, their husbands, then nodded yes. "Dad, can you?"

"Yep."

"Wait, I have something to say too," Kathy said, and grinned. "And, yes, five words or less."

"Okay."

"Kent?"

"What?" he barked, then softened the blow by winking at her. Kali turned and looked at Kurt. "Is he always like that?"

"Yep." Kurt grinned, then leaned in and whispered loud enough for everyone to hear. "So are Kam and Kyle."

"Oh lord." She grinned, then held up her hand. "Okay, we're going to play a game. Everyone who had something to say, say it when I say go. The others, let's try to figure out what everyone says. We ready?"

"Yes." Everyone laughed, and Kali leaned back, closed her eyes, and said, "Go." Suddenly, several things had been said, and Kali frowned as she sat up. She looked at everyone and they looked at her.

"Well?" Karen, always the impatient one, asked.

"Why?"

"Why what?"

"Why are you and Chuck and the kids moving back here? I thought you had wonderful jobs and a life in Houston."

Chuck stood and started to pace. "We did. We had everything we ever wanted. Terrific jobs, a wonderful family, a beautiful home, but we lost it all."

"How?" Keith frowned at his son-in-law. "And why am I just finding out about this?"

"Because, we thought we could get above it."

"What happened?" It was Kent who asked.

"Harvey."

"But, you said you weren't in the path." Kathy sat up in surprise.

"The reports lied. From where it was headed, we weren't in the path, but just before it hit, it turned and we were practically directly in it."

"Who's Harvey?" Kyle asked.

"Harvey was that big hurricane that went through Texas last year," Kam told him.

"But I thought that was Irma."

"Irma was a couple weeks later, and that went through Florida, but we still caught some of that," Chuck said. "The company we both worked for was flattened, and we lost everything in the house, except for the clothes we packed when we evacuated, but we stayed as long as we did, because we had to be there for the insurance and all that jazz, and because we helped with the office and their paperwork, but we're moving here, because we both had job offers, and came to interview for them this last week, and were accepted."

"Damn," Kali said, then waved at Kelsey. "I knew you'd be here."

"Wait, why did you say that?" Karen asked.

Kali grinned and pointed to her sister. "You said you were moving home. So did you." She pointed to Kelsey. "Dad said he bought Dusty Hill, Mom said she sold her business, Kent said he's done with the military, and wait..." She stopped and whipped her head back and forth between Kam and Kurtis. "Both, at once?"

"Yep."

"Oh lord. And Kam and Kurtis said they want to both date me."

"How the hell did you get all that from what we said?" Kent frowned at her. "And apparently, you're right. You scare the shit out of me, young lady, and I've just retired from serving thirty years in the Marines."

"So, you're done?" Kerri looked at him.

"Yes, for good. I'm not going back. I didn't tell you I was coming home, because I didn't want to have to go back and do the paperwork. I've signed on the dotted line. I'm free from the government's clutches." All the Kilbournes hugged him, and then Kali frowned and stared at her father, and started laughing.

"Sons, you sure you want to date her? She doesn't seem to stable to me." Kent grinned, and then laughed when Kali stuck her tongue out at him, but she looked at Ken.

"You knew, didn't you?"

"I don't know what you're talking about."

"Liar," she said, but grinned to soften to blow.

"What are you talking about this time, Kali?" Karen sighed. "Maybe it's good we're moving back. Being alone seems to be making you loopy."

"Ha." Kali laughed. "If you think I'm loopy, didn't you hear what Mom and Dad had to say?"

"Not really, something about a hill."

"For your information, Dad bought a race track, and Mom sold her business. That means they'll be moving to within ten miles from here."

"Why?" Karen asked, and stared at her parents in shock.

Kali laughed and waved her hand. "Oh, Kar, you should have seen him this past spring. He called me up on a Friday and wanted to come over."

"But, you're not available on a Friday or Saturday. Haven't been for five years." She looked at her father and rolled her eyes. "Even I knew that, and I live in Houston." She grinned at her sister. "Go on."

"I told him that I'd be there for Sunday brunch. I showed up, and he's like Kel used to be."

"How?" Kelsey asked, and Kali actually shoved him out of the chair he sat in at the table, and sat down and hung her shoulders, her hands and arms down at her sides. She grinned at her sister, and said, "I swear to god, this is the way he was." She dropped her head and rolled it back and forth on the table, and moaned, "I'm so bored. There's nothing to do," she whined, and grinned when her mother laughed.

"He did that almost every day."

"What happened to that speech when you retired?" Karen asked, and stood and held her glass up high. "I've worked twenty hours a day for thirty years. I built this business up from scratch." Kelsey laughed, and joined in and held up his glass.

"I've worked so much that my poor wife had to raise our three children by herself, with no help from me, and keep their schedules straight along with mine. It's time to let her shine. I'm retiring and becoming a househusband."

"Don't househusbands do the laundry, cook, and the dishes?" Kyle asked.

Kali giggled. "Yes, but our dad had a pair of black jeans on that day, and he stood, and one leg from here..." She turned and put her hand in the middle of her ass cheek and grinned. "All the way to the bottom was white."

"Mr. Kilpatrick. Don't you know you're not supposed to put bleach directly on dark colors? Even I know that," Kyle said with a grin.

"Yeah, after you ruined all our jeans," Kam said, then grinned to lighten the blow.

"It was only one bottle, it wasn't that much bleach."

"But, it was a gallon bottle, and it was only four pairs of jeans."

"Boys," Kerri said, and they shut up, but stuck their tongues out at each other, and then grinned.

"So, what happened next?" Karen grinned.

"I told Dad to meet me here the next Friday by four. Any later and I wouldn't wait. I told him I'd introduce him to what I do on the weekends. After that first time, he was on his own, and he went out and freaking bought it."

"What? I don't understand. You never told me what you did on weekends. I thought it was a hot date, and if you don't take those sexy hunks up on their offer, I'll be banging your head against the wall."

"We still have to talk, but I go to the races."

"Horse races?"

"No, dirt-track races." She looked at Kam and Kurt in frustration. "Help me out here."

"I got one better," he said, and looked at his family, and they grinned and jumped to their feet. "Follow us."

CHAPTER TEN

Everyone followed them and the Kilpatricks stayed back, while the Kilbournes worked like a well-oiled machine, and it was Karen who was the first one to walk forward. "And you race this on asphalt?"

"No. Dirt."

"But, don't you need traction? Won't you slide all over with those tires?"

Kevin grinned, and he was the one that explained everything, and she looked at her father, and said, "And you bought the track these drive on?"

"Run," Kevin said. "We run on the track."

"Oh, so you bought the track these cars run on?"

"Yep, and the one that one runs on." He pointed to the go cart Ken and Kent had pulled out.

"Cool. Mom, can I race one of these?" Charles asked, and Karen looked scared.

"I don't know. I don't know if you're old enough?"

"How old are you?" Kyle asked.

"Eight."

"I'm ten and I've been racing since I was three. All of us have. We started that young and worked our way up." He grinned, then leaned in, and whispered loudly, "Even girls race these."

"Wow. And if Kal thinks you're moving closer to here, where is this track?"

Kali laughed and walked up to her, then took her hand in hers. "See that tree up there."

"Up where."

"On the hill, it's summer, so it's hard to see, but it's the tallest one."

"Yes. What about it?"

"That's it."

"What? I don't understand."

"That's where the track is." Keith grinned. "And your mother and I looked at a house yesterday. We like it. It's not as big as the one we have now, but there's room for us and the grandkids. We can show you later, but right now I have to ask your mother something." He turned and stared at his wife. "Are you absolutely sure you want to sell?"

"Already done, and yes. I never let on, but Kali's a bad influence on her parents. I was hooked the minute we walked the pits that first night. I know you might not remember, but my grandfather used to race, and I loved going to the races."

"Where?" Kent and Ken asked.

"It was in the southern states, the Carolinas, and it was asphalt. But, the smells, the noise, the crowds, the everything, brought it all back, and I realized that no matter what I said or did, you were going to buy it anyway. So, I finally sold out to that big conglomerate that's wanted to buy me out for years, and I got a really good deal. I mean *really* good, but from now on, no more secrets. We do things together."

"Agreed." He grinned and kissed her. The cars were loaded back up, and everyone made their way to the back yard, and before long everyone was hustling around, and cooking on the grill and cooking in the kitchen, and when

Kali found she didn't have enough plates and silverware for everyone, she panicked.

"What?" Kam asked, when he saw her shocked expression.

"I don't have enough plates for everyone. I only have four. It worked this last week, because Missy's only six months old, and didn't need one. What am I going to do?"

"Breathe," Kam said, and looked up, and Kurtis was right there beside them.

"What's wrong?"

"Mini meltdown. Kali says she doesn't have enough plates to go around."

"Oh, that's not a problem." He grinned and he wrapped his arm around her, and hugged her tightly to him, and Kali sighed and relaxed into him.

"That's right. Relax, we've got you covered," Kurtis said, and nuzzled the side of her face and her ear. From behind her, she felt Kam's chest and groin against her, and she sighed again.

"What are you guys doing to me?"

"Showing you that you can rely on each other," Kam said, and actually sucked on her ear, and she felt it to her core.

"Kali!" someone called, and they broke apart, and Kali saw that the men adjusted their erections. "Kali, where's your plates?"

"Working on it," she called back, and looked at them in panic.

"Where's your back door?" Kam said as he breathed deeply, and adjusted himself again.

"Um, back there," she said, and then giggled when she realized it was where everyone was.

"Your front door. I am not walking past your family with this boner."

"There." She giggled, and pointed to the door that was only three feet away.

"Thanks," they both said, then leaned down and kissed each cheek at once. "We're going to have to sit down and have a talk later."

"I'm not really available until next weekend. After the filming tonight, Brian and I are going to have to work every night to get it ready for presentation on Friday."

"And we're racing Thursday, Friday, and Saturday. Will you be at McKay Saturday?"

"Probably."

"Okay. Then, we'll plan for that. I know we can talk later, but I want to nail a date down, but until we meet again, I want you to think of anything you want to ask us, and I mean anything. This won't work if you don't ask."

"Okay," she said, and pushed them to the door when her sister called her again. She shook her head and slipped into her bathroom, and splashed water on her face. She went out and saw that Kam and Kurtis came in with several packages of paper plates, napkins, cups, and boxes of silverware. She sighed in relief.

They sat around and ate, and at four Brian arrived, then he and Kali conferred in her office about the equipment he was going to use, and after putting everything together, and letting Brian load it in her SUV, she went out and stood in the shadows, then watched the two families interact, and it felt so relaxing.

"Excuse me." She stepped forward and everyone turned and looked at her. "It's time. Brian and I have everything I think we'll need, so if you want to head out."

"Okay," Kam said, and looked at the others. "Last chance to back out."

Everyone grinned and jumped to their feet, and the clueless ones just went along for the ride. Kent jumped into the RV with Kam, leaving his truck at the Kilpatricks'.

"What's going on?"

"Ever heard of Dillard?"

"Our engine backer, or the company we get our engines from?"

"Correct. They're now our sponsors."

"How the hell did you pull off that one, and which one of you are they sponsoring?"

"All four of us, even Kyle."

"How?"

"Kali."

"Is she related to them?"

"No, she's an ad executive. She makes commercials. She's in some type of competition at work, and Dillard's the client. When she called and asked what he wanted, he said new ideas, and his dream was to sponsor some local race-car drivers, like they did when they first started over thirty years ago. She told him about us, and he arrive here at Dusty Hill. He actually gave Kurt a new motor this year. Free of charge."

"Why?"

"Kurt kept shearing off the tranny bolts. Come to find out the tranny guys lied about being able to work with the engine he bought before you shipped out this last time. Old man Dillard was there, and he gave us the engine, and brought his own crew up to put it in."

"But, they're in California."

"No, well yes, but they moved here. They're in Arcade at that fabrication shop. That's their new factory."

"And all this is due to Kali?"

"Yes. And she had this bitching idea for a commercial, and we agreed, because it's for Dillard, and Dillard is on our hoods."

"I missed that," Kent said, and shook his head. "All I know is that I'm finally home, and I can't wait to get back into the thick of things. I think this last deployment was my longest, because I knew it was my last."

"I'm glad you're home, Dad."

"Thanks, and I see you're still keeping the others together. You know that's what Dad is for, right?"

"I know, and when it comes to the tough stuff, I let him take over." He grinned, then burst out laughing as he pulled into the pit at Dusty Hill. "Ask Dad about why he had to give Kyle the talk."

"What talk?"

"Son." Kameron deepened his voice, lowered his chin, and mocked looking over a pair of glasses. "Do you know about the birds and the bees?"

"Oh, shit. Ky, little innocent, eight-year-old Ky?"

Kam whipped his rig around, and snorted. "Innocent, hell, and he's ten and a holy terror." He parked, then bent his head, and Kent winced when he saw the stitches on the top of his head.

"What the hell happened?"

"Ky, I'd show you the bruise on my ass, but I don't swing that way, and you are my father. Your time of seeing my ass passed when I outgrew diapers." He grinned and hopped down. He knew he hadn't overstepped his bounds when his father was laughing when he joined them.

"So, what's the plan?"

"We drive on the track, park, jump out, and say a few words, but for right now, we're going over to park at the entrance, then we'll walk over and meet up with Kali and Brian."

"Who's that?"

"Her techie."

"Do I even want to know?"

"The cameraman."

"Oh." He grinned and helped all his sons with their cars, and then he and Ken walked over when the cars drove off. "So, what do you know of this Kali person?"

"Not much. I know her Dad better. And before you ask, no, we don't know what's up with her. Figured they'd let us know in due time."

"Figured as much. She seems like a strong-enough woman to be able to handle the boys, especially after seeing her dealing with her siblings. I pictured her doing that to the boys."

"Me too." Ken laughed. "Can't wait to be a fly on the wall when and if that happens. So, before we join the others. Want me to sleep in the RV tonight."

"What the fuck for? She's your wife too."

"But, you've been gone for a year."

"So, never stopped us before. Besides, if you sleep in the RV, what will Kerri think? That because I'm home, you don't want her anymore."

"Oh, shit," he said, and rubbed his ear. It still stung from when she'd wrenched it several years ago.

"Exactly. So, what's going on here?"

"Kali's making a commercial for Dillard, and the boys, all of them are featured in it. She explained it all to us a couple days ago." He paused and grinned. Together they rushed forward, then jumped the wall, and hurried to Kali's side.

"Are you hurt? Did you twist anything?" Kent demanded when they squatted down on each side of her. She looked at them and giggled, then waved her hand in front of her face, then suddenly Ken and Kent were replaced by Kam and Kurtis, and she laughed so hard, she gripped her stomach and rolled into a fetal position.

"Kali?" Kam said. "What's wrong?"

"It's stupid."

"What?"

"Do you know how long I've been coming to the races?"

"You said five years?"

"Yes, for five years I sat up in the top row, first section off turn four." She pointed over her head, and everyone looked up.

"And?"

"And, for five years, I thought the track was flat. Imagine my surprise when I step out on it, and take three steps and land on my ass. It was either that or face plant. Figured the ass plant was a better cushion."

Ken and Kent looked at each other, grinned, and slowly backed away.

"One, you don't have a fat ass," Kam growled.

"Two," Kurtis said. "We couldn't stand it if that beautiful face was damaged." And together they helped her up, and asked where she wanted to go.

"I don't know. I wanted to walk around and see what angle was the best." Just then they heard a beep, and Kyle came riding up on an ATV. "Here." He jumped off and the men helped her on and drove around. On the third pass they picked up Brian and drove slowly, and listened to them talk, and it was another six laps before they were satisfied.

They arrived back, and since Brian had hung the storyboards, Kent had walked them with Kerri and Ken, and Keith explained to everyone what they were going to do, and Kent looked at Kali. "You came up with this idea?"

"Yeah. Is it okay?"

"I love it, but what's this?" He pointed to the last scene, and Kali grinned. "That's your part."

"Mine?"

"Yeah, if you agree, Ken and Kerri's doing this part, and don't think I'm hitting on you, because you're old enough to be my dad, and I don't have Daddy issues and need another one, but your voice is deep and sexy, so here, read this." She dug through some huge posters, and pulled one. "Slowly."

Kent frowned and said, "Dillard's, where you can trust your family to be safe."

"Nailed it." Brian grinned, looking up from his camera, giving them the thumbs up signal.

"That's it?"

"That's it. And I'm not showing your face. That will be the tag line when the logo appears."

"Don't they have their own people for that?"

"Nope, that's my job." She grinned, then conferred with the drivers and Brian. When they had their instructions, she looked at her family, and said, "Can you wait in the stands? And, please, be quiet?"

Kathy grinned and corralled her family, and Keith hugged her, and said, "I'm proud of you, Kali." Then, he disappeared somewhere. Kali looked at her watch and saw it was going on five, and looked at Brian and asked if he was ready. At his nod she waved her hand in the air, but Kent came over and showed her what to do, and when she did that, she heard the cars start up and grinned at him. She put her finger to her lips, and pointed to Brian, and Kent grinned and nodded. By the time they had everything she pictured, it was ten at night, and as the last light turned off, she yelled, "CUT!"

"Oh my god," Brian said. "I love it. I'm so getting an A+ for this. I know you are. Now, we only have to splice it all together. When and where do you want me tomorrow?"

"Because I signed up ahead of time, can you meet me at the AV Lab at U of B at two tomorrow afternoon?"

"I can. Make sure I have your cell number." They exchanged numbers, and the first people to come to her were Kent, Ken and Kerri.

"It took a couple takes, or whatever you call them, but I think what you did was excellent," Kent said. He looked up and Kali saw her father. "If you bought this place for real, you're going to need someone like this to do your advertising."

"I know, but she loves her current job. I'm not going to pressure her." He grinned and hugged her. "It was great, I can't wait to see it. We'll have to have a party like we did for Red Solo."

"Great. But, we have to wait to see what Dillard thinks first."

"I know, but I have faith in you."

"Thanks, Dad," she said, and hugged her family who walked by, the adults carrying the young sleepy children, and Kali told them to stay at her house. As long as they didn't sleep in her bed, she didn't care where they flopped.

CHAPTER ELEVEN

Kali pressed her hands into her jittering stomach and took several deep breaths. They were all standing in the huge conference room, and seated at the table were four Dillards. She wondered which one was Max. Even though Maxwell had called her, she had never met Max. Everyone looked up as Tony Wright walked in, and made a production of shaking the Dillards' hands, then he stood at the head of the table.

"Gentlemen, thank you for coming in today."

"You're late," the oldest Dillard barked. "And we're here, because we want to get the show on the road."

"Dad, give the guy a chance."

Tony cleared his throat, and said, "I'll get right to it then. With your account, I did things differently, to stir things up. Normally, I'd get a proposal and pass it along to an ad exec, and they'd make the team and do the work, then present it. But, with your proposal, I had four teams to work on it. Two teams of five, and two teams of one."

"Why one?"

"Because, they are the best ad exec and tweaker I employ, and I wanted to see if they could do it without each other. As a matter of fact, I even told the teams that if a techie isn't on with them, they had to sink or swim, same with the teams of one. So, gentlemen, you will be presented with four ideas today, and hopefully by the end you'll be ready and willing to sign on the dotted line. So, without further ado, I'd like you to sit back and prepare to be wowed. I know I will be." He went to the back of the room, and before he sat, he said, "I'll let you guys decide who's to go first."

"I will," Matt said quickly from beside Kali, and grinned at her. He stepped to the front of the room, and grinned. "Hi. I'm Matt and Mr. Dillard, I would like to sincerely apologize to you for what I'm about to say, but after giving it a lot of thought, I being one of those teams of one Mr. Wright mentioned, I respectfully declined the offer to present to you today, and before you get all upset, there's a reason for it. Briefly, I am a techie, which means that I take someone's ideas, and put them to film, then I tweak that to their specifications. But, to come up with the initial concept, nope, sorry, nothing there." He actually knocked on the side of his head with his knuckles. "I hope you accept my sincere apologies for me wasting your time."

"Thank you for being honest with us, young man," the oldest Dillard said. Matt nodded and stepped back to stand next to Kali.

"Is that true?"

"Yep. Never even opened the file."

Kali giggled, and then Heather, the team leader of the team stepped forward and basically said the same thing Matt had. Them being a team of five techies, then Suzie stepped forward, but suddenly, Roger stepped forward, a member on Suzie's team.

"Before Suzie begins with her presentation, I'd like it be known that four of us on her team had nothing to do with what she's about to present to you. Even though she had a team of five, we couldn't get her to listen to reason, and we told her if she went forward, then we were going to say we had nothing to do with this. Right?" He glared at Suzie.

"He's right. They kept telling me the concept wouldn't work, but I know it will. So without further ado, my name is Suzie Miller, and I'm going to present you with the best new product that will make your business soar into the stratosphere, so if you'd kindly pay attention to the screen, I'm happy to present you with my new, and innovative idea. I'm surprised this hasn't been done before, it's so exhilarating, and on the cutting edge of what you need." She stepped to the side, and called for the lights to be dimmed. As soon as they were shut off, Kali pulled her phone along with Matt, and they grinned as they filmed what she presented, and by the end of it, everyone but the Dillards, Mr. Wright and Suzie had their hands over their mouths, trying not to snort their laughter too loudly. When the lights came back on, everyone straightened and coughed, but stopped laughing.

Kali watched as the Dillards blinked several times, looked at each other, and then at the same time all four of them pounded on the table, burst out laughing, and put their heads down.

"Mr. Dillard! That's uncalled for." Suzie actually stamped her five-inch heel and stumbled as she glared at them.

"Young lady," one man said, and Kali thought she recognized the voice as Max. "I specifically told Mr. Wright to leave the place for what we were looking for blank, and only one person from this agency called me asking what I wanted. What you forced us to watch for the last four minutes and forty-eight seconds is garbage, utter garbage."

"But it's new and innovative."

"Missy," Maxwell barked out. "What happens when you mix liquid and electricity?"

"I have no clue."

"And you had no clue when you put that garbage together." Maxwell stated as he pointed to the now blank screen.

"I beg to differ."

"You can beg all you want, but I will never put this crap in my stores, because it doesn't exist. For your uneducated mind, turning signals take light bulbs, which take wires, which take electricity."

"Oh, but I'm not talking about turning signals, I'm talking about blinkers. See, its blinker fluid." Suzie picked up the mock-up photos she'd had taken of gallon jugs of fluid.

"Dad," the three men said, and held him down. One of the men looked at Suzie and glared at her.

"Blinkers and turning signals are the same thing, they run off the battery, I don't know where you got your idea from, but you were set up." She looked at Roger who held up his hands and shook his head.

"That's why we refused to work with her. We told her and told her that it didn't exist. I even brought in the owner's manual to my Jeep to read, but she refused to listen. She said she had the next best thing since fire and sliced bread. Her words."

"That's enough," Tony Wright said as he stood and glared at everyone. "Suzie, thank you for that presentation. Now who's left?" He sat back down and Kali waited until Suzie walked away, but not before shooting daggers at her, and

Kali just grinned. To get her creative juices flowing, Kali had drawn up pictures of bottles of fluid, and labeled them blinker fluid. She'd thrown them in the garbage, and after seeing Suzie leaving her office that one afternoon, Kali had noticed the joking pictures missing from her trash basket.

"Gentlemen. Welcome. I'm sorry you had to watch that painful presentation. My name is Kali Kilpatrick, and I'd like to present you with a three minute and thirty second commercial. I believe that after talking with you, Max?" She looked down the row of men and the man she suspected was Max raised his hand and nodded. "You personally told me you were looking for new ideas. After giving it a lot of thought and talking to a lot of people, I hope you like what I have to offer you." She stepped back, said, "Lights," and started the presentation.

When the lights came back on, Kali looked at the Dillards and then around the room. You could hear a pin drop into the silence. She looked at Matt, scared, and he put his hands in his hair, bugged his eyes, and mouthed, "Oh my god." She didn't know how to take it, until suddenly the whole room burst out in a round of applause, and the Dillards actually stood and rushed forward. They hugged her and when everyone settled down, Kali noticed only two people weren't happy, and that was Tony and Suzie.

"I only have one question," Max said.

"Okay."

"Can you change it?"

"What?" Matt jumped away from the wall, and stalked to Kali's side. "That was brilliant! Do you know Kali's an award-winning ad exec, and she's even had her ads in the Super Bowl? Why would you want to change perfection?"

Kali reached up and used her three working fingers to cover Matt's mouth, and said, "Matt, stop, give them a chance to explain."

"Oh, sorry," he said, then kissed the back of that hand. "For what it's worth, that was brilliant, and I want the name of your techie, so I can punch them out. I think they might be just as good as, or better than me."

"We'll talk." She giggled, then turned to the Dillards. "What would you like changed? And I'd like to know why?"

"Can you go to the beginning?" Max asked, and when she did, he had her play it and then yelled stop. He jumped to his feet and grabbed his father's cane. "Sorry, Dad." But, he hurried forward, and even though there were several people in the room, he talked to only her. "This is us. The Dillard Family. Dad, Paul, Andy and me. I don't know how I got in there, I don't mind, I like it, but I don't remember posing with them and our employees."

"Techie." Matt grinned.

"Okay, now go to the end where the boys are all standing together," he said, and pointed when she stopped. "Our logo shows on all four cars, which is great, what we want. And all their other sponsors, which is also great. And on their fire suits. But, see here." He pointed four times, and Kali frowned.

Max turned to the room, and asked, "How many seeing this thought these four were Dillards?" Everyone raised their hand, and Kali slapped herself on her forehead.

"Because, you sponsor them, they were their sponsors, and because of the location, it looks like it's a name on a uniform, so it looks like their name is Dillard."

"Exactly. I don't know, maybe you can techie." He grinned at Matt. "Their name over our logo. They need recognition also. I'm not so stubborn or proud that I wouldn't share."

"So, you'd be okay if I had Kilbourne there."

"Or their first names. But, I don't think that would work." He leaned in, and whispered, "Too many women would know who's who." He winked when she snorted, then he went back and sat down. "That's the only flaw I see."

"I want to see it again," Maxwell said. "Ms. Kilpatrick, come back and watch it from this angle." Kali asked for the lights to be killed when she was in position, then started the commercial and saw it from that angle and nodded.

"I understand now. I'm so sorry about that."

"Don't be," Maxwell said.

"So, you liked it?" Tony Wright asked. "Would you like to go to my office and draw up the contract?"

"Not until we see the changes," Max said. "Call us when you have them and we'll come in to view them."

"I'm sure it'll only take a few minutes for that to be done."

"You can't rush perfection," Maxwell said. "Call us when it's done," he said, and headed toward the door. He paused just before he opened it, and glared at Tony. "You have a gold mine in that one." He pointed to Kali with his cane. "And if I was you, I'd fire that one." He pointed to Suzie and opened the door and exited. Tony followed them out, and Kali had just slipped the disk with the only copy of the commercial into her pocket, just as Suzie attacked her.

"You bitch. You set me up."

"What are you talking about?" Kali asked, and she saw the others in the room had their phones out and aimed their way.

"I found that blinker fluid ad on your desk. I'm sick and tired of you thinking you're all that and getting all the good clients." She paused as the door was whipped open, and Tony stormed in.

"Will someone tell me what the fuck just happened?"

"Suzie was just telling Kali that she saw the blinker fluid ad on Kali's desk."

"And?" Tony glared at Suzie.

"Uncle Tony."

"Don't Uncle Tony me. What did you do?"

"I took it, alright," she practically screamed. "I'm sick and tired of her getting everything handed to her on a silver platter. I want the good clients."

"Do your job and maybe you'll get some?" Roger called out. When Tony glared, he shrugged. "Hey, I speak the truth, I've worked with Kal on several accounts, and she's brilliant, which that video we saw showed." Kali noticed Tony didn't agree or disagree with the statement, but as she continued to gather her things, ignoring everyone, she saw Suzie round on Matt with all her fury.

"And you."

"What?"

"How could you?"

"How could I what?"

"How could you let that touch you?" she screamed, and several people sucked in their breath, and Kali looked up and saw Suzie was pointing at her.

"Just exactly what are you saying?" Kali asked.

"You're a cripple." She sneered at Kali and glared at Matt. "How could you let a cripple like her touch you. It's disgusting."

"Mr. Wright," Kali whipped around and demanded. "Are you going to do anything about what this intern just said?"

"Um, ah, I, I."

Kali glared at him for a full minute, but he continued to stammer, and Suzie came up to him and actually put her arm around him and her hand on his chest. When he didn't say anything, Kali stiffened her spine, pulled her phone and put it on speaker. She pushed one more button, and everyone heard the ringing.

"Dillard."

"Max, this is Kali Kilpatrick."

"Kali, hi. I have to say again that was a brilliant presentation. I can't wait to work with you. Did Tony tell you that we're offering a million dollars for the first six months for the account, but only if you're the ad exec."

"I'd hold off on signing anything with Mr. Wrong right now."

"Excuse me, did you say Mr. Wrong?"

"I did. As of two minutes ago, I quit working for The Wright Group, and because you haven't signed any contract with them yet, the presentation is still in my possession, so I have control of it. So, I'm putting it out there that if you want what you saw today, you'll have to hire me personally."

"Yes! Done! You're hired. I can't wait to see what else you come up with. Actually, I have to say I'm relieved. I didn't really trust that Tony guy, especially when he allowed that twit to show us that video. Blinker fluid. Seriously." He laughed, and then said, "Call me next week."

"I will, thank you, Max."

"Any time." They hung up and she turned on her heel, and the crowd parted as she stormed past.

"She can't do that, can she?" Suzie asked. "Make her give me that account, Uncle Tony." She heard Suzie and kept going to her office. She stopped at the supply closet and grabbed several empty boxes, and continued down to her office. The first thing she packed were her awards, then the pictures of her family, then she opened her bottom drawer, pulled a file and after flipping through it, she held them in her hand and stormed back down to the conference room.

"Mr. Wright," Kali barked out, and held up the papers. "I'll be out of here in fifteen minutes. Before I leave here, I'll have a check for twenty thousand along with three weeks' severance pay. I won't leave without it. And before you deny it, these contracts state otherwise. Is that clear? And if I don't have it, then I'll be calling my lawyer." She turned on her heel, and stalked to her office, and continued packing.

"Take me with you," Matt said as soon as he entered her office and shut the door behind him. He automatically began to help her pack. He let her do the desk, while he did the things on the shelves. She shook her head or nodded when he called her attention to something.

"Why don't you leave on your own?"

"Will you hire me?"

"Maybe." She grinned at her best friend. "Brian was pretty good. You saw his work."

"Brian who?"

"Meyers."

"How much did it cost to hire him? What type of equipment did he use?" Kali let him go on and on with the questions, then burst out laughing when he began to pout.

"What?"

"Brian is my brother-in-law Lyle's brother. He's twenty-two and a senior in the AP Tech class at U of B. His final exam is Wednesday of next week. Last week I met him for only the second time in our lives, and he said the girl he was dating took all their work when he broke up with her. He was strapped, so he did the tech stuff for a grade."

"Damn. And he's going to use the commercial you just did as his final grade?"

"Yes, and the equipment he used belongs to the school."

"Oh. I feel better." He grinned. "So, what are you going to do now?"

"Convince you to take this stuff to my truck." She grinned at the boxes. "Then, I'm going to go out to lunch and go home and clean my house. You wouldn't believe it, but I had a house full this last week."

"You, Miss private person, Miss I work sixty hours a week, Miss I don't date anyone, Miss shy, Miss introverted. Which is a crock, by the way. You don't have a shy or introverted bone in your body, and when are you going to take those godawful fake glasses off, and show the world the real you. Oh, sorry, went off on a tangent there. You had company? Anyone interesting?"

Kali threw her head back and laughed. "God, I'm going to miss you. Why don't you stick it out here, and I'll call you when I get my first client? I know I possibly have the Dillard account." She grinned.

"Why don't I like that grin?"

"Because, I might have another account, but I'm going to make them beg me first. But yes, I had a house full. My brother and his family showed up, and my sister and her family."

"Damn, that's a lot isn't it?"

"Eleven if you count my parents. Then there were the Kilbournes, and there were seven of them."

"Who are they?"

Kali grinned, and said, "The four at the end of the commercial."

"They're real? Real live race-car drivers? They weren't actors?"

"Nope, real live race-car drivers. Remember that day we caught Suzie snooping in here? You asked why I was dressed in jeans."

"Yeah, you said you were going to go get dirty." He grinned, then laughed. "You went to the track."

"Yep, have for the last five years, and what if I told you the first two drivers that arrived on scene asked me out, each, together."

"You go girl. I don't swing that way, but I'd tap that. One question. Are they twins?"

"Yep." He laughed, then paused at the knock on her door. Matt opened it and ignored the glare Tony gave him.

He walked in and handed her an envelope, before he stalked back out.

She opened it, and called out, "Will this bounce if I take it to the bank?"

He sighed and his shoulders slumped. "Not if you go today. After today I'm not sure," he admitted, then walked out. Kali and Matt exchanged surprised looks, then Kali frowned and quickly tapped the keys to her computer.

"I knew it." She grinned and pointed, and Matt came over and read over her shoulder.

"I don't understand."

"His bio says he's an only child. So, why in hell would he have a niece that would hang all over him? I bet she's his mistress, and what better way to keep her close than to employ her."

Matt tapped several keys, and laughed as he pointed, and they grinned. "So, if he's going through a messy divorce, get your ass to the bank and cash that check." They hurried up and finished packing up her office, and Matt and Roger helped carry them down. Kali was shocked when everyone in the department hugged her and wished her well.

As she walked past, she saw Tony standing there, and because she could, she walked up to him, and said, "You're a disgrace. I could have you brought up on charges with the EOE but I won't. But, if I ever catch your mistress calling anyone names like that again, I'll sue both of you. And, if this check bounces, I will take you both to court."

Kali turned on her heel and headed to the door, and Tony actually threw the coffee cup in his hand against the wall. "You bitch. You can't threaten me like that."

"Then grow a fucking pair, and man up that what she did was wrong. It's not my fault I was hurt in a car accident when I was three. And let's hope your wife doesn't find out about your little piece you have stashed away at the office. I read online you're going through a divorce.

"Don't you dare tell that fucking bitch of a wife of mine that I'm fucking Suzie here at the office."

"Don't have to," Kali said, and walked away. She turned the corner and saw Tony's wife step out of the office she'd been in while she'd been yelling at Tony, and the last thing she heard was.

"Hello, Tony."

"Oh, fuck me."

"No thanks, been there, done that. I hear Suzie gets that privilege now," Tony's wife said, and Kali heard another crash as she exited the building.

She hugged Matt and made sure she had his phone number, and then headed to the bank. It didn't bounce and she took the cash and put it in her own account, then headed home. She only made one call, to tell Brian how to fix the end of the commercial, and wished him luck. He had to turn his project in later that day.

CHAPTER TWELVE

On Wednesday afternoon, Kali hurried through the parking lot, and had to pause to look around to get her bearings.

"Kali?" She turned when she heard her named called, and frowned when the Kilbournes approached. "What are you doing here?" Kameron asked, and because it felt right, and because he wanted her to get used to it, he kissed her cheek, then stepped back, and Kurtis did the same thing. The other two brothers, and Ken and Kent only shook her hand. Kameron took that huge, thick black case from her, and offered to carry it for her.

"Brian asked me to meet him here. I have no clue why."

"Us too," Kam said, and stepped closer to her. They looked around and then from behind them, the door opened, and Brian appeared.

"Good, you're all here. Come this way."

"What's going on?" Kali asked as they entered the building, and found herself walking down a hall between Brian and Kam.

"I only know a little of it, but my professor has questions about the video, and he asked if he could talk to you and them." He pointed to the Kilbournes. "Then, if his questions are satisfied, he asked if you could stay for some special thing. I have no clue what's going on, and I'm nervous as fuck." He held out his hand, and everyone saw it shaking badly.

"Breathe," Kent said in that deep, deep voice of his, and he placed his hand on Brian's shoulder to halt him. They waited until his breathing was under control, then started forward again. After several turns he stopped before a door, and knocked on it.

"Come in!"

Brian drew in a deep breath, let it out slowly and opened the door. "Professor Emmerson."

"Meyers. What can I do for you?"

"You said you had questions for the people that helped me with the project I submitted. They're here," Brian said, and after everyone was standing there, he said, "This is Kali Kilpatrick, it was her idea and I only filmed and edited it. And these are the Kilbournes. Kenneth, Kent, Kameron, Kurtis, Kevin, and this little scamp is Kyle. And they own and operate The Kilbourne Racing Team."

Everyone watched as the professor stared at them and his eyes were huge. "You're not actors?"

"No, Sir." Kameron took one step forward, and said. He held out his hand. "Kameron. I have no idea what Brian turned in for you to view, but if the cars are on it, I'm number eighteen with the green and black. And I'm the oldest brother." The others introduced themselves the same way, and Kali noticed that Ken said he was the mechanic in charge of all of them, and that Kent was in charge of the schedule. Neither one of them mentioned that they were the father.

"And you?" Professor Emmerson asked Kali.

"What about me?"

"Meyers said he knew you, and that you were the one that came up with the concept. Do you have any proof of that?" he demanded, then sighed. "Sorry, I didn't mean to bark at you, but the videos the students turned in count for one hundred percent of their grade. It's too important to mess up."

"I can imagine," Kali said, and pointed to a table. "May I?"

"Sure." They watched as she took her portfolio from Kameron, set it up and laid everything out. "Until last Friday I was employed as an ad exec for The Wright Group in downtown Buffalo. I worked there for seven years. Almost two months ago everyone in my department was given a challenge to come up with an ad for a potential new client. However, the way the teams were made up, Tony, the boss and owner said that if we didn't have a tech on our team, we were on our own. I didn't have one. I was at my wit's end to know what to do. Sure I can operate a camera, but not as good as a professional, but when it comes to developing a concept, I'm a pro."

"It wasn't until my brother and his husband showed up that my brother-in-law pointed out that his brother was in the AV program here. I called him and talked to him. We've received written permission from the client and the Kilbournes for Brian to submit his video," she said, and dug through the papers and handed them over.

Mr. Emmerson didn't say anything, but he read them, then walked the boards and frowned. When he sat back behind his desk he looked at them, and said, "Thank you. I needed to ask these questions, because even though the students have been doing this for four years, the video Meyers submitted was of professional quality. I was wondering also why there wasn't the disclaimer at the bottom on the screen that the race-car drivers were paid actors and they were on a closed course. You know that stuff you see on TV in the car commercials?"

"Yes. But, I felt that wasn't needed, because it wasn't paid actors, and it wasn't a closed course." Kali frowned. "Is that a problem?"

"Not at all, but I needed the verification." He held up the release papers he still had in his hand. "Thank you. Now that I know he didn't hire a professional, not that I'm not calling you a professional, but did any money exchange hands during this video?"

"No," Kali said. "I asked for his help for my presentation, and he asked me and my client for permission to use it for this project. We basically helped each other out, and he is my brother-in-law's brother, so he's family."

"Good. Now that's cleared up. I'd like to invite you to the auditorium to view the top five videos that have been submitted. We take a vote here today to see who the winner is. Normally, the winner would get the help to make it a public video, but since you've already done that, then if Meyers wins, he'll get first pick on places he'd like to work."

"I don't understand." Kameron frowned.

"Today the whole department of AV and advertising will be viewing the videos submitted. There are five classes of thirty students each that submitted their videos this year."

"That's a hundred and seventy-five videos," Kyle said in shock.

"It was. The other professors and I viewed them all weekend, and only one person per class was picked as the top one. Now, with the whole department, along with the top twenty advertising firms from the surrounding areas about to view the video and pick the number-one winner, those ad executives would normally work with the winner to get their concept on screen, for pay."

"But, because I was a professional already, with a real potential client, Brian isn't eligible for that if he wins."

"Correct."

"I'm sorry."

"Don't be, I'm not," Brian said. "No offense to you, Professor Emmerson, but I learned more from working with Kali for two weeks, than I did in the first year of college. All I want is a grade. If I win, I win, I don't care about getting it published."

"Wait," Kent said, and the professor stared at him.

"Oh my god, you did the voiceover. Brilliant. But what?"

"Kali you said you don't work for The Wright Group anymore. Did they fire you?"

"No, I quit, but..." She grinned, blew on her knuckles, and rubbed them on her upper chest. "I did my presentation in front of all four Dillards last Friday. There were a couple things they wanted changed and then they'd sign a contract, but not until the changes were made. That happens all the time, so it was no big deal, but the policy The Wright Group had was that the ad exec whose presentation was accepted had full possession of the ad, until the contract was signed by the client. Once they signed the agency was the owner of the presentation."

"That's a good practice." The professor grinned.

"Correct. So, something happened five minutes after the Dillards left, and when my boss didn't back me up, I quit. Right there in front of everyone, with my phone on speaker,

I called Max Dillard and told him not to sign the contract with The Wright Group, which I am no long employed by them, and I was in possession of their commercial. He hired me on the spot to run his ad campaign. It hasn't sunk in yet, but I'm my own boss now, but this won't help Brian, because I'm still a professional, and I have possession of the video he presented to you."

"We'll work something out," the professor said, and sighed.

Kali giggled and when they looked at her, she held out her phone. "Want to see the competition I was against?" She handed her phone to Brian, and he worked his magic by hooking it up to a screen, and Kali told him what to access. The lights were dimmed and everyone saw Suzie's presentation, and after it finished, again you could hear a pin drop in the room, then every man in the room snorted, then burst out in laughter.

"Blinker fluid? What a twit." Kyle laughed. "Where did she get that idea from?"

"She stole it from me. I was at a loss as to what direction I was going to take the ad, and I was just doodling one day at my desk, trying to get the creative juices flowing. After I finished it I threw it away. That's the only thing I can think where she would have gotten it from. And a couple days later, I caught her trying to open my portfolio. After my presentation and the Dillards left, she confronted me calling me a bitch, and that I set her up. She did this in front of almost twenty people.

"Tony returned and some other things were said, and when I demanded Tony fire her, or at least say something to her, he stood there totally clueless, and I quit right then and there, but not before calling Max. So, I guess I'm a freelancer now."

"Okay, we'll work this out. No one knows who the top five videos are, but I guess Meyers knows he's a contender and we'll be showing them. I'd like to invite you to view them." He looked at the Kilbournes. "Have you seen it?"

"No," Kameron said, and frowned when the professor grinned.

"If I was you, I'd hire this young lady right now. I don't know if you need to get your name out there, but once you see what she and Meyers did, it'll blow your mind," he said as he stood, and ushered them out. He went one way, and Brian told them where to go, and when they settled in their seats, Kali was between Kameron and Kurtis, with Kevin on the other side of Kurtis, and the other three behind them, which left Kyle sandwiched between Ken and Kent. The lights went on and off several times, then people were taking their seats, and several men walked out onto the stage.

"At least we're high up, so we can see," Kyle said from behind them. The others grinned and listened to the statements from the people on the stage. It turned out that it was the head of the department that had said the opening statement, then the professor from each class got up, and introduced the students responsible for the upcoming video. They were called onto stage and told to explain how they come up with their concept. Kali leaned forward and paid close attention, but when the lights dimmed and the video played, she sat back to watch. Afterward, there was immediate applause and they took five minutes for questions, then went on to the next.

Finally Professor Emmerson stood and walked forward. He gave his statement and called Brian up on stage. He gave his speech and Kali nodded through it, and when they were about to play it, she sat back and nodded. After the video was played, there was dead silence from over three hundred people present. The only voice heard was from Kyle behind them, who jumped to his feet and screamed, *"PLAY IT AGAIN!"*

Several people throughout the room seconded that, and they ended up sitting through it twice more, and at the end of the third time around everyone jumped to their feet and clapped, whistled and hooted. Kameron turned to Kali, who had remained seated, and gripped her upper arms, pulled her to her feet and kissed her. Kali was so shocked she responded, then she was taken away from Kameron, and Kurtis did the same. When he released her, she sat down stunned.

The head of the department walked back out on stage with his hands in the air, and a huge grin on his face. When it quieted down, he informed them they were voting on the best video, and the first one flashed on the screen. There was some reaction, but it wasn't the best. The same for the next ones, but as soon as the Kilbournes appeared on the screen again, everyone jumped and applauded, whistled and made a lot of noise. Afterward, they made their way down to leave, but Professor Emmerson asked them to stay for the reception.

The Kilbournes answered a lot of questions, while giving autographs, and Kali was approached by several of the ad execs. She realized she knew half of them.

She was standing with several of them, and didn't hear Kameron or Kurtis come up behind her, when one of the other executives asked, "Is the rumor we heard true?"

"What rumor?" Kali frowned.

"You quit The Wright Group."

"I did."

"And was it because Tony's side piece he had working for him called you a cripple?" another one asked. Before she could answer Kameron and Kurtis had the guy pinned against the wall.

"What did you call her?"

"Nothing. It's the rumor going around as to why she quit, and that asshole of a boss of hers let her go, which was the biggest mistake of the universe," he said, and the boys let him down and smoothed his shirt and jacket, then stepped back to sandwich Kali.

"Is this true?"

"Yes."

"So, why was it a mistake?"

"You guys worked with her, I just saw the video, and that student said he worked with her. Don't you know that Kali's an award-winning advertisement executive? That since she started in the business, she's had three commercials in the Super Bowl. Ask any one of us here who is the best in the Buffalo area, hell, the whole Western part of NY, and they'll tell you Kali Kilpatrick. I can't tell you how many times I've called and begged her to come work for me."

"Me too," several of the others said.

"So, what are you going to do now? Who are you going to work for?"

"Myself."

"Shit," another man said, and threw up his hands. "We might as well sell our businesses and retire. No one will hire us now if word gets out Kilpatrick's a free agent." He grinned. "Just remember us little people working in the trenches, and throw us some scraps every once in a while?"

"I will." Kali laughed, and Kameron frowned when she didn't seem offended.

"So who has the Dillard account?" another one asked.

"Me." She grinned, then they groaned. "They wanted me to tweak a couple things before they signed, and I called Brian about it, and I see he did it, and now I know why they wanted it done, so I'll call Max on Monday and get him to sign on the dotted line."

"Damn," several said, then they shook her hand, and wished her luck as they slowly walked away.

Kali turned and saw all the Kilbournes were there, and she said, "I think I'm going to head home. It was good seeing you again."

She started to leave, and was surprised when it was Kyle that came up and held onto her hand as they walked back to the parking lot.

Next to her SUV, the little boy asked, "What did you have to change on the movie and why?"

"First it's a video." She grinned and saw everyone was interested. "When you four are all standing there at the end, before you climb back into your cars?"

"Yes?"

"Max understood, and so did I after I saw it a couple times. But when you were standing there with your arms crossed, the Dillard logo was prominent on your chest. We understand it's because they're your sponsor, but Max was concerned that people would think you were the Dillards, so Max asked if I could put your name over his logo, but only for the video."

"That's it?" Kyle frowned.

"Yep. And I told that to Brian, and I see he fixed it."

"I never would have given it a second thought," Kameron said. "But, I can understand why he had you change it. So, are you going to put that on TV?"

"I still have some bugs to work out, but I think so. I'm sorry, but I really have to go," she said, and quickly got into her SUV, and they all stepped back to let her leave, then Kameron swore.

"What's wrong?"

"I didn't get a time we could see her again."

"Don't rush it," Kent said, and they all went to the trucks they arrived in, and it was on the way home where Kent was driving Kameron and Kurtis, he asked what had happened to make them rough up that one guy. When Kameron told him what was overheard, the only reaction Kent showed was his jaw locking up and his knuckles were solid white over the wheel. They were silent the rest of the way home.

CHAPTER THIRTEEN

"Kilpatrick," Kali said breathlessly into the phone. She had lost track of it, and was busy, and it took several minutes before she found it and answered.

"Kali?"

"Yeah, who's this?"

"Your mother."

"Oh, hi, Mom, what's up?"

"Are you coming up the hill tonight?"

"For?"

"The races."

"Yeah, on Friday night." There was silence on the other end of the line, and Kali frowned. "Mom? You there?"

"Yeah, I was just wondering why you weren't here. It's Friday and hot laps start in two minutes."

Through the phone Kali heard the engines start, and she started swearing, "Shit, shit, shit. I'll be right there. Crap, I should take a shower first."

"And just get dirty again? Wash your face and hands and come on. I've saved your seat."

"Okay, I'll be right there." She hung up and literally started throwing things around to find her sandals and slipped them on, then grabbed her keys, and purse, and rushed out the door. Fifteen minutes later, she was hurrying up the steps, working her way to her seat, and sat down with a huge sigh.

"What in the world?" Kathy scowled at her daughter, then laughed as she reached up and began pulling pens and pencils from Kali's extremely sloppy bun that looked like she'd gone through several tornados. Kathy giggled as she took her daughter's purse and started going through it, then stood behind her and actually brushed her hair out, and put it in a quick braid.

"Mom."

"What? At least it looks better." She sat back down and handed the brush and seven pens and pencils to her daughter. "What on earth have you been doing, and do I want to even know?"

"I've been cleaning out my office."

"Damn." Kathy laughed. "Say no more, I understand."

"How you doing on the house hunting?"

Kathy sighed and slumped. "Terrible. The house you all saw fell through, but I've been so busy at the nursery, I haven't had a chance to go with your father to look at any more."

"But, I thought you sold it. Why are you still working there?"

"Because, I have a clause that says I can finish out this season. They take possession October first. And since it's not quite July, I still have a few months left, and I hate to mention this, but since you seem to be in a cleaning mood, I'm putting it out there that you need to come home, and clear out your old room, plus your stuff in the attic and basement."

"But, I thought I got all that when I moved out and bought my house."

"From your room, but your father's been going through stuff and helping get the house ready for when we list it, and found a few things in the attic. Boxes with your name on them. Luckily your brother and sister should be here for the Fourth, I thought we could all get together then."

"Let me know when you want me to come up," she said, and together they put their earplugs in, their face shields on, and settled down to watch the race. At the end of the night, Kali didn't stick around. She was almost one of the first ones out to the parking lot, and was home before the winner, which happened to be Kameron, was done giving his victory speech. She took an extra-long shower, and actually whimpered when she took her braid out and sighed. That was the thing she missed the most, being able to style her hair. She was in bed by one, and it felt great to sleep late, but she was right back to cleaning her office an hour after waking.

A week later, she walked into her parents' house at ten on a Sunday morning, stood, and observed her family. At last night's race, her mother told her that her brother and sister had arrived, and said it was time for them to tackle the house they grew up in. Kali didn't know how she felt about that.

"Aunt Kali!" Chuck yelled, and everyone turned and hurried over to her, and hugged her. She hugged them back and jumped in to help with the cooking for brunch, but suddenly she was whipped around, and she was staring at an outraged father.

"You are a brat," he said as everyone paused, and stared at him in shock.

"Keith!" Kathy said, and when he continued to glare at Kali, he threw up his hand to hold his wife at bay.

"I've been known to be, but what did I do this time?"

"Nothing." He sighed and deflated. "I take possession of Dusty Hill after this season, but I've been going over ideas of what I'm going to do, and how I want to advertise the hell out of it over the winter. I don't want to bother you, because you have a job you love, and I can deal with this, but I've contacted twelve ad agencies, and each and every one says the same damn thing."

"What do they say?" Kelsey frowned, then grinned when his father put his fingers to his face in the 'call me' fashion.

"Hello, I'm starting a new business, and I'd like to talk to the best ad exec you have in your company," he said, in his normal voice, then in a falsetto, "I'm sorry, Sir, but if you want the best in this area, you're going to have to contact Kali Kilpatrick over at The Wright Group." He hung up his phone, and sighed. "Twelve times, Kali. Twelve freaking times they said the same damn thing."

"So, call her." Kali bit the inside of her cheek to keep from giggling. Her father frowned at her, then grinned at the merriment he saw in her eyes. He picked up his 'phone' and said, "Ring, ring."

"Kilpatrick," Kali said into her 'phone', and grinned at her family.

"Is this Kali Kilpatrick, ad executive?"

"It is, how may I help you?"

"I'm starting a new business next year, and I need to hire an ad exec to promote the heck out of it over the winter. Unfortunately, it's a seasonal business, and I've called several other agencies, and they told me to contact you."

"So, you want to hire me?"

"Yes."

"Would you expect exclusivity?"

"Excuse me?" Her father frowned.

"Would you want my company to only work for you, or could my associates and I work with other clients at the same time we work for you?"

"Oh, no, you can work with others."

"So, what are you looking for?"

"Advertisement."

Kali laughed. "TV ads, newspaper, radio, promotions, contests, that's just some of the things I'm thinking. But first, what type of business?"

"It's a dirt race track."

"Is it active? Will you have races?"

"Yes."

"Do you have sponsors? Do you have special sponsor races planned? Promotions." She grinned when her family stared at her in shock, and Keith actually dropped his 'phone.'

He looked when Kathy handed him a piece of paper and frowned, then looked at Kali, and demanded, "What did you say the name of your company was?"

"Kilpatrick's." She grinned and hung up her own 'phone.' "I quit The Wrong Group last week. I've been cleaning out my office at home to get ready for any new business I can pull in. I already have a huge account, and then I'll have yours. I would have helped you out, but I wanted you to call me."

"I'll pay you. What's the other account?"

"Dillard."

"Holy shit, so what happened at The Wrong Group? Wait, I thought it was The Wright Group."

"It is, but it was all wrong for me. Something happened, and I quit on the spot, and since Dillard hadn't sighed yet, I called Max right in front of Tony, and told him I was now independent. He fired Tony and hired me over the phone. We're getting together tomorrow to discuss the video I made, and when it'll hit the airwaves."

"Can we ask what happened?" Chuck asked as he came back from directing the kids outside to set the table.

"Since you're all family, I'll tell you, but I won't tell anyone else. Understood?"

"Yes," they all said.

"I didn't know where I was going with the ad, so one day I was doodling and came up with this absolutely, stupid idea, but I went with it. I never had any intention of using it, because it wasn't real. But, it helps me clear the cobwebs, so the next day I was able to come up with what I did, but that doodle I threw in my garbage before I left for the day, an intern at the office, who I later found out was Tony's mistress, stole it from my garbage and made a whole presentation out of it. Thank god she went before me.

"Afterward, after the Dillards left, she accused me of setting her up. She admitted she stole it from my garbage can. But after my presentation, Max asked me to change one thing. Matt was upset and came to my defense, I covered his mouth, and told him to let the Dillards speak. When that intern attacked me, verbally, she turned on Matt and basically asked him how could he let a cripple touch him? It was disgusting and vile to look at, let alone have it touch someone. Tony heard everything, and when I asked what he was going to do, he said and did nothing. I called Max right then and there, and quit in front of everyone."

"Did you get severance at least?" Kelsey ask.

Kali grinned. "Actually, I demanded he cut me a check for three weeks plus twenty grand, the commissions he owed me from the last three accounts I landed. When he gave me the check before I left, I asked if it was going to bounce, he said only if I cashed it after that day. I packed up my office, went to his bank, took the cash, and went to mine and deposited it. That was a week ago this past Friday. I've been cleaning and reorganizing my office at home. For now, I'm going to hire Brian when and if I need him. Then later, Matt."

"Will he leave?" Karen frowned, having met the man several times.

"Yep, he asked me to take him with me when I left, but he decided to stay and see what would happen. He's going to give it six months. He called me yesterday and said that the intern has my office, and the person who passes out the new clients won't give her any, and two ad execs gave new clients my number."

"Good," Keith said, and hugged her tightly. He looked at his family over her head, and he all saw the anger on their faces for Kali's benefit. He gave his daughter an extra tight hug, then stepped back, and everyone's face went back to normal.

To break the silence, Lyle asked, "So, Brian was a big help?"

"Oh, my god, that brother of yours is a genius. Did he call you after his judging?"

"He did. Had to hold the phone away from my ear for the whole conversation. One of these days you have to show us the commercial."

"It's in my purse," she said, and Kelsey held up his hand.

"After we eat," he said, and started passing dishes to the others to take outside. Two hours later, the adults in Kali's family took their eyes off the large-screen TV in the family room, and as one they stared at her in shock.

"Holy shit, where's the nearest Dillard store?" Chuck asked. "I want to go get the parts for Karen's car."

"But that's still in Houston." Karen grinned. She stood and went to her sister and hugged her. "That was awesome." As they hugged, she whispered for Kali's ears only. "You talk to those hunks yet?" When she shook her head, she said, "Do it." Then, she backed up and grinned. Kali shook her head and took the congratulations from her family, knowing she was going to be okay.

CHAPTER FOURTEEN

"Hey." Kameron looked up when Kurtis came out of the bathroom with a towel wrapped around his waist, and stopped him before he headed to his room to dress.

"What's up?"

"I've been thinking."

"Oh, shit." Kurtis grinned and held up his finger. He disappeared in his room to come out minutes later with jeans on, and pulling a shirt over his still-wet chest. He sat down and took the cup of coffee Kam handed him as he dressed his feet. "What's up?"

"I was thinking about driving over and talking to Kali."

"About fucking time," Kurtis said as he sipped his coffee, and grinned at his twin. "If you didn't say anything before we left in three days, I was going to have Dad drive my rig, and I was going to ride with you and nag you the entire way. Ten whole hours of me nagging you."

"Hell, that'd be worse than Kyle. At least after a hundred miles, he falls asleep."

"But, then he wakes and is worse than before he fell asleep."

"Don't I know it, just remember, he's yours next season."

"Ah, hell," Kurtis said, but he laughed and shook his head. "I love the little guy with every fiber of my being, but he's a corker. Never know what he's going to come up with, and it amazes me he's better at one-line comebacks than you are."

"I know." Kam grinned and finished his coffee. They finished dressing, jumped to their feet, rubbed their hands together, and headed to the door. Twenty minutes later, they slowed and frowned. "Okay, I don't want to drive through her lawn, how do we get to her driveway without doing that?"

They looked around, Kurtis started giving him directions. They sighed in relief and grinned when they pulled in her driveway. They frowned when they didn't see any vehicles there, but they got out, and before they were twenty feet from their truck, they looked back and saw a black SUV drive in and slam on its brakes.

"Must have parked in her spot." Kameron grinned, he waved to her and made hand motions that he would move. They switched spots, Kali jumped out and went to the back of her truck.

"What are you guys doing here?" She started pulling grocery bags toward her, but was gently put to the side, and four strong hands and arms reached for the bags. Kali shut the tailgate, and they followed her into the house. Kameron and Kurtis frowned when they realized it wasn't locked, but then again, they never locked their doors either.

"Guys?"

"Oh, we thought it was time to have our talk. It's been several weeks."

"Oh," she said, and bit her bottom lip as she began unloading the groceries. They helped her put everything away. She sighed when it was done, and she couldn't stall any longer. "Where do you want to have this talk?"

"We can sit outside if that makes you comfortable," Kurtis said. "Would you like something to drink?" he asked as he opened her refrigerator, making himself at home. She only stared in shock as he pulled three bottles of water. Outside they didn't sit as close to her, but she was still in the middle of them, though she was able to see both of them from the position of her chair. They both stood and pulled the low table over, and tested it with their hands, then sat on it facing her.

They sat leaning forward with their arms on their thighs, and their hands clasped between their knees. As Kali suspected, Kameron began, "As we told you a few weeks ago, we both want to date you. Dad said a little about the way they and Mom live. That's what Kurt and I want with you."

"Marriage?"

"Not right now, but if this works, then possibly down the road, but for now, we'd like to get to know you and for you to know us. Just dating at first, and hopefully, that will lead to sex, but we have to get to know each other first, and the only way I can see that happening is to talk, ask questions. Does that make sense?"

"It does. So, are you always the one in charge?"

Kameron looked startled, and Kurtis snorted. "Yep, he is. It's his personality, but I don't mind." Kurt grinned. "How old are you?"

"Twenty-four. You?"

"Twenty-seven next month."

"What day?"

"Excuse me?"

"What day? I'll be twenty-five on the eleventh."

"The thirteenth." Kam grinned. "Are you wearing contacts?"

"No."

"Where are your glasses?"

"Oh, I don't need them. I've got twenty-twenty vision. I only wore the glasses to hide in public." At their frowns, she sighed. "Not a whole lot of people want to talk to, let alone be friends with redheads, but add a disability, and its worse. So, to stop the stares I started wearing clear glasses, but I made sure they were the ugliest ones I could find, and all of a sudden people didn't see me anymore."

"So, why take them off now?"

"You overheard, and I told you what happened to make me quit my job. It's time to stop hiding and be myself."

"Good for you," Kam reached out and took one of her hands gently in his, and Kurt did the same. "Would you like to show us?"

Kali took a deep breath, and turned her hands over into theirs. She watched closely as they studied her hands intently. They moved her dead fingers, ran their hands over the scar that was on both sides. When they were done, they still held her hands, and looked at her.

"Can you talk about it?"

"Yes and no."

"No pressure," Kam said, and sighed.

"I'm not being stubborn. I can't remember, and my family won't tell me. They are under strict instructions from the doctor to let me remember on my own, but I can tell you what I know."

"Okay," Kurt said, and Kali could tell they were confused, but it only showed when they exchanged looks. "But only if you're comfortable sharing."

"It's not much, and I'm not being smart or callus. I know I was three when it happened. I remember being at Grandma's house. Dad and Mom had gone out of town for the weekend, and us kids stayed with Grandpa and Grandma. They lived in the same school district as us, but not the same neighborhood. If that makes sense?"

"It does. Go on."

"It was a Friday, Kelsey and Karen left for school. As I said I was three, Karen was six and Kelsey was nine. On their way out of town, Dad had an expo for his business, and Grandma convinced him to take Mom with him, so as they got Kelsey and Karen on the bus, then packed up, dropped me and our suitcases off at Grandma's. I remember playing on Grandma's front porch. The school bus dropped Karen and Kelsey off. Grandma went over their schoolwork and asked about their day.

"Kelsey went in to use the bathroom, Grandma went in to fix us some milk and cookies. I was tired and was dozing off on the swing. Next thing I know I'm waking in the hospital with my arms wrapped in bandages up to here." She touched her shoulders and moved to the side, turning around. "Later after the bandages came off, I saw these."

Kam and Kurtis sucked in their breath at the scars radiating out from her elbows and all over the back of her forearms. When they were done inspecting them, she sat back and faced them again. "Oh, I forgot when I woke in the hospital, I couldn't talk." She waved her hand in front of her throat, and shrugged. "That's all I know. I did have several surgeries, but this is the best they can do."

"Do you know what's wrong?"

"All they said was that the nerve and tendon that is under these scars." She held out her hands and touched the scars as they each took one and rubbed the wounds there. "Are severed. It was either live like this..." She flipped her hands over and showed them the permanently bent fingers. "...or have them removed. Dad and Mom opted to keep them. But they don't slow me down. Dad even went out and had a set of, I guess the only way I can explain it is, like compression socks for your legs?"

"Yes, I remember my grandfather wearing them," Kam said.

"Yeah, Dad had two hand ones custom made for each hand. I wear them if I have important presentations, or know I'm going to be in very public places, and can't always hide them, but there's really nothing I can't do." She frowned. "No, that's not right. I can't braid my hair, but I can put it up." She pointed to her head, and they laughed as they reached up and each pulled a pen out of it.

"Oops, I wondered where those went." She giggled, then frowned. "So why do you want to date me?"

"You're beautiful." Kam frowned at her.

"Smart," Kurtis said.

"Funny."

"Sexy." Then they looked at each other, grinned, turned to her, and said at the same time. "And you like to get dirty."

Kali snorted. "So are you saying I'm a dirty girl?"

"Only a couple days a week." Kam grinned back. "But, time will tell how dirty you are." And just like that, Kali's girl parts woke and started screaming. "I see you like that idea. Now, I know we all probably have lots of questions, but I thought I'd go over the fundamentals of what our relationship would be like."

"Okay."

"At the end of this conversation, if you agree to go forward, this is what we expect. First, you will be dating both of us. We are a team."

"You can't play one of us against the other," Kurtis said. "I mean, if you and Kam have a fight or disagreement, don't come to me and expect me to take your side. The same if you and I have a disagreement, Kam won't take your side. We will take our side each and every time. I'm saying this, because we had a relationship years ago that almost tore us apart as brothers, but when it ended and we started talking to each other again, we realized we'd been played."

"The woman at that time was all for dating the both of us," Kam said. "But as it continued, we realized she only wanted Kurt and not me. Then, when we started talking again, we didn't talk for three months afterward. We realized that she only wanted to be with us for the bragging rights."

"What? That she bagged two hot, sexy guys at once."

"Yes. But she always pushed me away if we weren't in the bedroom. In the bedroom she was all for me touching her, but outside, she wouldn't even look at me."

"Why? You're a hot guy."

"Too demanding, she said. But I didn't and still don't think so. I have an opinion and I tell it, if that's too demanding, then so be it."

"To me that sounds like you're direct. Something I wished I would have had under my belt years ago, instead of finding my backbone only two weeks ago. But..."

"But what?" Kurtis asked, when she hesitated.

"Do you expect me to move in with you, or you move in here?"

"Do you move in with every guy you date right away?"

"No. Hell, I've never dated, and since we're putting everything out on the table, I'm a virgin." She was surprised when she didn't see shock, but grins on their faces.

"So, we can teach you everything we like from the beginning," Kam said. "But, no, we don't expect anyone to live with anyone."

"You're kicking me out?" Kurtis looked at his brother in shock, and winked at Kali when she giggled.

"What? No." Kam looked at his twin in shock, then punched him as he got the joke. "Ass."

"Thank you. But no, Kali, if this goes anywhere, time will tell if we move in with each other."

"Are there any restrictions?"

"Only that you don't play one of us against the other, and under no circumstances do you push one of us away in favor of the other. That's an automatic breakup for us. We won't do that again."

"Can I put a restriction on this?"

They frowned, but nodded. "I found out a couple days ago that Dad takes possession of The Hill, that's what he's going to rename it by the way. But he takes possession after this season. I've been going to Dusty Hill, State and McKay for five years. Well, this is my fifth year. Not once except for that day I asked you to participate in my commercial, have I ever gone into the pits. If we do this, I'm going to continue not to. Not that I'd be embarrassed to be seen with the both of you, but that's your job. I don't expect or want you to hang out at my job, so I'll give you the same courtesy, and not bother you at yours."

"Can we negotiate that?" Kurtis asked.

"What are you thinking?" Kam frowned at him, and then they stared at each other for several seconds, and Kam's face split with a huge grin.

"Oh, hell, do I even want to know?" Kali grinned.

"Have you ever had an adrenaline rush?"

"A couple times, the last time was at the showing of Brian's video, and when I've won some awards for my work."

"And you feel like you want to celebrate, you're on the top of the world and..."

"Yes. It's hard to explain, but you want to do something crazy and reckless."

"Exactly. We feel the same way every time we win. There are times when we get out of the car, and hear the roar of the crowd, we want to grab someone and kiss them. Pass our excitement onto them. But, it has to be someone we're going to be, or already are intimate with, and the sex that night would be out of this world."

"What Kam's not putting politely is that eventually, when you're comfortable with the idea, we'd like you to join our family and friends at the finish line. You've seen the people come onto the track to get their picture taken with us?"

"I have, but I'd like to put that in a to be discussed later column."

"Deal." Kam grinned. "Anything else?"

Kali nodded.

"Tell us. This is the negotiation stage. Let's get everything out on the table now."

"Okay, I just said that I'd never go into the pits, but that's a lie, only when it comes to The Hill. Dad hired me to be his ad exec to get word out it's under new management. So I'll be in the pits for that, but not for enjoyment. I want you to know that if you see me talking to other drivers, but ignoring you, I'm not playing you or anything like that."

"As long as we know ahead of time, we'll be fine with that," Kam said.

"Okay. Only one more thing I can think of for now."

"And that is?"

"Can I have two of those cards, the black one you gave Kyle?" She saw their expressions and burst out laughing.

"Oh, shit," Kam said. He looked at Kurtis and grinned. "This is going to be fun."

"I know," he said, and looked at her and nodded. "Yes. But, be prepared to receive one from us."

"One or two?"

"One, but you'll know it's from both of us."

"Fair enough. I'm not being snide, but at this time, I can't think of anything else. Though, I'm sure I'll have questions to ask along the way."

"And we expect you to ask, anything. Don't assume anything. This time you don't have to wait for the both of us to be present. Asking for clarification on anything that concerns you, isn't playing one of us against the other," Kurtis reassured her. "I know we haven't even started, but as long as we're on the one against the other thing, I have to say that if you can't do this and want to walk away, you walk away from both of us."

"That's why we didn't talk for three months." Kam pointed to Kurtis. "That woman said she was done, and she walked away, but she continued to call and see Kurt afterward. We fought, Kurt and I, and I walked away. It took several weeks for him to realize what that girl was doing, then several more to come talk to me about it."

"Have you always shared a woman?"

"Not always. When we first started dating we dated separately. It was a few years, three or four until we realized that something was missing in the relationships. The first time we shared a woman, I can't speak for Kam, but something clicked for me."

"Me too. And no, we are not gay. Yes, when we're in the bedroom with a woman, we're all naked and we see each other's cock, but in no way do they touch. So, if you do this, you'll be getting two cocks to give you pleasure."

"And four hands." Kurt grinned. "And twenty fingers."

"Along with two mouths, and two tongues." Kam grinned.

"Oh, Lordy." Kali waved her hand in front of her face. "So, if I say yes, we won't go inside to my bedroom right now?"

"No, but we might cuddle with you and kiss you," Kam said, and no one said anything until Kali drew in a deep breath, pressed her hands into her stomach, and slowly let it out.

"Yes."

CHAPTER FIFTEEN

Kali braced herself when the guys suddenly stood before her, reached down and gently helped her to her feet. They stepped closer to her, boxing her in, but Kali didn't feel trapped. She actually felt safe.

"We don't expect or plan on having sex with you today. We'd like to keep getting to know you," Kam said as he began rubbing her back.

"But we're going to start you getting used to being with two men," Kurtis said, and ran his hand down her back and over her ass.

"The first thing you need to know is that we're touchers. We like the feel of a woman, and we'll be constantly touching you. Something as simple as a touch on your arm as you walk by." He demonstrated, then leaned closer. "A kiss on the cheek, or the neck. A little nibble on the ear," he said, and put action to words.

Kali sighed and turned her head to the side to give him better access. She closed her eyes and enjoyed the attentions they were showering on her, and then she felt Kurtis behind her, and he gently pulled her to his chest. In front of her, Kameron stepped into her personal space, and gently, slowly so as to not scare her off, he took her face in his hands, and leaned in to kiss her. Just before his lips touched hers, Kali quickly licked her lips, and was shocked at the contact of their lips. What surprised her was that even though this was her first kiss, well, not really. They did both kiss her in the back hall of her house weeks ago, but this kiss was nothing like that.

That one was a full-on assault, while this one felt like Kameron was teasing her. He'd suck on just her top lip, run his tongue along it and then release her, then quickly released it, only to do the same thing with her bottom lip. Sighing in frustration, Kali lifted her arms and wrapped them around his neck, and suddenly the kiss changed. She heard Kurt mumble something from behind her, but she was too busy having her mouth devoured to understand what he'd said.

Kameron looked at his brother as he kissed the woman between them, and he saw the relief he felt on his twin's face. The same relief he felt. With just his eyes, he directed Kurtis to step closer, and when the woman in his arms moaned against his lips, he closed his eyes, stepped closer, and deepened the kiss by rubbing his tongue across the seam of her lips, and when she opened them his tongue slipped in, meeting hers. He lost himself in the taste and feel of Kali, and at first he was shocked when he was suddenly kissing the back of her neck, but he went with the flow and moved her hair, and kissed her neck, stepping closer and rubbing his aching erection against her ass. When she jerked forward Kurtis looked at him with widened eyes and a raised brow, because when she'd jerked forward, she'd slammed herself into his erection.

Kali groaned and slowly released Kurt's lips, and took several deep breaths. She put her forehead on Kurt's chest, and just went with the feelings that were coursing through her. She'd always wanted a boyfriend, and had listened intently to her female co-workers talk about their experiences, having always been envious. Not any longer. She now had a live and in Technicolor boyfriend. *Oops, make that two.*

"Penny for your thoughts," Kameron asked from behind her, and she tilted her head back when his arms came around her, and his hands slowly traveled up to cup her breasts, while Kurt's hands cradled her hips.

"Nothing."

"Kali," Kurtis said firmly. He didn't continue, until she opened her eyes and looked at him. "No lies. For this to work, you have to let us know how you are." He stepped back, and once Kameron steadied her, he also stepped back, and together the two of them faced her.

"Kali?" Kameron asked after several minutes of silence from her. He sighed and instead of standing over her, they sat down, so she was standing over them, and suddenly her breathing evened out, and the panicked look on her face slowly disappeared.

"God, I'm so sorry," Kali said on a rushed exhale. She sat down and grabbed the bottle of water and downed half of it. "All I could think of was that all my life, or at least since I noticed the opposite sex, I wished I had a boyfriend. Karen would tell me about her dates, and I'd listen to the girls at school, and even my co-workers, never expecting to experience the things they discussed. Then, I realized all my dreams were coming true, but I get double the pleasure and experience that were only in my dreams." When they continued to stare at her, she grinned. "That's it. Double the trouble, double the pleasure is all." She grinned when they gave her a stunned look, then huge grins spread out over both their faces.

"Okay," Kurtis said, and looked at his brother.

"Ditto." He grinned. "But I think we've given you a taste of what's to come. And as much as I want to strip you naked and sink my cock in you as fast and hard as I can, we have some things to discuss."

"Damn. I thought the talking was over." Kali sighed and settled back in her chair and sighed again. "Go ahead, hit me."

"Never." They both said at the same time. "We would never hit you."

"I meant with what you have to say."

"Oh," Kurtis said, and took several deep breaths and sat back down. "Sorry."

"What race tracks do you go to?" Kameron said, and put his hand on his brother's shoulders, but then sighed as he explained, "That women we told you about earlier, the one that played one of us against the other?"

"The one that pushed you away, but wanted Kurt?"

"Yes. She accused me of hitting her when Kurt wasn't around, because she'd been with him."

"Damn, why didn't you kick her ass to the curb right then and there?"

"We were only eighteen when it happened."

"Ah. I understand, and no, I don't think either one of you would hit me or any woman, especially not the way you treat your own mother and Kyle. I can see the love and respect you have for your family. You'd carry that over into any relationships you had. Now to answer your question, I only go to Dusty Hill every Friday they have races. Same with McKay. Then I go to State every Saturday."

"Any others?" Kurtis asked as he moved the chairs, so they were sitting in a circle of three.

"No, there aren't any closer to home. State's two hours away."

"So, you've never been to Eriez?"

"Where's that?"

"Erie, Pennsylvania."

"No. What are you saying?"

"It's the beginning of July, and our schedule is about to get busier. Eriez Motor Speedway experienced some problems this spring, and closed for a couple months, but they're back open, and we've been racing there for years. Starting this weekend, we'll be going back there."

"When do they race?"

"Sunday nights and its three hours one way from here," Kameron said.

"Then I won't be going. I don't think I'd get much sleep before I'd have to go to work on Monday."

"But, don't you work for yourself now?"

"Oh crap. I do." She giggled. "But, I still don't think I'll go. New unfamiliar places are hard for me." She looked down at her hands and stiffened slightly when two strong, tanned hands covered them.

"We understand," Kurtis said, and gave her hand a squeeze, then sat back.

"We're only asking, because there's no racing at Dusty Hill this next week. So we'll be racing at Port Royal on Friday, then Dog Hollow on Saturday, and swinging up to

Eriez on Sunday to come home for the week and do it all over again. We'll be doing that the entire month of July."

"But, there will still be races while you're gone?"

"Yes." They grinned when her panic cleared. "I guess we're just saying that you won't be seeing us at the tracks you go to for July."

"So, you'll be gone the whole month?"

"No, we'll be home during the week. Well, at least Monday, Tuesday, Wednesday and some Thursdays. We leave between nine and ten on Friday morning for Port Royal. Unless we get our shit together and leave the day before."

"How far away is this track?"

"Six hours. Then, we go over to Dog Hollow on Saturday. We'll get a map and show you, but we'll be here during the week, so we can go out or stay in, whatever you'd prefer. We can even cook a meal for you."

"You cook?" Kali asked in shock, then gave them both the stink eye. "Or, are you calling grilling, cooking? That's what Dad does. He can't boil water, but he can grill a mean steak, but he calls that cooking. Two totally different animals."

"Yep. We cook and we grill." Kurtis grinned.

"And if you'll allow us to hang out with you this afternoon, we'll cook dinner for you."

"Sure, but let's grab a sandwich first." She grinned. "I went grocery shopping without eating breakfast, and I'm hungry." They went into the kitchen and she got everything out, as they ate she frowned.

"What?"

"So, if we're doing this, we'll be considered boyfriend/ girlfriend, right?"

"Yes."

"Then, does that mean as my boyfriends, you'll be helping me if I need it?"

"Of course," Kurtis said, then laughed at her expression. He looked at Kam. "We've been had."

"I do believe we have." They let it go until they finished lunch, and once everything was cleaned up, he said, "What do you need us for?"

"Follow me." Kali grinned and went out the back door, then out to the garage. She opened the door and went in to turn on the lights, and they followed her in.

"What are we doing in here?"

"I've never used this garage, except for some lawn stuff." She pointed over to where the lawn mower was parked off to the side, and a couple rakes, shovels, and other gardening tools.

"Okay, but I don't understand." Kameron frowned as he looked around. "It's a big space, clean, but it doesn't look like you park in it."

"I don't. I had an idea when I drove home from my parents' house yesterday. If I'm going to open my own business, I'm starting out slow, but I already have two huge accounts." When they frowned, she grinned. "Dillard's and Dusty Hill. My office in the house isn't going to be big enough. I'm going to have to hire someone like Brian. I was thinking I could turn this into an office, and check this out." She walked over to the corner and they helped her up a set of rickety steps.

Upstairs in the garage, the twins stood in the middle and looked around at the huge empty space. They both were six foot three, and they had room to walk without hitting their heads. "So what? You want to make this space into your office?"

"I was thinking I could get a shed for the lawn stuff to be stored in, then make this space up here for the tech stuff, and my office would be downstairs, but it's cold in the winter. Would it make sense to have insulation put in? I know nothing when it comes to construction, but I do know that those stairs will have to be replaced. I guess what I'm asking is, would you be willing to help me, or give me pointers, or tell me who to call?"

"Sure," Kameron said. "Do you have a tape measure?"

"What for?"

"To know how big this place is?"

"I went over the paperwork I got when I bought this place, and the garage is listed as thirty by fifty."

"Damn," Kurtis said, and looked at his brother, and grinned. "Bigger than the place we live in." He looked over at Kali and grinned at her frown. "We own and operate a garage over in Sandusky. A few years ago, we built on the back of it. It's this size, but not two stories. It's small, but it works for us."

"Oh."

"And Kevin and Kyle still live at home."

"Would you mind if I call Dad in?" Kameron asked as he pulled his cell. "He's pretty good at construction. The way he's been lately, don't be surprised if the rest of the clan shows up, and Kyle. I'm warning you, he'll be here in fifteen minutes if I call him."

"Why?"

The twins looked at each other, and mimicked Kali herself as she'd been a few weeks ago. They sighed deeply, hung their heads, and sighed several more times.

"What's wrong?" Kali asked in concern.

They grinned, and said at the same time, "I'm bored, there's nothing to do."

Kali snorted and covered her mouth with both hands. "Oh my god, who says that?"

"Dad." At her frown they grinned harder. "Kent. Thirty years in the military and he's done."

"When he'd be home between deployments, he worked in the garage with us, but it takes some time to get into the swing of things. Ken black carded him from the garage yesterday."

"Oh my god. Why and for how long? Does this mean he doesn't go to the races with you?"

"No, just the garage for a week, and it's because he was barking at the new guys like the Marine he is. When five guys went up to Dad and threatened to quit, longtime seasoned guys, who happen to be the crew chief for each of us. Dad Ken gave Dad Kent a black card. Told him to get his act together before he comes back."

Kali grinned. "And Dad Kent knows construction? Do you think he'd give me good advice and maybe help me?"

"Hell, if Dad Ken knows about this, he'll give you the money to pay Dad Kent." Kurtis grinned at Kameron. "He only gave him the black card an hour before we showed up here."

"Go ahead and call him then. Maybe by now they're going to need a break from each other. Because somehow I don't see Kent taking that black card seriously."

They grinned, and Kameron dialed as Kurtis walked around with Kali, listening to her ideas.

CHAPTER SIXTEEN

"You can't be serious!" Kent yelled at his brother as they entered their house. "I'm talking to you, Ken!"

"No, you're bellowing at him," Kerri said from the end of the hallway with her hands on her hips. "What are you bellowing about now?"

"Woman, I don't bellow." Kent bellowed at her, then realized what he'd just said, and when he saw only one of her eyebrows quirk up, he knew he was in trouble. And when Kyle giggled from beside his mother and yelled, he knew he was done for. But, being a Marine most of his life, he stood tall and proud, ready to take his beating, so to speak.

"Kevin!" Kyle bellowed. "Daddy's in trouble."

"What else is new?" Kev asked as he joined them, and looked between his mother and fathers, and quickly put his hands on Kyle's shoulders, and started to back away.

"Don't move," his mother said, and the two younger boys froze. She stared at the two men before her, but addressed her question to Kent. "Seriously, you want to use that tone of voice with me?"

"Well, no," Kent said. "But, I don't bellow," he said proudly, and frowned when the other four people present snorted.

"Bullshit," Kyle said. "You don't talk, you bellow."

"I do not!"

"You just did." Kyle sassed back. "Didn't your Mama ever teach you to use your inside voice? Because, I love you, Daddy, I really, really do, but you've been walking around here and bellowing since you got back this time. Something's different, and you're taking it out on us. Use your inside voice, and maybe you'll get better results."

"Since when do you talk back to your father like that?" Kent bellowed.

"Since he's being an ass," Kyle said, and stood his ground. When he took one step forward, Kent was shocked when Kyle stood in front of his mother and brother, and held out his hands.

"Back off. Go cool down, then we can discuss this. Go on." He waved his hand and pointed to the door. "Walk it off, that's what you always tell us boys to do, now take some of your own parenting advice." Kyle stood with his hands on his hips and stared up at the huge man in front of him.

"Christ." Kent sighed, and deflated before all of them. He looked at them, and said, "I'm sorry. But Ken gave me this." He pulled the black card out of his back pocket and showed them.

"So, what's the big deal, I get one almost every week."

Kent snorted and grinned at his wife and brother. He looked at Ken and sighed. "I'm sorry."

"You're forgiven, but the card is still in effect. I don't know where your head is, but it's not here. You can't go around bellowing at the employees like you have been since you returned." As they talked, they made their way into the kitchen where Kerri poured coffee for the adults, and Kyle retrieved glasses of juice for him and Kevin. When Kent went to say something, Ken held up his hand.

"I'm not done. I love you brother, you know I do, but when the best employees come to me and tell me they are going to quit if you continue, I had to black card you."

"Who?" Kyle asked. "Who was going to quit?"

"Peter, Larry, Carl."

"Dad!" This time Kyle bellowed at Kent. "They're the fucking crew chiefs for the guys. How the hell can you make them quit?"

"Kyle," Ken said calmly. "First, stop with the swearing. Second, I handled it, they aren't quitting. Third, the black card is for one week away from the garage. Four, I'm handling it. You know the rules with the black card. We discuss it, you can add your input, but you don't get to become angry with the person that received the card."

"Well, that sucks," Kyle said, and when Ken glared at him, the moment was broken by the sound of a cell going off. Everyone reached for theirs, and Kent grinned.

"It's mine. Kilbourne," he barked into the phone, and the others looked around at each other and rolled their eyes, and snickered at the way he answered. Kerri shook her head at his frown.

"Kam, what's up?" Kent listened and frowned, then made a motion of writing and took the paper and pen, and began making notes. Finally, he said, "I won't know until I take a look at it." He paused, and said, "Hold on." He put the phone at his chest, and said, "You guys have any plans this afternoon?"

"No," everyone answered.

"Want to go over to Kali Kilpatrick's?"

"Sure," they said, and Kent smirked when Kyle jumped off his stool and ran up the stairs. He put the phone back to his ear, and said, "We'll be over soon." He hung up and grinned, then coughed when Kyle came back down with his hair slicked back.

"Don't say anything." Kerri said as she walked up, and put her arms around his waist, and he knew all was good with them. "He's got a huge crush on Kali."

"How much aftershave did he use?"

"Probably only a handful. It gets better. At first he used a whole bottle at once, but he's getting better."

"Does he know that Kam and Kurt are talking to her this afternoon to start dating her?"

"Yeah," Kerri said, and turned her head into her husband's chest and giggled.

When Ken came up behind her and wrapped his arms around them, he leaned in and whispered to Kent, "He says he's going to give Kam some competition."

Kent snorted and shook his head. He hugged his brother back, and said again, "I'm truly sorry."

"Forgiven, but you'll have to apologize to the guys when you return."

"I will." He lifted Kerri's chin, and whispered, "We good?"

"Yes, but you'll have to make it up to me later tonight for bellowing at me."

"With pleasure," he said, and kissed her.

"Daddy, we don't have time for that shit, time's a wasting, and we gotta go," Kyle said, and he slammed out of the front door, bellowing over his shoulder, "SHOTGUN!"

"Damn, I think Kali's right. I think he might be mine."

"Yep," Ken slapped him on the shoulder. "Because, my kids are perfect angels." He grinned when Kerri slapped his ass.

"All our children are perfect angels. Some are more challenging than others." She grinned, then frowned. "Do you know why Kameron asked us to come over? Do you think they want us to help them convince Kali to date them?"

"No, he didn't get into everything, but I took some notes. Something about moving Kali's office, and making another one and a shed and insulation."

"Oh," Kerri frowned, then gathered her things, followed Ken out, headed toward the SUV, and at the last minute, Kent went into the garage, and came out with several items that he put in the back, before he got behind the wheel and headed out. Thank god it was summer out, and everyone automatically rolled their windows down, to get the smell of Kyle's hair out of their nostrils.

Less than thirty minutes later, they pulled in behind Kameron's truck, and everyone disembarked from Kent's SUV. They saw the three people walking in the back yard, and they were pointing and nodding, or shaking their heads. Kyle was the first one to take off, and when he reached them he threw his arms around Kali and hugged her, then he looked at Kameron and grinned. Kent admired Kali when she didn't reel away from the strong smell of his son, but actually kissed the top of his head. He grinned when she turned her head and wiped her mouth. They caught sight of each other and grinned.

The adults and Kevin made their way over to them, and after hugging his sons, because that was the way the Kilbournes greeted people, they even hugged Kali. "So what's up?" Kent asked.

"We'll let Kali explain it," Kameron said. He knew he was almost throwing her under the bus, but if they were going to have a relationship, she was going to have to learn to talk to his father.

"Might as well come into the house and I'll start there." She motioned for them to follow her, and she stopped in the kitchen and asked if they wanted anything, but they declined. Kameron kept Kevin behind and pulled his wallet, and after asking if he wanted to go to the store, he gave his younger brother money, and told him to pick up stuff for the grill. He actually threw several suggestions out, and Kevin wrote them down, grinned, then took the money and keys to Kam's truck.

"Dad's parked behind you." Kevin frowned.

"Are the keys still in it? Move it over behind Kali's, then take mine."

"Okay." He grinned and disappeared. Kameron went down the hall and stood in the doorway, and watched as Kali began talking to Kent.

"This is my office. You saw what I do. I'm starting my own business, and if I'm going to have someone like Brian work with me, this isn't big enough for both of us, and I don't want the business to take over my house, so I thought I could convert the garage to an office. I've got two clients already, and I'm going to have to get started, but I don't want to rent office space right now," she said, and waved them out, taking them to the garage. Once inside she turned and held her arms out. "This is thirty feet by fifty feet, and take a look upstairs."

She watched as Kurtis took them up, and Kerri and Kali slowly followed. "I was thinking of having this floor for the tech stuff, but Kameron pointed out that I'd have to beef up the electricity."

"And downstairs would be your space?"

"Yes, and as I grow, or if I grow, I could have a small section as a receptionist, but I think if I get that big, then I'll be able to rent a bigger space. But, what I'm asking is, if it's possible to winterize the garage, so it's warm in the middle of the winter, and if I'd have enough power now, and how would I go about doing it, and who do I call?"

"Sh," Kent said as he put a hand to her lips, then he gently put his hands on her shoulders, and said, "I understand what you're trying to do, and yes, it can be done. Just ask Kam and Kurt how warm their place is."

"What's that mean?" Kameron asked, then looked at Kali. "It's warm, we only keep the heat at sixty-five in the winter, and sometimes it's so warm we turn it down, or crack a window."

"That's because the outside is brick and I insulated it. I can help you get this to what you want, but we're going to have to sit down and talk about what you want." He indicated for them to go down the stairs. Once down he looked around, and went out and brought a tape measure and hammer from his SUV. Kerri handed Ken a pad of paper and pen from her purse, then she stepped back with the boys as Kali walked around with them.

"What about that stuff?" Kyle asked as he pointed to the corner at the lawn equipment.

"That's what we were doing out in the back lawn," Kali said. "Walking around to find the best place to put up a shed." And then everyone went out and began walking, and both Kent and Ken agreed with the location Kam had pointed out.

They were sitting around on the patio, but didn't start their discussion, because Kevin had returned. He took everything in the kitchen, and when Kali frowned Kam grinned. "I figured Dad would get his teeth dug into this, and I sent Kevin to the store to pick up food for everyone, figured after we talked we could have a BBQ. How far away do your parents live?"

"They're up in Norton, but Kelsey and Karen are there also with their families."

"So, call them." Kerri grinned as she pulled her phone. "Or, I can call Kathy. Maybe Keith would want to know what's going on. Have you talked to your parents about this yet?" she asked, then looked at her in shock. "Oh shit, I didn't mean you had to have your parents' permission to do something with your own house. I'm so sorry."

Kali laughed. "Don't worry about it. I didn't think that. I only came up with the idea yesterday when I drove home from there, but I could call and see what they say. Dad owned and operated a heavy equipment company for thirty years, but he also put in huge buildings. I guess I should call him."

"Let me." Kerri grinned and dialed. "Kathy, hi, it's Kerri. I'm calling, because we've invaded your daughter's place, and we have a project going, or starting. Thought you'd like to know and come join us." She paused and grinned and nodded. "Let me check." She lowered the phone and frowned at Kam. "She wants to know if she needs to bring anything."

Kam looked at Kevin and he grinned. "Plates? Glasses?"

Kerri laughed and relayed the message and hung up. "They're actually halfway here. Jordan wanted to come see all the green stuff at Aunt Kali's house, because there's not enough at Grandma's house. I have no idea what that means."

Kali laughed and pointed to the ground at her feet.

"What?"

"Grass. When Jordan was here for the first time a few weeks ago, as soon as Lyle got him out of the car, he asked what the green stuff was. I was shocked he didn't know what grass was. That week he stayed here, he'd even take a nap out here, and he tried to sleep out here at night. See, they live in a small two-bedroom apartment in San Diego, and what little grass they do have, it's brown."

"Yuck." Kyle shuddered. "So, Chuckie's coming too?"

"Yes, but don't you mean Charles?"

"He likes to be called Chuckie."

"He does? Or, do you like to call him that?" Kam asked sternly.

"He does, he said it himself. He thinks Charles is an old man's name." When Kyle held up his hands in defense of their looks, he said, "Honestly, ask him." They sat around and talked, discussing everything under the sun for the next hour, when they were invaded by the Kilpatricks.

CHAPTER SEVENTEEN

"And why didn't you discuss this with me yesterday?" Keith asked his daughter as they settled back in the lawn chairs, after walking the garage and back yard with Kali's family.

"Because, I never thought of it until I was driving home. I was thinking of some ideas for The Hill, and it dawned on me that I didn't have the room for me and a technical guru. Earlier I mentioned what I wanted to do to Kam and Kurt, and they called Kent, and Kerri called you." She grinned. "So, now you know."

"Smartass."

"Yep, you taught me well." She grinned again. "So, what's the next step?"

"Who you thinking of hiring for the tech work?" Keith asked. "I don't care, but I'd like to talk to them about the amperage their equipment would need. See if the location would work for them. Then, after we have that information we can make up some plans, and go to the town for a permit."

"Sorry, I forgot about a permit," Kent said. "I'm used to just doing it, in the military where we didn't have to worry about stuff like that. Most of the stuff was done on base."

"That's fine. Lyle, do you know if Brian's home?"

"He's not. We were over there and he pulled out and went camping for a month. Said now that he was done with school, he was taking time off to unwind." He laughed. "I had to repack his bags, because he had video cameras and regular cameras and film in his bag. No clothes."

"So, his idea of unwinding is going into the woods and taking pictures?"

"Yep. I'm sorry, but he left for the Adirondacks an hour ago."

"That's fine. I know of someone else I can call." She excused herself and went into the house. In her office she sat at her desk, and nodded when she saw Kam and Kurt standing there. "Come in. I'm calling a former co-worker. His name is Matt Clayton. He was my techie at The Wright Group."

"The one that asked you to take him with you?"

"Yes. I'm telling you this, because I think once I tell him what I'm asking, he's going to beg me to come work with me, and as much as I love and appreciated Brian's help, Matt knows me, it's like he knows what I'm looking for before I do, and I didn't want you to be jealous if you saw him around here."

"As long as he knows you're with us, it shouldn't be a problem, and we'd like to meet him."

"Sure, but you have nothing to worry about. He's only a friend. We worked together for seven years, no six. I was there a year before he was, and he's like Kelsey, a big brother." She saw their nods, and she put her phone on speaker and dialed.

"Thank you for calling The Wright Group, how may I direct your call?"

"Matt Clayton please."

"One moment."

She was put on hold, then a gruff voice answered, "Clayton."

"Matt?"

"Yeah, who's this?"

"I'm hurt, I've only been gone a little over a week, and you've forgotten me already."

"*KALI!* Wait." He disappeared off the phone, but they heard rustling, then a door slam and he was back. "The twit's lurking. Please, tell me you're calling to get me out of this hellhole. I finally realized why I used to love this job, it was because of you, your mind, your ideas, putting those to film, the way you challenged me. But, Tony has me working with the twit, and we're at a standoff. I refuse to take direction from that twit."

"What does she have you doing?"

"Remember her presentation?"

"The blinker fluid?"

"Yeah, she still believes she can tweak her video, and get clients to buy her concept. I won't put my name on garbage. But, I digress, what's up?"

"Can you get away?"

"I can. Why, where am I going?"

"I'd like you to get to my house as soon as possible. And, yes, I'm going to hire you, but you might have to stay there for a couple more weeks. Depends on when what I'm planning is finished. I'm only saying this, because I don't know your financial situation."

"I'm good. I can even take a year off work and not be hurt, but I'll let you tell me what you're doing first before I decide," he said, then sighed. "Who the hell am I kidding, I'll work for you."

"With Matt, you'll be working with me."

"Whatev, give me your address."

"First where do you live?"

"A small town south of the office here, you've never heard of it, living in Norton."

Kali grinned and wrote on a pad, *'I never told anyone I bought this house'*. Then she turned it toward Kam and Kurt who read it, and grinned.

"Actually, I don't live in Norton anymore. I bought a house after the Bud commercial."

"Oh? And big brother's just finding out about this now?"

"No, big brother found out about it when I closed, but my honorary big brother's just finding out about it. So, where do you live?"

"Machias."

"Really. What way do you go home?"

"South on the four hundred to the sixteen, until I get to the four-way stop in Machias, turn right, and it's six houses down from there on the left. Why?"

"So, you drive through Devil's Nose?"

"Yes."

"That's where I live. When you get to where the DMV office, the new location."

"Next to the bank?" he interrupted.

"Yes, take that left, go to first stop sign, go straight, then take the first right and I'm at the end. Green house, you'll see several vehicles in the driveway. What's that noise?"

"I'm pulling onto the four hundred now. When I slammed that door, I switched you from the office phone to my cell and left."

"Holy shit, you can do that?"

"You'd be surprised what this techie can do." He laughed. "Okay, I'm on the four hundred. So, I head toward home, when I get to Devil's Nose I turn left at the DMV, go to stop sign, stop, go straight, take first right. What's the name of that road?"

"Elton Extension."

"Okay, turn right on Elton Extension, then go to the end. What number and color?"

"Green and eighteen." She looked at Kam and grinned, then she rolled her eyes when he looked at Kurtis and puffed up his chest.

"See you soon." And he hung up.

"Wow," Kurtis said. "He seems a little high strung."

"He is, but he's the best, and if it wasn't for him, I wouldn't be as good as I am."

"Bullshit," came the voice from the doorway, and they turned to see Kyle leaning against the doorjamb. "It's you that make them look good. Without your ideas and insights, they wouldn't know where their ass was."

"Kyle," Kam said sternly. "Language."

"It's the truth."

"We know," Kali grinned, "But, you don't have to swear."

"Sorry," he said, and actually blushed. They all went back out and told the others what was happening, and they sat around and talked until Matt arrived.

"KALI!" came a bellow from the front of the house, and she grinned as she jumped to her feet, and went around the front of the house. "My Darling!" he yelled, and ran to her and picked her up, then twirled her around until she begged

him to stop. He set her down and took her face in his hands, and kissed both cheeks, then her forehead. He stepped back and froze, then leaned in, and whispered, "Who are all these people, and why are three of them shooting daggers at me?"

Kali looked around and saw everyone standing there, and sure enough in the front were Kameron, Kurtis, and Kyle. She giggled and without saying anything, she linked her arm with Matt's, dragging him forward and made the introductions. She saved Kameron and Kurtis for last, and as they went to shake hands, she grinned as she said, "My boyfriend."

"Which one?"

"Both," they said, and stepped up on either side of her, and he looked at the three of them and grinned.

"About goddamn time. And you?" he asked Kyle.

"She's my friend."

"Good, she's a great gal to have as a friend. She's my friend too. Has been for six years."

"So, you're not her boyfriend?"

"Eew, that'd be like dating my sister."

"Eew, I don't have any sisters, but that would be creepy."

"I know." He grinned and turned to the others. "So, I'm here, what's up?"

"Follow me," Kali said, and rolled her eyes when Kam and Kurt were right beside her. She stopped so suddenly they went past her, and when they turned back to stare at her, she glared at them, leaned in, and whispered, "Knock it off, this is my job. I don't bother you at yours, so don't do it to mine. Matt is only a friend." They held up their hands and stepped to the side, and grinned when she actually slapped both of them in the gut, hard enough to hurt when she stormed past. To show they trusted her they stayed outside with the others, and it was only ten minutes later that they returned. They even stayed back when she explained how she wanted to set up her office, but they drew the line when Matt went upstairs with Kali, and they followed, but they stayed out of the way and watched the two work together, and realized they had nothing to worry about.

Back at the circle in the lawn, Matt was handed something to drink, the kids were further in the lawn playing, and Matt looked around, and asked, "So what do you need from me?"

Keith and Kent sat forward, and said, "We need to know that if you're in full production mode, or whatever you call it, when all your equipment is it full capacity, what's the voltage you're going to need?"

Matt sat forward, grabbed a pad of paper, and started jotting things down. It took twenty minutes, then he and the two older men went back to the garage, and started discussing everything. While they were planning, Kam and Kurtis disappeared into her house. An hour later everyone was back in the group, and the twins came out of the house with platters of meat. They grinned when Kali stared at them in shock.

"What are you doing?"

"We told you we'd cook you a meal. I sent Kev to the store earlier. I didn't want to use the food you'd bought. We've got burgers and dogs for the kids, pork steaks for us. We've made a couple salads that are cooling in the fridge."

Kali grinned and looked at her Dad. "See, Dad, that's what cooking is. Not just using the grill, but also cooking other things to go along with it."

"Yeah, yeah, yeah, but your mother won't let me near the stove."

"Why, because you almost burnt the house down when we were younger?" Karen called out to him. "Remember, we had to call the fire department."

"Yeah, and didn't your mother get a brand new kitchen out of the deal?"

"She did."

"But we had to eat take out for months," Kelsey said. "That's why Mom made sure all of us could cook."

"That's right." Kathy said as she and Kerri came out of the kitchen. She walked up to her husband and stood behind him, and leaned down and kissed the top of his head. "But, I don't mind cooking for you. You provided for us for all those years, it was the least I could do. You learning to cook wasn't really a bother. You were the one who did the work around the house in addition to working away from home. So, if our children are ungrateful brats to pick on you about it, don't think for a minute that it bothers me."

"I don't," Keith said. He looked at his children and grinned. "See, your mother thinks you're ungrateful brats."

"We are." Kali grinned. "But, we love you. If we can't pick on each other, then what's the sense of hanging out."

"Agreed." He looked over at the grill, and when he saw flames flare up, he called, "Need an expert's help there, boys?"

"We got it, but thanks," Kam called, and grinned when the men joined them at the grill, Keith, Ken and Kent all giving pointers.

"So," Matt said as he sat beside Kali, and grinned. "Both? And when did this happen?"

"Today, and yes."

"No judgment, just one question and I'll leave it alone."

"What's that?"

"Are they the guys from the video for Dillard?"

"Yes."

"Which ones?"

"The first and second ones that drove onto the track. And yes, they are twins."

"Cool. Now do you really have the Dillard account?"

"I do, Max sighed the contract yesterday. The commercial's going to hit the airwaves in two weeks."

"Do you have any other accounts?"

"I do, but it doesn't start until September 15th and it's huge. I want to start rolling out the ads February first."

"That long?"

"Yes, wait until you see what it is. I'll tell you when you come on board." She grinned when he called her a tease. They sat around and talked until almost dark, and after everyone left except for Kam and Kurt, they helped her finish cleaning up, and before they left they made sure she was well kissed, and knew that they were very interested in her, but again said they'd wait for the sex, until they knew each other better. It was a long time before any of them fell asleep in their own separate beds that night.

CHAPTER EIGHTEEN

On the second Saturday the guys were away, Kali was sitting in her usual spot in the top row in the last seat at the State Speedway, eating the supper she always had. Sandwich, a handful of chips, two cookies, and a bottle of water. It was intermission, and a lot of the people who'd sat around her had gone down to either smoke or get something to eat. She watched as a man dressed in pressed black dress pants, a white button-down shirt, and a purple striped tie walked down in front of the stands, back and forth, back and forth, several times, all the time looking up in the stands, and talking on a cell phone.

He finally looked up and then nodded, hung up his phone, and started up the first set of stairs. He came almost all the way to the top, one row down from where Kali was sitting. He sat down on the row below her, facing her.

"Excuse me, I don't mean to interrupt you, or be rude, but are you Kali Kilpatrick?"

"I am," she answered, then stared at him in shock. "Oh my god, did something happen to the Kilbournes?"

"What? Oh no. I'm sorry. It's nothing bad, I promise you. I'm sure you saw me walking back and forth down there. I was on the phone with your father, and there is absolutely nothing wrong with your family. I swear to you. I have a proposition for you," he blurted out, and when he saw her expression, he sighed and hung his head. "God, I'm not doing this correctly."

"First, take a deep breath and let it out slowly," Kali said as she packed up her supper, and hugged her hands to her waist. When he seemed calmer, she nodded. "I'm Kali Kilpatrick. How may I help you, Mr.?"

"Oh, Martin, George Martin." He held out his hand, and even though it didn't show, she cringed inwardly and shook his hand, and was relieved when there was no reaction.

"Well, Mr. Martin, what can I do for you?"

He looked around as people started to join them, and said quietly, "Can we go to my office?"

"Excuse me?"

"Damn it," he said and shook his head, and blurted out, "I want to hire you as an advertiser, I know your father from Dusty Hill, and he recommended you. But, it's a lot to discuss, and I know you live three hours away, and I don't know when I'll make it back to this area, so I was wondering if we could go to my office and talk."

"Sure, do you think it'll take the rest of the race?"

"It might. I hate to pull you away from the features."

"That's okay, my favorite driver's aren't here today."

"Oh, why not?"

"They're on some track called Dog Hollow, then they're going to Eriez tomorrow."

"Ah," George said, and when Kali stood, he actually picked up her bag and carried it for her, indicating she should go first. They didn't talk until they were down on the ground and he showed her which way to go. She frowned when they went around the stands and up the outside of the announcer's booth and in. He waved to the people there, walked to the other end, and into a small office. He closed the door and Kali could see the whole track from there. She went over and stared out the windows.

"Cool."

"Yeah, at least it's a little quieter in here, but we'll still feel the rumble as they go by. Here's a pad of paper and a pen in case you want to take notes." He passed them to her then loosened his tie, undid the top two buttons of his shirt and settled behind his desk. "As I said I'm George Martin and I'm in charge of the ULMS division, which encompasses several race tracks."

"I don't know if I follow what all that was."

"ULMS stands for United Late Model Series. That's why the Kilbournes aren't here tonight. They all follow Kameron, or not follow, but race on the same track he does. It's a family thing. And he runs all the ULMS sanctioned races. Last week, this, and next, he's running Port Royal, Dog Hollow and Eriez in the sanctioned races. If there isn't a sanctioned race he stays closer to home. But, in addition to being the head of the ULMS division, I own several race tracks." He stood and went over to a wall and motioned her over.

"I had heard Dusty Hill was going up for sale, but your father beat me to it, and that's okay, but his track will continue to be a sanctioned ULMS track, and I'm sure you've heard about them?"

"Not really, I don't know much about racing. I've only been going for five years and it wasn't until this past spring my parents were involved."

"I know, Keith told me. Have you ever been to a race at Dusty Hill and saw that there were more people there on some nights than others, and it was a night the Kilbournes were there? And the nights they weren't it was less fans?"

"I have, but I thought that was because they followed the Kilbournes."

"That might be the case, but not always. On those nights there are huge amounts of fans, there are more cars than usual. Say in the feature for the late models there are over forty cars, but on other nights there might be only twenty-five? Those nights with the larger number of cars are the nights of a ULMS sanctioned race. Those extra cars come from all over to run in those races, because they are on the circuit, along with Kameron Kilbourne."

He smiled when he saw Kali stare off into space for several moments then grinned when she looked at him. "Okay, but I reserve the right to ask lots of questions."

"Granted." He grinned, then pointed to the map in front of them. "This is Dusty Hill. The track your father owns. ULMS sanctioned. This is State, where we are now. I own this one. Then we have McKay, also ULMS sanctioned. But the county of McKay owns that one. That's why no race will be this next week, because it's their county fair. Then this is Port Royal." He slowly moved his finger down, over and the further he went the wider Kali's eyes became. "Also ULMS sanctioned, also owned by me. Then this is Dog Hollow." His finger headed back to the left and stopped. "Also owned by me and ULMS sanctioned. Then we have Eriez." He moved his finger up and to the left. "Again, ULMS and me."

"Wow, so how far are the tracks?"

"Six hours from here to Port Royal. Five from there to Dog Hollow, and five from there to Eriez, and four home from there."

"So, what do you need me for?"

"Coming up in August there's a huge ULMS sanctioned race over in Ohio, it's three whole days of racing. Late Models only, which is the car that Kameron drives. We're talking over a hundred and fifty cars and the purse to the winner is over a hundred thousand."

"Wow, that's a hell of a lot more than the three or five or eight grand they get at the local tracks."

"Correct. And the cars will be coming from all over the country to race. Then there is another huge one, but it's for all classes and for five days in Charlotte, North Carolina, and the winner of each class gets a hundred thousand. That's in November. Every year. The one in Ohio is new this year. Never been done before."

"Okay, but I don't understand what this has to do with me."

"Not this next year, but I want to do that here." He pointed to the map and his finger landed on the track they were standing at now. "Out of all the tracks I own, this is the best one for seating at this time, but your father and I are planning some things, he said he'll let you in on it when he officially takes over the track. That's why you're not doing anything yet."

"I know. So, what do you want from me?"

"I want to hire you to do the advertising for what I want to do, but first I want you to go to the race in Ohio and be a spy. Get as many pictures of the event as you can, ask questions, look at their layout. I'm not stealing their ideas, well, yeah, but not in a bad way. In a way that we'd know how it's done. Tweak what's weak there, you know, improve it." He went back to his desk, opened the drawer, and pulled out an envelope. He dumped the contents in the middle of the desk.

"This is two press passes to the event, the name of the person who will give you a tour, a blow by blow of what they did, and how they did it, and will answer all your questions. He's the coordinator in charge of that event, and this is him giving you permission." He handed her a letter, which she took and read.

"And you want me, to go and do this?"

"You and the man your father said is your cameraman. The race starts on a Thursday, but we, Mr. Bloom and I, would like you there the Sunday before. This way you can see everything before the drivers start to arrive, and it'll be less crowded. They will start arriving on Tuesday."

"Do you want me to stay for the whole event?"

"Yes, you and your cameraman. Mr. Bloom can explain everything until he's blue in the face, but I'm a visual person. I want to see pictures. And before you leave for Ohio, which I will pay you for your time, with the hopes that all pictures and videos you obtain can be used to promote what I want to do in a year or two. I'm hoping next year. But, in the meantime, I'd like to hire you for a couple other projects I have already got going."

"Which are?"

"I have websites and Facebook pages for the tracks I own. I had to fire the person in charge of them, because he was putting his own personal propaganda on them, and not the races. You've seen the guys in the infields taking pictures as the drivers go by?"

"I have."

"Those pictures are what I want on the internet, along with pictures of the winners getting their trophies."

"Okay, that would be a job for Matt, he's the camera guy and all that."

"That's what your father said. So, here's my card, have him call me. What's his last name?"

"Clayton, Matt Clayton. I'll talk to him tomorrow about it. Do you have a list of those sites?"

"I do." He stuffed the items back in the envelope, and handed her that, along with the list of websites. Kali asked a question which led to several, and when someone knocked on his door, they frowned when it opened.

"Boss, we're done, and about to shut off the lights."

"Oh, shit," both Kali and George said. They jumped up and George looked at Kali and said. "Give me five minutes and I'll walk you out." He hustled around and began throwing things in his briefcase, and after he closed it, he made sure she had all her things, and then he snapped his fingers, pulled open a drawer, and shoved some papers into a folder and handed it to her. Shocked, Kali automatically took it, and put it with the rest of her things. After leaving the office, she reached for her bag he'd placed on the outside of his office, but he waved her away, and carried it for her.

Kali expected him to leave her at the bottom of the stairs, but she was shocked when he walked her all the way to her SUV, then he put her bag inside and shook her hand. "I look forward to hearing from you and Matt soon. I hope we can work well together, Kali." He even leaned in and kissed her cheek, stepped back, and said, "Drive carefully." And he waited until she was in, buckled and had pulled out. In her rearview mirror she saw him turn to leave then. Kali's mind was whirling all the way home, so after her shower, she fell asleep with no problems.

CHAPTER NINETEEN

Kali spent all day Sunday going over the paperwork George had given her, along with the websites and Facebook pages, which made her wince when she saw them. "Hell, I can do better than this," she said to her computer, and started making notes.

She spent most of the morning working, and when her stomach started rumbling, she went out to make herself something for lunch, and saw a movement out of the corner of her eye. She grabbed a knife and hid to the side, and frowned when no one came to the door, but she heard the garage door open. She ran to her room to throw on some clothes, and with the knife in her hand she crept out of her house, and through the bushes to the back side of the garage.

"Stop right there," she said in the deepest voice she could, and when the man held up his hands, she said, "Turn around slowly." They did and she lowered her arms and glared at him. "Kent, what the fuck, you scared the hell out of me. Why didn't you stop at the house to tell me you were here? Un-cool."

"I'm sorry. It's Sunday and I thought I'd let you sleep in."

"Pff, I haven't slept in since I was ten. Hey, why aren't you at Eriez? Aren't the guys racing there tonight?"

"They are, but Kevin wrecked last night, and there's no way for him to get his car fixed in time for tonight's race, so he and I came home, and the others went on to Eriez. They'll be home early morning. I left Kevin home brooding and going over the inventory we have at home, then he'll go over to the garage. I left him to his mood, and came over here to work." He grinned and watched her. "You going to use that?" He nodded to her hand, and she blushed as she looked at the knife she still held.

"Oops. Sorry. So, you want to come in and have some coffee?"

"I don't want to bother you."

"You won't be, actually, I was wondering if I could talk to you."

"About?"

"Racing."

"Not my boys? Or the lifestyle they're asking you to partake in?"

"Maybe eventually, but I don't have any questions yet. But, I have to talk to them tomorrow when they come over, and I really want to get my shit together before I do."

"And you think I can help you?"

"How long have you been going to the race track?"

"Since my mother was pregnant with me, and I'm fifty-one."

"See, I've only been going for four and a half years, and Dad for only four months."

"Fine, you twisted my arm." He laughed and together they went up to her house, and she ended up fixing them both a sandwich, then after he cleaned up, he looked at her and grinned. "You're stalling."

"I don't know how to ask my questions without sounding dumb."

"Baby girl, the only dumb question is the unanswered question."

"Oh. What's ULMS?"

"United Late Model Series. Kam's a member, and after the last two nights, he's taken the lead in the series."

"Meaning?"

"Meaning, he's leading in points, meaning he's won all the ULMS races he's entered. Meaning, he'll probably be the champion again this year. Fourth year in a row."

"And that's good?"

"That's great."

"Have you heard about the Dirt Million?"

"Absolutely. It's a race over in Ohio next month, only Kam can race in it, but we're all going. We've already gotten our tickets and camping site. Want to go?"

"When are you leaving to go?"

"Tuesday morning, it's only a six or seven hour drive."

"That's what I thought." She sighed.

"Kali?" Kent asked in that deep voice of his, and put both his hands over hers. He left them there until she breathed easier.

"Wait here." She hurried away and was back with a thick folder in seconds.

"Last night I was at State Raceway. During intermission I was eating the supper I packed, and a man came up to the stands and talked to me." She wasn't looking at him, and didn't see the flash of anger in his eyes, but he did sit back away from her. She looked up, and sighed. "I don't know if you know him, but my Dad sent him looking for me."

"Who?"

"This guy, his name is George Martin."

"Georgie?" Kent frowned. "Why did he want to talk to you?"

"He wants to hire me." She laid out the contract, and watched as Kent slipped a pair of glasses from his shirt pocket, and he slipped them on the end of his nose. That's how she imagined Kam and Kurtis would look in the future. It took several minutes for him to go through everything, and the last thing he read was the contract George had given her before she left the night before. The one he'd gone back for.

"Wow." He looked at her in shock and admiration. "And you know how to do what he's asking?"

"Yes. Do you know this Mr. Bloom?" she asked as she handed him the envelope. She dumped everything in front of him, and handed him the letter.

"Damn."

"Good damn, or bad damn?"

"Excellent damn. Tickets are a hundred bucks a pop, for us, everyone but Kam had to buy a ticket, plus the cost of gas for Kam's whole rig, Kevin and Kurt's RVs, and Ken's truck and fifth wheel, then the cost of the camp sites. Not to mention the seats we'll be sitting in while we watch the race. This right here, is about a thousand dollars' worth of entertainment for two people. Granted, you'll be working, but still, and they're going to pay you to boot. I'd say go for it."

"I want to, and I don't think it'll be a problem, but when Kam, Kurt and I talked about starting a relationship, I set some ground rules. I don't want them to think I'm reneging on them."

"May I ask what they were?"

"I've been going to the races for almost five years. The only day I was in the pits was the day I asked the guys to do the Dillard commercial." At his frown, she giggled. "I know it's not funny, because Kam got hurt. It was the day Kyle hit Kam in the ass with the slingshot up at Dusty Hill."

Kent threw his head back, and laughed. "I know it's not a laughing matter, but Kevin got it on film, but why do you think that about them."

"I told them that I'd continue going to the races, but I wouldn't go to the pits. That was their job, and I wasn't going to disturb them at their job. Like I told them, I don't expect them to disturb me at my job."

"Okay, I can see where you would think you're going back on your word, but didn't you tell them you'd be in the pits once Keith takes over?"

"Yes, and I told them that I didn't want them to get all jealous if they saw me talking to other drivers."

"Ah, and you think if they see you at The Million back in the pits, talking to other drivers, they might get upset."

"Yes."

"I don't think they will, not if you show them what you just showed me, and you'd have a press badge. I only see one problem with all this and them."

"What's that?"

"They're going to probably want you to stay with them in Kam's RV or Kurt's."

"Oh, that's not a problem," she said, and sighed as she looked out the kitchen window into her back yard.

"Kali," he asked gently. "What is it?"

"It normally would be nothing, but I'm scared to drive all that way by myself."

"Aren't you going to have Matt with you?"

"I don't know. I have to talk to him about this yet."

"What if Kam and or Kurt drive down with you? Pete and Larry can drive their rigs."

"It's not who goes with me, it's just that I have a slight, teeny weeny problem, and for the life of me, I have no clue why I have this problem, or where it stemmed from."

"What's the problem?"

"I have to drive. It's not an ego thing that I'm a better driver, but if I'm not behind the wheel, I freak. When I was younger, I literally had to ride with my head out the window. It got better when I got behind the wheel. Hell, I won't even let Dad drive me up to the track. So, driving myself to Ohio won't be a problem, it's that I was going to ask the guys to go in with me early, but I can't see them sitting beside and behind me for six or seven hours."

"How bad do you freak?" Kent frowned when he saw her hands clenched into fists.

"It starts with me zoning out, then it slowly goes to like I'm in a trance, and I end up ice cold, shaking uncontrollably, and then sit there with my legs to my chest, my arms wrapped around my legs, and I can't move. I don't hear anything, I don't see anything. The last time that happened was when I rode with Dad from their house to here when I bought the place. We towed my SUV behind a U-Haul. Cheaper."

"What brings you out of it?"

"Being out of the vehicle, being warm, and Dad talking to me. Something about his voice. It's not *what* he says, but the tone. Hell, I don't even hear what he says, but it's like I go someplace deep in my mind, and it's Dad's voice that I'm looking for, and he brings me up from a deep, deep abyss."

"And, it only happens when you're a passenger? Even in the back seat?"

"Yes, the only time I don't freak is if I'm in control."

"I know this is none of my business, and you can tell me to go to hell, but have you had sex with my boys yet?"

"Not yet, they want to wait. I don't know why, they tease the hell out of me with their kisses and caresses, leave me all hot and bothered, and wanting." She sighed, then looked at Kent, and said firmly, "You really need to talk to them about that."

Kent laughed. "Why I was asking that was, I was wondering if being sandwiched between the two of them would freak you out."

"It hasn't so far, so it's not that. Nothing they would ever do, this has been going on all my life."

"Do you ever ask your parents why?"

"I do, but they say the same thing they say about my hands. They're under strict instructions not to tell me, to let me remember on my own. So, something must have happened when I was young, but as I told the guys, for the life of me, I can't remember."

Kent made a mental note to talk to the boys about this, but then remembered her immediate concern. "I'm sure if you explain everything to Kam and Kurt, they'll let you drive the entire way, but don't be shocked if they make you pull over and walk around every two hours. I would."

"Thanks for the warning. So, you think I should do this?" She used a finger to pushed the papers she'd had him read earlier around on the table before gathering them up and putting them back in their folders.

"I do. I don't know much about your profession, but I really do. But, talk to Matt, because from what Lyle's said, Brian's gone for the month, and you don't know whether he has plans for next month, or if he's having so much fun he doesn't come back when planned."

"True, and Matt's last day at The Wrong Group was Friday. I'll call him tomorrow and have him come over. So, what were you going to do on the garage today?"

"Drywall. The electrical and plumbing are done, along with the insulation, I was going to start hanging that and mud it, so that we can sand it tomorrow with the boys here, and then we can paint before we leave again. So, only a week left and you should be open for business."

"Can I help?"

"Sure. I'll teach you to run the saw, and together we can get the stairs to the upstairs redone."

"Cool." She grinned and grabbed two waters, and handed them over, but then gathered the papers and took them to her office. She caught something out of the corner of her eye, and grinned when she grabbed them and headed out after Kent.

CHAPTER TWENTY

Kameron pulled into Kali's driveway, and as he parked, turned his truck off, he looked over at Kurtis, and together they frowned. "Is that Kali?" they asked as they saw someone using a table saw.

"She can't be using that," Kurtis said as he reached for his door handle, but Kam's hand on his arm stopped him.

"And what do you think is going to happen if you storm out there and tell her that? Do you really think that's a good idea? Let's go in with a clear head, and find out what's going on."

"Fine." Kurtis sighed. They both slowly exited the truck, and made their way to the entrance of Kali's garage. They stood there and waited until she was done doing what she was working on, then when she shut off the saw, Kam's heart melted when she looked up, saw them, and the grin that came over her face was heart melting.

"You're here." She removed her safety glasses, and hurried around the saw and ran up to them. They circled her and shared a three-way hug, then they took turns kissing her. When they stepped back, but not away, they grinned at her, then reached up and wiped sawdust from her cheek.

"What are you doing?" Kurtis asked in a mixture of shock and awe as he looked around at the garage, soon to be Kali's office.

"Making the steps for the stairs."

They looked around and frowned when they didn't see the stairs, and where they had been, the hole wasn't even there.

"For what?"

Kali grinned, not bothering to turn around and look. She wrapped her arms around both of their waists, and used her chin to point out of the open door. They turned and saw their father pulled in. He must not have seen them or their truck, because he came out of his truck in his true bellowing fashion.

"Woman, I swear you're the biggest pain in the ass I've ever encountered. I gave you my number for emergencies."

"Oh, suck it up, buttercup," Kali said, and giggled as Kam and Kurt stared at them in shock.

"Dad?"

"What?" He scowled, then grinned. "Reinforcements. Get a handle on that woman of yours, she's getting out of control."

The boys held up their hands, and grinned. "Nope, you're on your own, but what's going on?"

"Come help me unload the truck," he said, and after everything was unloaded, Kent told Kali, "Yes, that's what you're going to need."

"Soundproofing?" Kam asked. "What are you going to soundproof?"

"Let me start at the beginning, which was only yesterday by the way. I came over here, because Kevin was in a mood. He was pissed at me, royally."

"What did you do?" Kam grinned.

"Nothing. I swear to god I only tried to reason with him." Kent held up his hands. "Honest. All the way home he was bitching, because he couldn't get online to order the parts he needed. I told him before he went out and bought new, he should, now mind you, I said *should*, go through everything at the house and the garage, to see if there were replacement parts. He told me that would be a waste of time, but when I pointed out the money situation, he got all quiet and started brooding. Didn't say anything the rest of the way home. Yesterday, when he got up, he went to the internet looking for parts. I told him he had to pay for it himself."

"Ouch," Kam said, then looked at Kali. "We've been a racing family all my life. Both Dads raced, and so did their father and uncles. They passed on the tradition to us, their father did to them. When we were first starting out, they'd pay for the parts we needed, and work with us to make any repairs."

"Teaching you as you went along?"

"Yes," Kurt took up the story. "As we advanced and started winning, all new parts had to come out of our winnings. Kam and I learned from the beginning to use spare parts that were lying around the house garage, or the work garage. Why pay hundreds of dollars for something you already had, but had a couple dents, right?"

"Makes sense, but why would that bother Kevin?"

"He's prissy," all three men said, then shook their heads. "That wasn't nice, and it's hard to explain." Kent sighed.

"Kevin has to have everything look perfect. No dents, no rust, hell, the first thing he does after a race is grab the hose and wash his car. He wants things to be spick-and-span at all times."

"He would have made a great Marine." Kent grinned. "I don't know if it was my fault, or if it's just a personality quirk of his, but when I told him that he had the quarter panels in the back of the garage that were in good shape, he freaked. He even called Ken to tell him what I had said."

"Is that why Dad was yelling on the phone?" Kam asked. "We thought you'd done something again." He grinned to soften the blow.

"Ha, ha, not funny." Kent sighed. "After he hung up with Ken, I told him that I didn't appreciate him trying to play one of us against the other. It wasn't allowed in our house. He made noise of moving out, and I said go ahead. And how much money would he have left in his account to move, if he bought new parts totaling almost ten grand, when we had the parts on hand."

"Holy shit," Kali said. "Parts are that much? And I don't mean to put my two cents in, but if he's such a neat freak, why does he run dirt and not asphalt."

"We ask him that all the time." Kam sighed. "It would be almost like a stab in the back if he did that, but lately I've been thinking, maybe he should give it a try. Sure, he's good, he's the leader in his class, he's great on the track, it's off the track he's arrogant and a pain in the ass."

"So, what did he say after you asked him about the money?" Kurtis asked.

"He glared at me, threw up his hands, and stormed out. When I left to come here to work, he was hauling things out of the garage." He grinned. "Did you see him this morning?"

"No, but we heard him," Kam said. "Swearing up a blue streak. Throwing tools. All the men were working outside."

"Damn, maybe I should go home."

"No, when we were pulling out, Dad was pulling in."

"Okay," Kent said, then looked at his two oldest boys, and grinned. "I have to say, this little lady has been having me questioning my own intelligence with her questions."

"Why? What's going on?"

"I came here yesterday to get away from Kevin. Thought I'd spend the day hanging drywall. Fine, right? But then, I failed to tell Kali I was here, and she snuck up behind me, and scared the shit out of me. Once that was cleared, she made me lunch, and asked if she could help, but she had some concerns about what I was doing."

"What type of concerns?" Kam frowned.

"I didn't like the way the stairs stuck out in the middle of the room like they did. So I asked Kent if they could be moved. Instead of having them here at the front, we were able to move them to the back against the wall. He went up and walked around to make sure it was feasible to move the hole. When he was walking around up there, I heard every step down here. Can you imagine if Matt's up there doing that, and rolling around in his chair, what it would sound like down here?"

"Shit. It'd drive me batshit crazy." Kurtis grinned at Kam's glare. "Kam's like Dad, a noisy person."

"Good to know." Kali grinned and winked at Kam. "I don't think Kent believed me, so I had him stay down here, while I went up and walked around. He agreed we needed to soundproof everything. The stores were closed by the time he decided what we needed, and we'd started the stairs. He left instructions on how to cut the treads, and he was picking them up. I just happened to call with questions. That's all, just questions." She grinned at Kent's scowl.

"Fine," he said, and grinned. "They were good questions, and I just happened to understand, and picked up the items she was talking about." He indicated the supplies.

"So, what do we do now?"

"As you can see, there's plenty of space with those I-beams. I was going to put the five eighth drywall directly on the ceiling here, then insulate to the bottom of the beams, then put up another layer of drywall." They were all looking up, and Kam and Kurtis were nodding. They looked at Kali when she sighed.

"What is it?" Kam asked as he put his arm around her.

"I sort of like the look of the beams."

"We don't have to go to the bottom of them," Kent said. "I was just saying that because it'd be easier, but we can put the drywall on top of the beams if you want them exposed."

"Thank you." She grinned, then crooked her finger at him, and when he bent down closer to her, she kissed his cheek.

Kam and Kurtis exchanged smirks when they saw their father blush, then he stood up and blustered, and said, "Daylight's a wasting. Kurtis and I will start on the ceiling, Kam put up the risers, and show Kali how to put in the treads."

"I know how to hammer a nail, you know."

"Fine. Is it alright if Kam gets you started then?"

"Yep." She grinned and turned to Kam. "Where do we start?"

"With this," he said, and he grabbed her and kissed her soundly, leaving her breathless when he stepped back. Before she could recover, Kurtis was there to do the same thing. He made sure her legs were steady, before he stepped back and grinned.

"Kent." Kali turned and glared at him. "Talk to them, dammit." She stomped her foot, turned on her heel, and before she left, she glared at the older man. "You have five minutes. I'm going to get us something to drink." Only the sound of Kent's bellowed laughter followed her.

"What was that about?" Kam frowned after the woman who'd turned him on his head.

"Yeah, I'm confused. I thought she liked our kisses."

"She does. But she's frustrated you don't follow up on it."

"But, we don't want to rush her." Kam frowned.

"I understand, son. Believe me, I do. But, take it from a man who's been there. If you wait much longer, she's going to find it elsewhere. You're leaving her hot and bothered, and sexually frustrated, and I'm sure she does the same to you. Do you want to see her with someone else?"

"Fuck no," they said at the same time, and Kent shook his head when they continued to stare at each other. He was close to his own brother, but he would never understand the twin connection. He started to get back to work, and the boys quickly joined him, so that when Kali returned with several bottles of water, they were all hard at work.

Thirty minutes later, Kam came up behind Kali, and stepped a little bit closer to her, so whenever she moved they brushed body parts. "I'm done, bring the first tread, and I'll watch you attach it."

Kali frowned, but did as he said, and by the time he'd stepped back, she had to take several deep breaths to cool down. Kam joined them and Kent just shook his head at him. "Just don't get pissed when she retaliates against you."

"Bring it," Kam whispered, and everyone settled in to what they were working on. At one point, Kam was up on a ladder, and he didn't see that Kali had gone back for another riser, when all of a sudden he felt a hand on the inside of his thigh, close to his balls. He jerked, and almost fell off the ladder when he heard a giggle from below, but when he looked down, Kali was several feet away.

"Damn it," he mumbled under his breath, and the only reply he heard was his father chuckling, and that was how their afternoon went. Each and every time Kurtis, Kam, or Kali were within arm's length, they touched, they fondled, and they kissed. It wasn't deep passionate, rip my clothes off now kissing, but just a subtle peck on the back of a neck, a bicep. Kent was amazed by the restraint they showed.

Finally, around five that afternoon, they stepped back and looked at their work. Not only had Kali put up the treads, but she'd also stained them and helped them, then once they were done for the day, they all stepped back, and admired their work. Kent smirked as he looked over, and saw that Kam and Kurt had wedged up on either side of Kali. They were done for the day, and everyone knew it, but he decided to play devil's advocate. As he picked up his tools, he smirked, and called out.

"Hey, boys, your mother's making lasagna tonight. Should I set a place for the two of you?" He looked over just in time to see Kali glare at him, and it took all his military training not to crack a smile. She glanced at the boys when they didn't say anything, and took a step back, and began cleaning up the already-clean area.

"Not tonight," Kam said, without looking at Kali. "We have other plans. Right, Kurt?"

"Yeah."

Kent frowned, but he nodded. "Okay. I guess that's it for the night. I'm going to take off. I'll be back around ten in the morning to finish up. Night, Kali."

"Night," she called out, but didn't look at him. He sighed and went to his truck, and he heard the garage door start to close. He quickly looked back and saw his boys had Kali trapped between them, and Kam was kissing her. With a huge grin, he whispered to himself. "Smart boys." Then, he climbed into his truck, called for a pizza delivery, then called his brother and told him of his plans. By the time he arrived home, his brother grinned when he walked into the bedroom, and pointed to the bathroom where they both heard the shower running.

"Boys are in the living room with the pizza." Ken grinned, and together they stripped naked, and walked into the bathroom and climbed into the shower with their wife. It was several hours before they all lay there well spent.

"Not that I care, because tonight was lovely, but what brought this on?" Kerri asked as she sat up in the middle of their bed, and rubbed her hands through both their hair as they laid their heads on her shoulders. Kent laughed and explained what he had witnessed all day, after telling him what Kali had said the day before.

"Oh god, I know it's not funny, but remember when Kali slammed her siblings' heads together? I can picture her doing that to the boys, especially if they didn't step up to the plate? What did you say to them to make them change their minds?"

"I flat-out told them that she told me she was sexually frustrated, and if they didn't do something, she was going to find it elsewhere."

"Oh god." Ken laughed. "Wrong thing to imply. The boys losing their favorite toy." Ken laughed. "Not that I see Kali as a toy, not in anyway. I see her as 'the one' for them, but I fear they're not there yet. I only hope if anything happens, they can keep their heads about them."

"Me too, but we're just going to have to let them know that we're there for them—all three of them."

"Agreed," Kent said, then started kissing his way up his wife's body, and it was several more hours before they were raiding the refrigerator in the middle of the night, eating the lasagna that Kerri had made for dinner, but Ken had put in the refrigerator so he and Kent could show their wife some loving.

CHAPTER TWENTY-ONE

Kali had stared at Kent with anger, when he suggested his sons go home with him to have dinner, and when they didn't answer right away, she'd stepped back from them, and began organizing the items she'd stacked earlier. She had heard them speak, but didn't really hear what they said. The garage door started going down, she was whirled around. Kam's mouth was on hers, that she was flattened to his front. Before the door was all the way down, Kurtis came up behind her, reached between them, and began massaging her breasts. Before, they'd only teased her, but now they were giving her a full-on assault. She sighed, relaxed, and went with it. She didn't know how far they would go. She hoped they'd go really, really far, because she was getting sick and tired of going to bed frustrated every time she'd been with them.

When Kam lifted his head and was breathing deeply, he turned her, and Kurtis took his place, but his hands replaced his brother's, and his lips played with her ear and neck. When Kurt lifted his head, Kali saw him nod, and suddenly she was picked up, and with Kurt leading the way, Kam carried her from the garage to the house, and directly to her bedroom. Kam lowered her gently, and he grabbed one foot and removed her shoe and sock, while Kurt did the same to the other one.

What she liked about this was that whatever they removed from her, they removed from themselves, so by the time she was only in her bra and panties, they were down to their jeans. Wait, jeans, what the hell? She rose on her elbows and frowned at them.

"Sorry, we don't want to scare you."

"So, why not remove your jeans?"

Kam actually blushed. "Commando. We were in a hurry to get here, and didn't do our laundry yet."

She grinned and reached between her breasts, flicked the clasp open, and shrugged her bra off her shoulders.

"No fair," Kurt said, but he grinned as he undid his jeans, and shucked them in one fluid motion. Kam had done the same thing, and Kali sucked in her breath at the beauty before her. Two men with wide shoulders, six-pack abs, and an inverted v. They both had a light dusting of chest hair, but the darker line that led from their belly button down, was like a magnet to their magnificent cocks, which were jutting, hard, long, and thick, from the apex of their thighs. She reached out toward them, and sighed when each set of hands gently traveled up her legs, and together they removed her panties and then climbed on the bed, to kneel beside her.

"We don't want to scare you. We're going to take this slow, as much as it might kill us, but we're going to go slow, but know this. We will be having sex tonight, and the nights to follow, but for right now, it'll be slow and easy."

"Can I touch you?"

"Oh, yeah." Kurt grinned down at her. "Just as much as we're going to touch you." To put actions to words, he reached down and gently took one of her breasts in his hand, began to massage it, and then played with her hard, distended nipple. As she arched into his hand, she reached out and gripped Kam.

"Easy, Baby," Kam said, and put his hand over hers, then released her grip. "It might be hard as steel, but it's still delicate." He began moving her hand up and down his length, causing him to clench his teeth, and breathe through his mouth. "That's enough for now," he said, and brought her hand up to his abs and breathed easier. He reached down and took her other breast in his hand, then together, the two men helped Kali to her knees, and they kneeled before her. For the next few moments, three pairs of hands explored.

When Kali held both of them gently in her clasp, she licked her lips, and asked, "Can I taste?"

"Yes," they both said through gritted teeth, and she slowly bent down and took one of those magnificent cocks in her mouth. When she closed her eyes, she didn't compare them, not one bit, and after licking the head of one and getting a taste, she turned and licked the other. When she felt her hair being tugged, she opened her eyes, and looked up into two beautiful faces.

"Take the head slowly into your mouth. Feel free to use your tongue wherever you'd like," Kam said, and swore when she licked the whole length of him, then played with the small bundle of nerves beneath the head. When she opened her mouth wider, he put his hand over his cock to stop her descent. "Kurt's turn."

Kali grinned and turned to Kurt, and did the same with him she'd done to Kam, but this time, when she opened her mouth and started to draw him in, he didn't stop her. She looked at Kam, and winked.

"Go slowly," Kurt said. "Don't force it, only go as far as you can." He closed his eyes, and groaned as she began to lower her head. He threw his head back and then looked over at his brother, and the further down Kali went on him, the wider his eyes became, until he felt her nose and chin hit.

"Holy shit," he said, and looked down and saw that she had all of his impressive length in her mouth. When she whirled her tongue, he reached up, gripped her head gently, and tried to get her off him, "Babe, I'm going to come, if you don't want me to come in your mouth, you'd better back off." But, she reached up, gripped the back of his thighs, and started going up and down faster on him. When he felt his release was imminent, he gripped the sides of her head, and as he tried to pull out, she tightened her mouth on him and went all the way down, and he lost it. It felt like hours until his release stopped shooting out, and when she slowly lifted her head, she cleaned him off as she raised her head, and when his cock slipped from her mouth, she sat back and frowned when he fell to the side, breathing deeply.

"You broke him." Kam grinned at the shock on her face.

"No, she didn't, you ass. It's just her mouth is amazing, and it's been a while since I've been with a woman."

"Really? I didn't break you?"

"Nope." Kurtis reared up and wrapped his arms around her, and kissed her senseless. When he let her up, he settled behind her, and said, "Now show Kam how amazing that mouth of yours is." And he reached around, and began playing with her breasts. Kali turned to look at Kam, and at his nod she looked at his cock and saw the head was a deep purple, and looked like it had its own heartbeat.

She slowly bent forward, and gently licked his throbbing cock. After she played, she licked the pre-cum from the head, moaning as she opened her mouth, and slowly enclosed hers over him, firmed her lips, going down on him. Again she didn't stop until she had all of him in his mouth. She felt him jerk, and as she slowly lifted her head, she also jerked and went back down on him.

"Fuck, Kurt, what did you do?"

"Pinched her nipples. Her breasts are super sensitive. Can't wait to get my tongue on that clit of hers."

"Christ, Kurtis, stop."

"What? I didn't do anything." But, he laughed and continued to play with Kali.

"Oh god," Kam said, and gripped the sides of Kali's head, and began working himself faster and faster. "I'm coming," he yelled, and didn't wait for her to say anything, or pull off, but he took his cue from her when her tiny hands dug into his thighs, and her mouth tightened on him.

"Arg!" he yelled, and forced his hips forward, then came hard. With his head thrown back, he saw stars, and in the back of his mind he made a mental note to punch Kurt later. After Kali was done with him, he went the same way as his brother, and fell to the side of the bed, breathing hard.

"Oops." Kali giggled, and lay down next to him, with Kurt snuggled up behind her. She didn't touch Kameron, but she watched him closely. It was several minutes before he turned his head and opened one eye.

He quirked his brow, when he asked hoarsely, "Do you even have a gag reflex?"

"Nope." She grinned and the two brothers looked at her in shock, then threw their heads back and laughed. Kam reared up and pushed her onto her back, then kissed her passionately. When he let her up for air, he grinned and looked at Kurtis.

"Your turn."

"Oh, yeah," Kurtis said, and with her still on her back, Kurtis kissed her, and Kam moved down her body, taking one nipple in his mouth and gently bit down, and as she jerked, they both held her hips down. "Told you." Kurtis grinned at his brother, and as Kam continued down her stomach, Kurtis worked his way down to her breasts, and spent a lot of time there.

"In case you couldn't tell," Kam said as he settled between her legs. "Kurt's a breast man." And before she could comment, he leaned forward and licked the length of her, and Kurt reached down, without taking his mouth from her breast, and helped hold her down.

"Oh god," Kali cried out. She felt like her body was floating above the action. Every place they touched brought more and more pleasure, but when her insides started to feel different, especially really low in her belly, she gripped Kurt's head and forced it up. "What's wrong with me?"

"What do you feel?" he asked, and looked at Kam who had stopped.

"My insides feel funny. Like there's a huge pressure building." She frowned when both of them grinned.

"It's okay, let it go. Follow your body's reaction. Let it come."

"But what is it?"

"This," Kam said, and bent his head, increasing his administrations to her, and because he'd only teased her for the past five minutes, he sucked deeply on her clit, and grinned against her when she exploded beneath him. He lapped up her juices and crawled up her body, and gave her a hug and kissed her gently. When he released her, he stared down into her beautiful blue/green eyes, and smiled. "That is what you call an orgasm, and I'm assuming it was your first one ever?"

"Mmm," Kali said, and smiled sweetly at him. She was so relaxed and limber that she put her arms over her head, and stretched. "Yes."

"But, not your last." Kurt grinned at her and worked his way back down her body.

"Wait, don't you have to wait between orgasms? I'd read somewhere... *OH GOD!"* she screamed, and jerked her hips up into Kurt's face. "I don't know what you just did, but keep doing it."

They chuckled and they both started working her over. After she had two more orgasms, they gave her a break, but not for long.

When Kam climbed between her legs, he moved her damp hair from her face, and kissed her gently. "You ready for more?"

"I think so."

"This next step is going to hurt, and I'm sorry. God, you don't know how sorry I am that I'm going to cause you pain, but I want you to tell me to stop if it gets too intense."

When she frowned, Kurtis moved her head, to the side. "We're not big into BDSM, and we can explain that later, but people use safe words."

"Like to tell you to stop? I've read some books with that in them."

"Then you know what we're talking about?"

"Yes."

"So, we're going to use the stop light. Green is your good to go, yellow you want us to slow down, and red..."

"Stop all together."

"Yes. Eventually, we'll both take you together, but we'll have to work up to that. This being your first time, Kam will be the one to introduce you to sex, and you'll be so busy sucking my cock while he's doing that, you won't feel the pain."

"Does it last long?"

"It shouldn't, no more than a few seconds. Kam will stop after he takes your virginity, so you can adjust to his size."

"And you're sure you'll fit?"

They both grinned, causing Kali to suck in her breath, and her eyes widened when Kam started working his cock inside her. He'd go in a little at a time, pull out, then go again, until he looked down at her and kissed her gently. From beside her, Kurt asked if she was ready, and when she tried to nod her head, Kam slammed into her so suddenly and hard, she screamed, but his mouth absorbed most of the sound. He immediately stopped and lifted his head.

"I'm so sorry."

"It's okay," she said, and after only a few moments she frowned. "Huh."

"What, what's wrong?"

"Nothing, but I thought that pain was going to rip me in two, but it's gone." She grinned. "You can continue, because Kurt looks like his cock's going to explode again any second now." Kali grinned when they grinned, and after going up on his knees, Kam wrapped her legs up over his elbows and started to move. In the meantime, Kurtis moved so she had access to his cock, and sucked in his breath when she took him in her mouth. He looked at his brother, and the thoughts and feelings passing through them intensified, and right at that moment, Kali had another orgasm, and after she came down they looked at each other, and nodded. They turned their attention back to the woman between them, and Kurtis gave his signal that he was about to come, and then together they let their releases go, and the most amazing thing was that Kali joined them. The two men fell down on either side of Kali, and the three of them took several minutes to get their breath back.

Both men rose up on an elbow, looked at her moving her sweat-dampened hair from her face. "You okay?" Kurtis asked with a grin on his face.

"Mmm," she said, and Kam chuckled when she barely moved. He got up and went to where he assumed was the bathroom, and after disposing of his condom, he decided to turn on the shower instead of just wiping her down. He went out and saw Kurtis was coming back into the room, with a bottle of water and an armload of sheets.

"Found them in the hall closet, didn't think we'd want to sleep on the sweat-stained ones."

"Good idea. You good doing this?"

"I am. Don't think the shower's big enough for three?"

"No, but there's room to add on." He grinned, already thinking of the future. He went to the bed and helped the exhausted woman sit up. "Come on, Babe, get something to drink. It'll help, then I'm going to take you into the shower."

"Can't," she said as she drank thirstily from the bottle he held to her lips.

"Sure you can."

"No," she said, and held up her hands and both the guys frowned at them.

"What? We don't understand."

"Have to take the fingers off," she said tiredly, and each man took a hand in theirs and saw that all of her fingers were extended. "Because I was helping Kent in the garage, I put them on. But it's not a pretty picture if you get them wet."

"Oh, Can we take them off?"

"Sure," She sighed and held out her hands. She kept her eyes closed as they removed her compression 'fingers', and she actually sighed when they massaged her hands, but after a couple minutes, she started to pull them away, and sighed in relief when they let go.

"Come on," Kam picked her up, took her into the shower, and after getting her hair wet, he massaged her whole body, then rinsed her off. Just then Kurt opened the shower curtain, and Kam blocked the water as he reached in and took Kali. Kam quickly washed himself, and with a towel around his hips he went out to the bedroom, taking Kurt's place when he went in to shower. Fifteen minutes later, they were all dried off and snuggled in bed together. It was only eight at night, but they were exhausted, and it didn't take long for the guys to follow Kali into sleep, but just before they closed their eyes for the last time that night, Kam looked at Kurtis and said quietly, "She's the one."

"I know," Kurtis answered, and neither one saw the smile cross Kali's face before she also fell asleep.

CHAPTER TWENTY-TWO

Kam woke the next morning with a smile on his face, he put his arm above his head, and looked at the woman on her knees between him and his brother. He looked over and saw that Kurtis was already awake.

"What do we have here?"

"Looks and feels like we might have woken a sleeping dragon," Kurtis said, and grinned when Kali's hand tightened around his cock. He had awoken to the feel of a tiny hand on him, and saw that Kali was on her knees between them, and was working both of them.

"Finally," Kali grinned.

"Finally, what?"

"You're awake, I didn't want to disturb you by getting up, but now that you're awake I can get up." She dropped her hands off them, and made like she was going to get up but suddenly Kurtis reared up, wrapped his arms around her, fell back on the bed with her on her back, and him on top of her.

Kali laughed and looked at Kam, and suddenly stopped laughing, when he saw the expression in his eyes.

"Uh oh."

"Yep," Kam said, and reached his hand out, and Kurt moved to the side and along with Kam reached down between them, and grinned. "So wet, so ready. You got this?" He grinned at his brother, rolled over and grabbed his pants, then pulled a condom out of the pocket and handed it to his brother.

"I do now," Kurt said, and after donning the condom he reached between them and gripped his cock, moving it up and down through her wetness. He looked into her eyes and slowly entered her, and when she tensed, he stopped. "Sh, it won't hurt this time. Just the first time. From now on we'll be giving you nothing but pleasure," he said, and grinned when she relaxed her inner muscles. "That's right, relax." He talked to her soothingly, and when he felt her completely relax, he kissed her and pulled out, then slowly entered her. When he lifted his head, she grinned up at him.

"Oh."

Kurt went up on his fisted hands to begin moving, and slowly ended up on his knees, but at a signal from Kam he pulled out, and quickly flipped her over, brought her up to her knees and slipped back into her. Kam lay down in front of her, and held his cock for her, and it didn't take long for her to take him into her mouth, and before long they were all groaning and moaning, finding their release at the same time. Heaped in a pile in the middle of her bed, she laughed when she saw that both Kam's head and legs from the knees down hung over the sides. And while Kurt lay next to her, his legs were the same way.

"I think if this thing goes any further, I'm going to have to look into getting a bigger bed."

She laughed when they only lifted their heads, and said in stereo, "You think?"

Kali laughed and rolled out of the bed, and headed to the bathroom. "Coffee's in the cupboard above the pot, I expect to have the pot done when I get out." Then, she ran away laughing when the pillows came flying after her.

"God, she's fun," Kurt said as he continued to stare at the bathroom door.

"She is. I don't know if you heard me last night, but she's the one for me."

"Me too. Hopefully neither one of us will fuck this up. I can't tell you how sorry I am for what happened before."

"Water under the bridge, bro. Water under the bridge." He did a backflip off the bed and grinned at his brother. "Now, I'm going to go take a shower, a cup of coffee sounds good."

"Bastard." Kurt laughed at him.

"Nope, I know who my Daddy is." Then, he hurried into the bathroom and climbed in behind Kali. By the time they joined Kurt in the kitchen, the water had run cold, but the coffee was hot. When Kurt said he was going to take a shower, Kali waited until he was at the other end of the house, and called out, "There's no hot water." They only heard the slam of two doors then several swear words.

"Don't worry, he'll get us or me back soon." Kam grinned, then without permission opened her refrigerator and began pulling items. "You don't mind, do you?"

"For someone else to cook? Hell no." She grinned. "Do you need any help?"

"Sure, I'm going to make omelets, you can cut up the veggies."

"Okay," she said, and when Kurtis joined them he leaned against the kitchen entrance, and a sense of calm came over him, seeing the two of them working together. He came in, took the knife from Kali's hand, then quickly kissed her. After he released her he turned and filled his own coffee cup.

"Problem?" He smirked as he sat down and watched them.

"No," Kali said, her voice slightly higher than normal. She cleared her throat and went back to cutting up the veggies. "Kurt, instead of sitting there watching us, why don't you make yourself useful, and go to the office and bring out that green folder that's on the center of my desk."

"Okay." He did and was back in seconds. "Here it is."

"Read it."

"Excuse me?" Kurt frowned, and saw Kam look at her quickly.

"I've got something to discuss with the two of you, and I thought you could start reading it, then Kam can read it. Or he can read it with you and I'll finish cooking."

"No, I'll cook and Kurt can read," Kam said firmly, and twenty minutes later they sat at the kitchen table, and as Kam began to eat, Kurtis pushed the folder forward, and when Kam frowned he only grinned. Kam read as they ate, and no one said a word. When they were done, Kurt quietly cleaned up their dishes, refilled their coffee cups and sat back down, just as Kurtis was closing the folder.

"Wow. And when did George approach you, and yes, we know him."

"Saturday during intermission at State."

"And are you going to do this?"

"I'd like to, but for what George wants for his tracks, I'll have to talk to Matt about it. I wanted to talk to you guys first."

"We're happy you want our opinion, Kali," Kurt said, and took her hand in his. "But, this is your job, we agreed at the beginning we wouldn't interfere with our jobs. And if you do this, it's your job."

"So, if I do this, you wouldn't have a problem with me talking to the other drivers? See me talking and maybe laughing with them?"

"No, as long as you know that you're with us, we have no problem with you talking with the other drivers. The only problem we'd have is if you started kissing and fucking them in front of us," Kam said, in his usual blunt fashion. "You know we're going to be there, right? That I'm racing?"

"Yes, Kent told me when I asked him questions."

"And according to this Bloom person, he wants you there on Sunday, and he's set you up in a hotel room?"

"Yes, actually if you read it, there are two rooms, I figured it was one for me and one for Matt. I'd really like to go. It's not like I have to put in for vacation time from a boss. Since I now own my own company, it's not going to be a problem."

"So what is?" Kurtis asked. "Because, from where we're sitting, it sounds like there's a problem."

"Maybe, maybe not." She hedged, then sighed at the look in their eyes. "It sounds stupid when I say it out loud."

"Let us be the judge of that," Kam said, and put his hand over one of hers, and Kurtis did the same with the other one, but she took them away, and sighed as she wrapped her arms around her middle, burying her hands in her sides, out of their line of sight. "Remember when I told you about these? That I don't know how it happened?" She lifted her hands, and wiggled her working fingers, then buried them in her sides again.

"Yes."

"Well, something else happened and I have no clue why, or what caused it. But, I told Kent yesterday, because he suggested that you two might want to go with me on Sunday, having someone by the name of Pete and Larry drive your rigs."

"They're our crew chiefs," Kam said. "Larry's mine, Pete's Kurtis."

"Oh. Well, I told Kent I didn't know if you'd like to ride shotgun, or in the back seat all the way to Ohio."

"Why would we do that? We'd share the driving."

"That's just it. I'm a pretty easy person to get along with, but there is one teeny weeny aspect of my life that I have to have complete control of. I mean a hundred percent or more control of this. If not, things don't go well. Matter of fact, things could get ugly in less than a heartbeat."

"What's the thing you have to have control of?" Kurtis asked gently.

"Driving. I have to be behind the wheel and in control. When I was younger before I learned to drive, if I rode in a car, I couldn't ride in the back, still can't. I had to ride in the front like a dog."

"Excuse me?" Kam asked in shocked anger.

But Kali quickly held up her hands. "It was me, you know how dogs stick their heads out the window when you drive down the road? That was the only way I could ride. For months before I turned sixteen, I'd have huge fights with Mom and Dad about me getting my license. I refused. I wasn't going to get it. I was going to go out and buy a bicycle and use that, but after Dad did something I said I'd try it."

"What did he do?"

"We lived three miles from a park. He and Mom took Dad's truck to the park, and left it there, then he asked if I wanted to go for a bike ride. We ended up at the park and he had me sit behind the wheel. That was the first time ever that the symptoms didn't start. We didn't even put the keys in the ignition. I just sat behind the wheel."

"What symptoms do you have?"

"I'm fine for about five miles, if the windows are open, then after that, even with the window open, I start to zone out. It takes a couple miles, but I start to stare into space, and everything around me disappears. My hearing, my eyesight. I don't see or hear anything. Then, I bring my legs to my chest and hug my arms around them. I start to shake uncontrollably, and I'm cold, but I don't move. I don't rock back and forth, or even blink."

"Damn. How do you get out of it?"

"Believe it or not, the only one that can bring me back is Dad. The last time it happened I wasn't gone as long afterward."

"What does that even mean?"

"My family calls these episodes 'gone'. That I've gone someplace where nothing exists. The first time these happened it was hours, and I'm talking twelve, thirteen hours to bring me back. As the years passed it was less time, but still long. I got my license when I was sixteen. Since then I drive everywhere. Hell, I won't even let someone drive me up to Dusty Hill, because we don't know when it'll happen. Five feet or five miles."

"You've never had one of these episodes since you started driving?"

"No."

"When was your last one?" Kurt asked.

She sighed and took each of their hands. "Four and a half years ago, the day I moved in here. I didn't have a lot of stuff to move out of Mom and Dad's. I could have put it all in my SUV, Dad's truck and Mom's car, but my parents went out and bought my living-room furniture, this table and chairs, and the beds and dressers in the spare rooms."

"Let me guess, they did it because they love you, and it would have been better to rent a U-Haul, tow your truck behind, and have you or your mom drive a vehicle behind, because then your dad could turn in the rental."

"Exactly, and not thinking, I jumped into the passenger seat of the rental. I had some things to say to my dad. I don't know if you know this, but they live on the northern end of Norton."

"Fuck," Kurtis said and gripped her hand. "How long before it happened?"

"According to Dad, we weren't even out of Norton yet."

"Do you know you're having one?"

"No. I only know I have them, because when I come back I'm in a different place, which is normally my parents' living room. But, when this last one happened, I was in my living room, and it was completely empty, but both Dad and Mom said that it wasn't as long. See when it happened, Dad only pulled over and grabbed the extra blankets he always carries behind the seat in his truck, and wrapped me up, but then continued driving here. So, if you have that hour and a half, it was only two hours after I arrived here that I came back, but I haven't had one since."

"Can you drive other vehicles?" Kurt asked. "Or does it have to be your vehicle?"

"Oh, I can drive anything. I drive Dad's truck or Mom's car, the actual vehicle isn't the problem, it's that I have to be behind the wheel and in control. It's when I lose that control I have an episode."

"Okay," Kam said after the two guys did their staring thing. "We'll take my truck then. It has a crew cab, and a short box, but Kurt and I can easily ride in the back seats. Is there any type of special blanket your father uses if something happens?"

"The fuzzy ones, thick and fuzzy. I think they're called fleece."

"Okay. We'll make sure we have a couple on hand. Anything else?"

"Not that I can think of, just the blankets, and maybe a bottle of water."

"Not a problem. We still have several days before we have to leave, and we'd like to go down with you. We know you'll be working starting Sunday. Maybe you can call this Bloom guy and say you'll be there on Saturday? You know, you'll be working, I'll be working, and we can have some fun before we start." He raised his brows up and down and Kali laughed, and as she stood to go to him, she was interrupted by the banging on her front door.

"Shit," they all said at once. It was Kurtis that went to the door and whipped it open.

CHAPTER TWENTY-THREE

"Hey, wakey, wakey, time for some eggs and bacey. I don't have any bacon, but I got those muffins you like," Matt said as he jumped to his feet from his sitting position on the front porch, and whipped around to stare in shock. "You're not Kali."

"No, I'm not. Who are you?" Kurtis asked gruffly. The guy looked familiar, but he couldn't place him.

"Matt Clayton. I'm the guy Kali is going to hire to be her techie."

"Ah, that's why you look familiar."

"Yep. Is she here?"

"Yeah." Kurt turned on his heel, and assumed Matt was following him. He entered the kitchen, and cleared his throat when he saw his brother and Kali with their lips locked and Kam's hands on her ass. They broke apart, Kali looking guilty, and Kurtis made a mental note to talk to Kam about it, then they could clarify to Kali.

"It's for you." He stepped to the side and Matt entered the kitchen.

"Matt!" Kali said, and went over and hugged him, but both men realized it was a side hug, and they barely touched one another. "What are you doing here?"

"I gave my notice and worked it out. Roger and the gang took me out Friday night, and I took the rest of the weekend and yesterday to recover. If you still want me, I'm here to start work, and I'm even willing to help get the garage together."

"Oh my god, you're really willing to do actual physical labor?" Kali laughed and looked at Kam and Kurt. "For the last six years, the most physical labor he's done is roll around in a chair, push some buttons, and carry a camera on his shoulder."

"Bitch," Matt said, and everyone knew there was no heat behind it.

"Yep." She grinned and looked out the window when she saw a flash. "Come on." She slipped her bare feet into her sandals, and told the others, "Kent's here."

"Oh," the guys said, and hurried down the hall to get their shoes from her bedroom. Matt only raised a brow, and when he caught Kali's eye, he gave her the thumbs up and grinned.

"Shut up." She slapped his shoulder and went out.

"Not saying anything," Matt said. He watched as a huge man exited a truck, came over, and hugged Kali, but when he saw Matt he scowled.

"Kent, this is Matt Clayton, my techie. Matt this is Kent Kilbourne. You guys met a few days ago. You asked him about the electricity he'd need for his equipment. Remember?"

"Oh, hi, I talked to you about putting my studio in. Sorry, I'm dressed for work now." He indicated his chinos and polo shirt. The last time he'd been here he'd worn torn jean shorts and a ratty tee. They turned and looked as Kam and Kurt came out of the house, and Kali rolled her eyes when the men grinned at each other. She shook her head, then went over, and opened the garage door.

"I can't wait to get started on this. I've pictured how I want to set up my studio," Matt was saying. "I'm hoping we can get in there in the next month. Holy fucking shit," he said as the door opened all the way, and the lights automatically came on. He turned in a circle, then ran over to where the stairs used to be. "What the fuck?" He looked around and saw four people grinning and pointing to the other end of the garage. He frowned until he saw the stairs, and ran to them and up.

Kali grinned when they didn't hear him running around. He came back down fifteen minutes later, and grinned. "So, what do we have to do to finish?"

"Paint the walls." Kent grinned. "And we got the overhead door guys coming in an hour."

"Why?"

"Don't you want windows to look out the door?"

"Oh yeah." Kali grinned. "Sorry I forgot," she said, and as the guys started gathering up the paint supplies, she said, "Matt, if you got a minute I'd like to talk to you at the house."

"Sure," Matt said, and followed his friend and boss. She sat him down at the table and pushed the folder to him.

"Read that." She went to her office for her laptop and booted it up, and accessed the websites. She went back out and saw Matt was almost done and waited.

"Okay, but one question or fifty."

"What?"

"What's State, Dog Hollow, Port Royal, and Eriez?"

Kali grinned and turned her laptop. "This is the website for State. Out of all of them, this is the best." She only pushed her laptop toward him, and let him look at his leisure, then he went through the list. When he was done, he grinned. "And this guy wants to hire us to redo his sites and pages?"

"Yes, but I told him you would be doing that, because you were my techie. I told him you'd be calling him in a couple weeks. Just tell him you work for me, and he'll see you."

"I have to say I'm a little scared."

"Why?"

"I've never been to a race. Sure, I've flipped through the channels, and saw some on TV, but never sat and watched it."

"This is totally different. For one, this is dirt, and the biggest track they race on is only a half mile around. I can't speak for the last three tracks, but I've been going to State for the last four and a half years, every single Saturday unless it's raining, and as long as they run, I go to McKay and Dusty Hill."

"Damn, I'd love to go to a track to see what it's like, especially before we go to this one." He held up the press badges for the Dirt Million.

"You can ride with us," Kent said from behind them, and he held up his hands when he knocked. "Sorry, but the door guy is here, thought you might want to be down there."

"Sure," Kali stood and headed out, and saw Kent sit down and wave her away. The last thing she heard was Kent asking Matt how he felt about getting dirty. She went down to the garage and saw she had no door at all. She stood to the side and watched as the new door was put in, and when it was down it was pretty, then she went in and stood and nodded when she looked out. She turned the lights out and saw it was bright enough and nodded. “I like it.”

“At least this way you can look out and not feel like you’re boxed in,” Kam said, from her side. She laughed and reached up and saw that he had paint on his cheek, but when she went to wipe it off it was already dry.

“Don’t worry, its waterproof, so what did Matt say?”

“He’s interested, very interested, but I don’t think he’s going to commit until he knows more, which I totally understand, and I agree with him. I know how Matt works and he needs to connect the dots, then he can run with it, but it’s more than connecting the dots.”

“How so?” Kurt asked as he came up and kissed her, then stepped back and grinned at her flustered look.

“I guess you could say he has to experience it, hear it, taste it, and feel it, and he just admitted to me that he’s seen NASCAR on TV, but he flipped the channel and never watched it. Before I came out here, Kent said that Matt could go with you guys this weekend.”

“Sure, that wouldn’t be a problem,” Kam said as he dipped his paint roller in the pan, and started painting the ceiling again.

“Are you agreeing, so you can help him understand dirt-track racing? Or so you can grill him about me?”

“Will Matt spending the weekend with us be so bad?” Kurt frowned at her. “You don’t know it yet, but Kam and I are pretty nice guys. We’re only offering to help the guy out, and that will help you out. Won’t it? You’ll know the longer and deeper this relationship becomes, you’ll learn that our number-one objective will be to help you in any way we can.

Whether it's educating your associate, or giving you all the orgasms you can handle."

"And anything in between." Kam grinned at her shocked expression.

"Oh. I'm sorry I jumped to conclusions."

"Don't be, just don't do it again. We told you to ask, and you did. Now are you going back to the house to work, or are you going to help us with the painting?"

While she decided, Matt and Kent joined them, and as the four of them began discussing plans for the upcoming weekend, she automatically picked up an angled brush, poured some paint in a small container, and went over to the wall and started doing the trim. She listened intently to what they were discussing, nodded when she knew something, and paid close attention to what she didn't. All the while she was making story boards in her head.

"Hello!" someone called out, and Kali ended up jerking and swore when she took the paint up the wall, but then realized it would be covered with the other paint. By the time she stood and hurried forward, the other men were standing in the doorway, and she pushed her way through them.

"Hello, can I help you?"

"I'm looking for Kali Kilpatrick."

"That's me. And you are?"

"Gregg Middleton, I'm the town code enforcement office. I'm here to inspect the new build."

"Oh, come on in." She stepped back and introduced the others. Kent took charge, walked around and showed him what they had done, and then he questioned what type of business it was going to be, and after he took several notes, he said she'd passed and would send the paperwork to her. What surprised her was that he asked if she had a business card, because the town was looking for a new advertiser. She ended up giving him her name and phone number, until she had new cards made, then Gregg quickly left.

"Hey, boss," Matt called out.

"Yeah?" She picked up her brush and got back to work.

"What's the name of your business?"

"I was thinking of Kilpatrick's. At least for now."

"Sounds good. I'm done painting upstairs. Only the trim has to be done. I don't mean to leave you in a lurch, but I was wondering if I could slide on out. I want to go home and go through my equipment, and get it ready to bring over tomorrow. I can start to get set up."

"Sure. And when you come back tomorrow, I'll have a set of keys for you."

"Thanks, Kal," Matt said, then hurried away. Shortly after that the guys had finished with the big painting areas, and all that was left was the trim.

"Kali," Kam said as he walked up to her. "I hate to leave you with all the trim work left to do, but Kurt and I have to get back to the garage. If it's alright with you, we'd like to come back later tonight."

"Sure, but how much later?"

"Between six and seven?"

"That's fine. I'll finish up here, and then get some work done in my office. Want me to cook for us when you get here?"

"No, we'll bring something with us. Later, we can sit down and work out some type of schedule."

"Okay," she said, and before she could put the brush down, he reached out, pulled her to him, and kissed her senseless. He stepped back and Kurtis was there. They both made sure she was steady on her feet before leaving. She looked at Kent, and at his smirk she grinned. "I don't know what you said to them, but thank you."

"Not a problem, and unfortunately I have to leave too. It's not good to leave Kyle with Ken at the garage all day. He gets bored and then little things start happening. Not a pretty picture."

"You should bring him over here sometime. I've ordered furniture online for here, and it's supposed to be delivered in the next couple days. We can always have him put it together."

"Oh god," Kent said in mock horror, but grinned. "Maybe I will, call me when it arrives and I'll let you know."

"Okay. And I want to thank you for all your help. Please do up the bill, and I'll cut you a check."

"Sure," he said, and kissed her cheek before making sure she had his number, then he left, knowing full well that he wouldn't be sending any type of bill to her. As far as he was concerned, she was family, and family didn't charge other family.

CHAPTER TWENTY-FOUR

"There's an exit five miles up, can we pull over there?" Kurtis asked from the back seat of Kam's truck. They were all headed to Ohio for the big race, and he and Kam had discussed how they would get Kali to pull over every few hours. It wasn't that they didn't trust her driving, but after spending the last seven weeks with her, spending every night with her, they knew she would drive straight through without stopping, since she'd questioned Kam several times on how big his gas tank was, along with what was his miles per gallon ratio.

"Why you gotta pee?" Kali laughed from the driver's seat. "Didn't you go before we left home?"

"I did and no, there's something up here we want you to see." He grinned as she whipped her head up, and frowned at him in the mirror.

"What?"

"Pull off there," Kam said, both ignoring her question. She followed his instruction then at the stop sign he told her where to go. Ten minutes later he had her pull over and put the truck in park.

"Where are we? It's the middle of nowhere."

"It is, but look to your left."

Kali looked and didn't see anything, until she noticed the tall light poles. She frowned and looked harder. "A race track?"

"Yes, this is Eriez Speedway."

"Oh wow." She looked at her watch. "So, it's a little over three hours from home to here."

"Yes. Thought you'd like to see where it was. Now turn the truck around and go back the way we came, but instead of getting back on the expressway, go past it for about seven miles."

"Why?"

"Because, there's a restaurant there we go to every time we race here. Great food, good company, good prices, and we're halfway to our destination, so why not stop and get some lunch?"

"Sure. I didn't eat much for breakfast. Someone kept me busy during the night, so I slept late."

"Brat," Kurt said from the back, but he grinned. "Keep up that attitude and you might not be able to sleep all night tonight."

Kali didn't say anything, but both men saw her do a happy dance in her seat, and she had a faraway look in her eyes.

"Pay attention to the road," Kam said sternly from beside her, and he laughed when she stuck her tongue out at him. Ten minutes later, they pulled into a small restaurant and were greeted like long-lost family members, even though they'd been there just two weeks ago. After using the facilities, Kali joined them, and they placed their orders, sat around talking and enjoying a good meal. Kali felt several eyes on her, brows furrowed in confusion. When the waitress continued to flirt with both men, she was about to say something, until Kam leaned back in the booth and put his arm around Kali.

"Sorry, Rachael. We told you we were in a relationship."

"What's she have that I don't?" The waitress demanded. "I've been waiting on you for years, and you've never taken me up on my offers. Why the hell not? I want to know what she has that I don't."

"Manners for one," Kali said snidely from beside Kam, and she felt Kurtis nudge her foot. She frowned at him and talked like Rachael wasn't even there. "What, she's been coming on to both of you since we sat down. You both ignored her, except to place our order, and she didn't get the hint." She looked at Rachael, and asked, "Didn't it ever occur to you that your customers only want to come in and have a nice leisurely meal without getting hit on all the time? Or do you take the term customer service a few steps further?"

Rachael didn't know what to say to that. She slapped their bill on the table, and hurried away. When the two men didn't say anything, but just stared at her, she asked, "What?"

"Nothing," they said, and she didn't believe them, so she opened her purse threw a twenty down on the table, pushed Kam until he let her out, then she went to the ladies' room, then back out to the truck.

She was sitting behind the wheel when they came out, but instead of getting in, Kam opened the driver's door, and said, "Turn it off, Kali."

"Why?"

"Because you're pissed, and one very important lesson to know is to never drive pissed."

Kali sighed as she reached up and turned it off, then Kam reached in and unbuckled her seatbelt, turned her to face them as they both crowded in the small space, not giving her any room to move.

"We are not mad or upset with you," Kam began.

"We're in awe of you." Kurt grinned and reached up, took her head in his hands and kissed her. When he was done, she frowned at them.

"We've been in relationships off and on since we were fifteen. Separately and together. You are the first woman to ever come to our defense when some other woman was hitting on us. We love coming here, but Rachael has become a problem. A year ago, we told the owner how much we loved and enjoyed coming here, but we wouldn't be coming back because of Rachael. Several other drivers had said the same thing."

"Instead of firing her, because she is a good waitress, her hours were switched so that she didn't work when we had a race. I never suspected she'd be here on a Saturday, not until she came up to our table, but I want to thank you for speaking up."

"Hey, I was only protecting what's mine," she said, and was suddenly grabbed and kissed by Kam, then again by Kurtis. They stepped away and grinned when she sighed.

"Better hit the road," they said, and this time Kam climbed in the back, while Kurt climbed in the passenger seat beside her. Kali didn't leave until she had herself under control. When she looked at them before putting the truck in gear, they only smirked at her.

"Shut up," she groused, then took off. The rest of the trip was uneventful, and Kurtis gave her directions from beside her. She was able to go directly to the hotel, and once parked, she exited and stretched, twisting this way and that to get the kinks out.

"You okay?"

"Yeah, just getting the blood flowing. So how we going to do this? Matt's coming in tomorrow, so that'll be fine, but the room is registered in my name, what if it's not big enough for the three of us, and do you check in with me?"

"Are you embarrassed to be seen with us?"

"No, why would you say that?"

"Then, we'll be together," Kam said as he began taking suitcases from the back of the pickup.

"Why do you guys have only an overnight bag when you're going to be here for a whole week?"

"Because, this is only until our rigs get here on Tuesday. That's where the bulk of our clothes are," Kurtis said, and jerked her suitcase away from her when she went to get it.

"Fine," she said, but had him stop, so she could get the information Mr. Bloom had sent her that was in the front zippered pocket of the case. With that, she strode forward and into the hotel.

"Welcome to the Mansfield Marriott, how may I help you?" the woman behind the counter asked, she didn't look at Kali at all. She was looking over her shoulder at the men standing behind her.

Kali wrapped her knuckles on the counter, and when the clerk startled, Kali pushed the reservation forward. "I have a reservation. Kali Kilpatrick." It seemed like it took forever and a day with the tapping of the keys, but finally she looked up and smiled, again looking behind her. "You're all set. Here's your key, you're in room ten twenty-eight. Will that be all?"

"Could I have two more room keys please?"

"Why?" she blurted out, then sighed. "I'm sorry, that was unprofessional. I should have asked you how many keys you needed. Forgive me," she said, and quickly programmed the key cards, slipped them into their individual envelopes, and passed them across to Kali.

"Thank you," Kali said, and stepped away. She was three steps away when the clerk said.

"May I help you?"

"We're with her," Kam said as he came up behind her, put his arm around her waist, and right in front of the clerk Kali handed them each a card, then walked toward the elevators. Once inside they turned and saw the clerk looking at them in stunned shock.

Once the doors were closed, she sighed. "That was rude."

"But, effective," Kurtis said. "So now we know she won't be hitting on us every time we come and go."

"Does that happen often?"

"More than we like." Kam sighed and held the elevator to allow her to step off. They followed the signs to their room, and Kurtis was the first one in. When he whistled, they hurried in behind him, and stopped to stare. They had entered into a sitting room that held a chair, a couch, a loveseat, then there was a huge TV, a refrigerator and microwave and even a desk. Leaving their bags there, they saw a bathroom off to the left, and going further there was the bedroom. Which held a king-sized bed, two dressers, a table and chairs, a desk, two side chairs, and an even larger TV on one of the dressers.

"Damn," Kali said, and frowned at a door off to the right, and saw that it was another bathroom. She came out and grinned at their stunned expressions.

"I think I'm going to like this." She laughed. "If I'm working, I won't keep you two awake and vice versa. I like it."

"So do we." Kam grinned as he came out of the bathroom off the bedroom. "Comparing the two, this one is a whole hell of a lot bigger. While I don't think this is luxury, but it is high-end business class."

"Yeah." Kali agreed, and began turning on lights, but Kurt opened the drapes and bright sunlight poured into the bedroom, and they stood there looking out at the skyline. "Eeh, view's not very impressive." She shrugged, tossed her suitcase on the bed, and started unpacking and the guys joined her. It didn't take long before they were all unpacked, and stood around looking at each other.

"It's almost five, want to go for a walk and see what the neighborhood has to offer?" Kam asked.

"I have to call Mr. Bloom first, and let him know I've arrived and find out what time and where I meet him in the morning."

"Go ahead," they said, and stepped out of the bedroom, so she could make her call. Twenty minutes later she joined them in the sitting room, and grinned.

"Noon tomorrow at the track, and he gave me some recommendations of the surrounding area within walking distance."

"Okay." They clicked off the TV and started toward the door, but Kam stopped so suddenly that Kali ran into the back of him, and Kurtis into her.

"Before we leave, I have one thing to say."

"What?"

"What happened at the restaurant earlier was fine, perfect, I had no problem with it, except for one thing."

"What?"

"When you are with us, you pay for nothing. Understood?" he demanded, then suddenly from behind her came a hand holding a twenty-dollar bill. Without saying anything Kurtis stuffed it in her bra and patted it.

"Yes," she gulped.

"Good," Kam said, and kissed her, then whirled her around, and Kurtis kissed her.

She sighed and as they left the room, she said, "I don't think I'll ever get used to that. Maybe I'm so mind-boggled, because you turn me around so fast."

"Or, it could be because we're good kissers." Kurtis grinned and when they stepped off the elevator they were laughing, and all three of them waved to the front-desk clerk as they left. Outside she gave them the information Mr. Bloom had given her, and it was almost midnight when they arrived back to the hotel, and the three of them stayed awake only long enough to shower and crash on the bed. Within minutes all three were sound asleep.

CHAPTER TWENTY-FIVE

Kali slowly awoke, and moaned when she felt four hands massaging her back, from her neck all the way down to her ankles. "A girl could get used to waking this way."

"And she speaks," Kurt chuckled in her ear, and circled his tongue around the outside shell. When she did a whole-body shiver, the four hands flipped her over. She could only get a squeak out before both of them covered her from the sides. She felt both their hard cocks along her hip, but her hands were trapped, and she couldn't reach them, then she was too busy exchanging kisses with both of them, and when she was breathless, they moved their hands down and made sure she was ready for them. When she opened her legs further, they looked at each other, and grinned.

But, then Kam looked at her, and said in all seriousness, "It's time."

"Time?"

"For you to take both of us, together."

"Do you think I'm ready?"

"We do." Both of them looked down at her, and saw the emotions flitting across her face.

They were just about to tell her they could wait, when she looked at them both, and asked, "How do we do this?"

The brothers looked at each other, and did their silent communication thing, then after kissing her senseless, they moved her so that Kurtis was under her. She straddled him and when she went to reach between them to guide him into her, her hands were suddenly put behind her back, and she felt a slap across both of her ass cheeks.

Kali stared at them in shock, and didn't know what to say, but when Kam began massaging her ass, she moaned.

"We told you we don't often do BDSM, but we've been known to spank every once in a while." Kurt grinned up at her, and grinned when she squirmed as Kam reached down and fondled her inner folds.

"She likes it." He grinned, then got off the bed and walked around to the nightstand. He handed his brother a condom, then put one on himself, and pulled out a tube of lube, and tossed that on the bed beside Kurtis' knees. Once Kurt brought his legs together, they lifted her and settled her over him, but they held her up until just the head of his cock was inside her. She wrinkled her nose at their laugh, then moaned when Kurtis took one breast in his mouth. She was so busy being overwhelmed by what Kurtis was doing, she didn't pay any attention to Kam, until she felt the cold lube run down the crack of her ass, but they held her steady, and didn't allow her to jerk away from them.

"Easy," Kam said. "Relax, and soon you'll be feeling nothing but pleasure. You've been good so far when we played with you here. After today, you'll be able to take both of us at once. I'll go slow, you just have to relax and enjoy," he said as he began massaging her rosette with his finger, then slowly worked it in. He went as slow as he could, and kept adding more lube. After he'd worked two fingers, he looked at his brother and nodded.

Kam removed his fingers and the glove he'd put on, then put more lube on both Kali and himself, and helped his brother slowly lower her onto his shaft. When she groaned, Kurt reached about and held her ass, and nodded up to his brother. He lifted Kali back up, so only the tip of his cock was inside her, and Kam began pushing inside her.

"Oh god."

"Breathe," they both said, and Kurt played with her breasts, while Kam began to slowly advance. He had to grit his teeth and breathe deeply through his nose. He paused and had to catch his breath. "Just a little bit more. God, you're so tight. This is killing me."

"I can take your place." Kurt grinned and laughed when they both yelled no. Kam started moving forward again, and breathed easier when he breached the ring of muscle, and was able to slip all the way in.

"What's wrong?" Kali froze and tightened up, clenching both of them tightly.

"Nothing, I'm all the way in. Now we can slowly lower you back onto Kurt, and all three of us can have some fun."

"No, what's on my back? I feel something dripping."

Kurt frowned, then looked at his brother and chuckled. "It's Kam. He's sweating."

"Oh." She relaxed and as she did they lowered her onto Kurtis, who swore and gritted his teeth. "Oh god, I feel like you're going to rip me in two."

"Relax," Kurt said, and Kam saw his hands tighten on her hips. They began with their normal rhythm of Kam pulled out, then as he pushed back in, they lifted Kali and Kurtis slipped almost all the way out. It only took seconds to get back in the rhythm, and then Kali stared at Kurt in shock, and he reared up and slammed his mouth over hers as she screamed out her first orgasm. Both men swore and had to pause when she'd tightened up all her inner muscles on them. They waited for her to come down from the orgasm, then because she'd just had hers, they couldn't wait and doubled their efforts, and minutes later the three of them came. Afterward, Kali fell on Kurtis, and Kam on Kali, all of them fighting to catch their breath.

It took everything Kam had in him to pull out, dispose of his condom and fall to the side, still breathing deeply. Kurtis reached between them to hold onto his condom and nudged Kali and looked at his brother, and grinned. "Little help here?"

Kam reached over and rolled Kali off his brother and into his arms, then smiled when he realized she was asleep. He glanced over and saw it was only seven in the morning, and decided to wrap her tighter in his arms, and they fell back asleep.

Around nine Kali jerked awake, and saw she was alone in the bed, but she heard the shower and only winced twice as she rose from the bed, and headed toward the bathroom. She opened the door and saw Kam in the shower, and because she could, she opened the door and climbed in, reaching for the soap.

"Morning."

"Morning. How do you feel?"

"A little sore, but good. You?"

"Happy."

"Me too." She sighed and hugged him. When he reached for her, she shook her head. "If you don't mind, I'd like to hold off on more sex, I think I might be more than a little sore."

"Not a problem. Want me to wash your hair?"

"Please?" She ducked her head, and after her head was completely wet, she turned and moaned several times as he washed and rinsed her hair. Afterward, Kali was brushing her teeth when Kam went out to the bedroom, and saw Kurtis sitting on the bed waiting for them.

"What are you doing?" Kurt asked as Kam started dressing.

"She's sore, we didn't do anything."

"Oh," Kurtis said, and stood and started dressing. He studied Kali when she came out and started dressing. "Are you okay?" he asked when she winced a couple times. "Maybe we should have waited."

"No, I'll be okay. I'm just not used to having two redwood trees in my private parts at the same time." She grinned when they sputtered. Kam actually spat out the water he'd just taken a drink of.

"What did you say?" He looked at her in shock, then at his brother. "What did she say?"

"She compared our cocks to redwood trees." Kurt laughed.

"Oh, well," Kam grinned and went over and hugged her. "About today, we're going to stay here, and you can take the truck." He handed her the keys. At her frown, he said, "Because, this is your job, and I'm not allowed at the track until Tuesday. Neither is Kurt. My only question for right now is, do you want to order room service, or go out to eat?"

"I think we'll have a better time or faster service if we go out. I know my appointment is for noon, but I'd like to get there a few minutes early, and I'm not exactly sure where the track is."

"Okay. There's a restaurant downstairs."

"Then, let's go there," she said, and grabbed a piece of paper, and quickly wrote, then pushed it to the side along with five dollars.

"What are you doing?"

"Leaving a note for the cleaning lady to leave extra coffee, and the five is for her tip."

"Oh."

"Haven't you ever stayed in a hotel?"

"No, we've always stayed in campers, then when we started making money we bought our own rigs. Hard to find a hotel around some of the tracks we run on."

"All right then. It's common courtesy to tip the housekeeper, and have you seen the coffee?"

"No." They frowned and followed her. "What the hell is that?"

"It's supposed to be a four-cup pot, but these packs only make two cups, but with the way you two drink the stuff, it'll be one cup, and there's only two."

"Damn." Kurt said, and grinned at her. "What are you going to drink?"

"Ass, why do you think I requested more coffee?" They laughed and went to leave, but Kali quickly ran to the bedroom, then grabbed her purse and a briefcase and the truck keys. "I'll leave for the track from the restaurant downstairs, then you guys can do what you want. Are you sure you don't want the truck? I can always get a cab."

"No, you take the truck," Kam said, and frowned when Kurtis went the other direction when they turned the corner, but they waited for him at the elevator. When he joined them, he had a huge grin on his face.

"What did you do?"

"Saw a cleaning lady and told her I was in ten twenty-eight, and drank a lot of coffee. I gave her a twenty to leave lots and lots of coffee."

They laughed and went downstairs. As soon as they stepped off the elevator and started toward the restaurant, the front desk clerked called out. "Miss Kilpatrick."

Kali frowned as did the guys, and went over to the desk. "I'm Kilpatrick."

"A note for you," she said, and handed it to Kali, but made sure she eyed Kam and Kurtis, and actually sighed when they stepped closer to Kali, but she only thanked the clerk and turned and laughed as she pushed them out of her way after slamming into them.

"Personal space, guys." She grinned and they went into the restaurant, and after getting coffee, they decided on the buffet. Finally, she read the note and frowned.

"What?" She passed the keys to Kam and the note.

"It seems that starting at eleven thirty today, I'm going to have my own personal driver for the week."

"Damn," Kam said as he took the keys from her, and pocketed them. "We don't know when we'll see you again, especially if you have your own driver. So I want to say that that if you come home Tuesday and don't find us in the room, and all our stuff is missing, it's not because we've left you. It's because we left to go to the track."

"But, we'll leave you a note, and we won't be leaving until we get the call from Pete and or Larry that they have arrived, or are so many miles away, then we'll be leaving."

"Oh. I know I shouldn't be disappointed, and I know you were going to the track, but I'm going to miss you."

"Maybe one night you can sleep in the RV with us, depending on your schedule."

"I'll have to let you know. We have each other's phone numbers, so I'll let you know when I'm done for the night."

"Sounds like a plan," Kam said, and dug into his breakfast. They all looked up when someone called her name, and all Kali did was kick the chair across from her and grin.

"You made good time." Kali told Matt, who reached over and grabbed the coffee pot and a cup off the table next to them.

"I was too excited to sleep, so I left at three this morning. Took my time and only got lost trying to find this place. So where are you?"

"Ten."

"I'm on seven." He paused and told the waitress he'd do the buffet, then quickly filled a plate and rejoined them.

"We have a meeting with Bloom at noon, and here," she said, and gave him the note.

"Cool, so I can leave my car here?"

"Yep, I'd say for this first meeting today, take your camera for stills, and maybe a small video camera, not something you'd use later for video, but then again, that's your department."

"I know." He grinned and they discussed what they would be looking for, and the setup of the pits. "Hey," he said, and looked at Kam and Kurtis. "I've been meaning to ask this. Do you have assigned spots at the pits? I noticed you park in the same spot, or close to it at every race."

"If you remember from riding with us, we're almost always the first ones there, but no, our pit spots aren't assigned. It's first come first served. And remember last week at State? How crowded it was? That's why we like to arrive early, so we have a spot to set up."

"Yeah." They finished their breakfast, and Kali stayed and lingered in the restaurant with her men, while Matt ran up to his room, and after he took a quick shower he gathered the equipment he thought he'd need for that day, and arrived with only seconds to spare before their driver arrived. Kam and Kurtis both kissed her goodbye, but they kept it PG rated, by only kissing her on the cheek, but with the promise they'd see her that night.

CHAPTER TWENTY-SIX

Thursday afternoon, Matt and Kali were in the pits talking to drivers, taking pictures and were working their way down the line, when all of a sudden Kali, who had been walking backwards and instructing Matt on the shots she wanted, bumped into someone. She whipped around to say she was sorry, then grinned. She started to throw her arms around Kam, but he only looked around with his eyes and she nodded.

"Oh. God, it's good to see you. How are you doing?"

"Good. So can I ask you a question?"

"Sure, what's up?"

"I heard there were almost seventy-five cars here, what have you heard?"

"Bloom said total that sent in their entrance fee was eighty-nine."

"Damn."

"Yeah."

"Want to hear what I heard?" Matt grinned as he joined them, and began snapping pictures, acting like he did with all the other drivers, not letting on they knew him.

"What?"

"Two things, people who know you are bitching, because they're saying there's no way they can win."

Kam only grinned and puffed up his chest. "What was the other thing?"

"Other people are asking who the hell Kilbourne is. They'd never heard of him. And something about money on the website, you're in the lead by more than ten grand."

"Damn, last time I looked it was only four grand, but I'm in the lead?"

"You are. Can you tell me what that means?" Kali asked, and clicked her pen.

"A year ago, Bloom sent out an e-mail to all drivers across the country to see if there was interest in a race like this, but as you know, it's only super late models," he said, and looked over as Kurtis walked up and joined them.

"He had enough interest to put this together. We put this race on our websites, and then started talking about it at the tracks we ran on. When fans bought their tickets for this event, they had to pick a driver. Every ticket sold, the driver they picked received certain points. You could also donate extra money to that driver. Once the preliminary races are done, even if I come in dead last, I still get to race in the main qualifying, because I'm the leader in the fan pick. The top five advance no matter what, unless they wreck."

"You're number one? I thought you were second?" Kurtis asked in shock.

"According to what people are saying in the pits, he's ten grand over everyone."

"Damn."

"Do you get that money? In addition to what the winnings are?"

"I'm not sure how the purse is divided. That's something you'll have to talk to Bloom about. All I know was that when I unpacked my car, the purse was almost two hundred grand.

Who knows what it'll be at the end of the race. Or how they even figure it."

"Okay. I'll do that. We've discussed everything but the money and how that works. Maybe I can catch Bloom and ask him."

"Have you eaten?"

"This morning at the hotel."

"And it's three in the afternoon," Kurtis said, and when he reached for her hand, Kam clamped his hand down on his forearm and shook his head.

"She's working."

"Oh, sorry." He grinned and looked around at the other drivers. None of whom he knew. He sighed, and asked instead, "Have you been everywhere?"

"I have. Are you looking for anything in particular?"

"I was thinking that if you were hungry, maybe we could go out to the vendors."

"No thank you," she said, and shuddered.

"They suck." Matt grinned. "For something this big and with this many fans, you'd think they'd have better choices than French Fries, fried dough and dried hamburgers. On a scale of one to ten, the food rates about a point five. Trust me, a peanut butter sandwich would taste better, and I'm allergic to peanuts."

"Damn," Kam said.

"So, you know of the fan boxes on the back straight away?" Kurt asked.

"Yes, why?"

"We have the first one from here. We've got coolers and a grill all set up. Why don't you swing by and grab a bite, and Dad wants to see you, said it was important."

"Okay. I'm almost done here, we can make it over in about an hour. I'm assuming Matt's welcome?"

"Absolutely." He grinned and they watched as she moved down the line. Kam and Kurtis watched until she was out of sight, then looked at each other and grinned.

"So does Dad really want to talk to her, or did you make that up to make sure she eats?"

"He really wants to talk to her." Kurtis grinned. "When he bought all our tickets, he had to request so many bands, in order to get in and out in the pit camping area. He bought extras and wants to give one to Matt and Kali."

"So, if it's late she can stay here." Kam grinned. "But he didn't know Kali back when he ordered them."

"We know that, but we don't have to tell her that they were just extras, and besides I don't think Kali knows that her family is here."

"They are?"

"Yep, rolled in about three hours ago."

"So, Keith and Kathy are here, that'll be good for her."

"It will, but I mean her whole family." Kurtis grinned and spread his arms wide. "Sister and her family, brother and his family, and Mom is practically kissing the ground Karen walks on."

"What's Kyle done now?" Kam shook his head and hung it low, then looked up and grinned.

"Believe it or not, he was teaching Dad how to shoot his slingshot."

"Which one?"

"Ken. Kent's marking out the distance, and several other people have gathered around and are taking turns. Dad's set it up like a firing range, and Kyle's taken all Mom's hair ties to make more."

"Oh lord."

"Yep." Kurtis grinned and asked how soon before he could leave his car.

"I'm done, I saw Kali on the other side of the pit, and waited for her to work her way this way, and you know after the first initial shock of seeing her shake a driver's hand, I was good with it. She's totally different with them than she is with us."

"Professional?"

"Yes. But, I'm starving. I have a drivers' meeting at five thirty." They told Pete and Larry to come over and grab something to eat at the fan box, before the drivers' meeting, and then they made their way there. They greeted the Kilpatrick's like long-lost family, and after everyone said hello, Kathy approached them.

"Have you seen Kali?"

"Yes, she and Matt are walking the pits. She's asking questions and taking notes, and Matt's snapping pictures."

"So, she's fine? She's not hiding in a corner? She's actually talking to someone?"

"Mom." Karen came up behind her mother and put her arm around her. "Kali's fine. You have nothing to worry about when it comes to her and her work."

"But you know how she always hid in a corner, and then those godawful glasses she wears that she doesn't need."

"When was the last time you saw her?"

"When the kids came back before they moved here. Just before the Fourth of July. Why? What should I know?"

"That your youngest daughter is a delightful woman. She's smart, savvy, fun-loving, and has one hell of a sense of humor," Kam said, and saw Karen nod in admiration and Kathy worry her bottom lip.

"I'm sure you've gotten to know Mom by now, and she'd tell you if we were dishonest," Kurtis said.

"I know, it's just that I worry so much about her. How did her hands look? How many people jerked away from her when she shook their hands? Did she shake their hands? Or did she keep them wrapped around her middle?"

"Mom," Kelsey said firmly as he joined them. "Stop. It's been almost twenty-three years. It's done, it's over, now stop. Kali is a bright, beautiful, fun-loving woman. You should be concentrating on her finding a husband, other than something that is out of everyone's control."

"I know, but I just worry."

"Well, you can stop," Kelsey said, and directed her to go join Kerri. As soon as their mother was out of hearing range, the siblings turned to the twins. "I'd like to apologize to you for that. Mom and Dad both worry about her, but Mom more so."

"Can you tell us what happened?" Kam asked. "She told us very little."

"But, she did say something?" Karen asked, and exchanged looks with her brother.

"About her hands was that she was at her grandparents, and fell asleep on the swing on the porch, and woke up with her hands bandaged from her fingers to her shoulders. Nothing more about that."

"And when we asked her to ride here with us," Kurt said. "She told us she had a teeny weeny problem with riding if she's not driving. Said she starts to go into a trance, then she gets cold and almost folds in on herself, and she doesn't even realize she does it."

"And she told you this?" Karen asked in shock. "Did she say anything else?"

"That she puts her knees to her chest, then hugs them and stares off into space. She called it zoned out, and that if that ever happens, then get a blanket and put it over her. She said a heavy fleece one. I don't know if you know this, but Kam and I have been dating her for almost eight weeks, and as soon as she told us that, we went out and made sure we have that type of blanket in each of our trucks, and in our home."

"I've noticed the dark green one in her living room," Kam said, and frowned when the two of them exchanged looks. "What's wrong?"

"We can't really tell you at this point, but if she told you all that, I'm pretty sure it won't be long before all will be revealed."

"Don't you think Matt should know if something happens? He's with her all day, and we're with her all night. Or does he already know?"

"He's clueless as far as we know, but we're not trying to be mean or evasive. It's just that the doctors said it would be better if she remembered on her own, and from what you've told us, she has never, ever said that part about sleeping on grandma's porch."

"Is it true?"

"Yes, everything you said is true. So maybe she is getting her memory back."

"If she is," Kelsey said firmly. "Then, we're doing the intervention. Has she said anything else?"

"Yes, she called the teeny problem an episode, and only her father can get her out of it, and the last one was the day she moved into her house."

"Ah, we didn't know about that one," Karen said, and pulled her phone. "I want you to get our numbers, and if anything happens, and I mean anything, you call me or Kelsey first. It's time to put a stop to this, and by the time everything is said and done, our baby sister will almost be whole again."

"We understand, but can I ask how much of a memory loss are we talking?"

"Technically it's about two hours."

"But, not technically?"

"Three months, but she was under medical sedation or a coma at that time, but the actual thing that caused all this was only two hours."

"Okay, we'll trust you for now," Kam said. "But, if we feel this is hurting her in any way whatsoever, we will be coming to knock on your door."

"Understood," Kelsey said, then nodded and they turned to see Matt and Kali approach. He looked at his sister. "Someone better tell Matt."

"I will," Karen said, and went over to greet the two newcomers with smiles and hugs.

"Should we be worried?" Kameron asked as he watched his lover greet her sister.

"Naw, but be prepared if something happens to call one of us. Preferable Karen or me." They watched and slowly made their way over to Kali, and as soon as they approached, first Kameron, then Kurtis kissed her, and grinned when she stumbled as they released her.

"Hey." Kent grinned as he approached. "Hold out your left arm," he said, and grinned when she was too stunned from her men's kisses to question him. She frowned when she felt something on her arm, and looked down and saw a bright yellow and white band.

"What's this?"

"The pass to get into the pit camping area. Thought you might like to join us one night and you can't get in without that band," Kent said as he put another band on Matt's arm. "I know you didn't order anything, but we always get extra, and see the shirt we're all wearing?"

She frowned and saw the front of their shirts were the same as hers and Matt's. "What about it? It's the same as mine."

Kent only grinned and had everyone turn around, and she saw on the back, it said, '*Kilbourne 18*.'

"Oh my god, you have driver's shirts? Mine only says, '*Event Staff*'."

"Yes, and where yours gets you where you need to be, ours show support for Kameron. I have one for you, but the boys have it. Didn't think you'd want to mix business with pleasure."

"Thank you so much, Kent." Kali actually hugged him, then grinned when she saw her parents there, along with Kathy and Kerri holding a plateful of food, which they gave to Matt and her, and everyone settled down to eat. When it was time for Kameron to go back to his car for the drivers' meeting, Matt and Kali left to go do what they had to. Matt grinned when he said that he was going to be in the infield taking pictures, and Kali was going to be up in the announcer's booth. They agreed to meet up after the race.

CHAPTER TWENTY-SEVEN

"Ohgodohgodohgod!" Kali said from the pit box on the backside of the track. She was jumping up and down and had a tight grip on Kurtis's forearm with one hand, and her father's with the other. It was Saturday night and the main feature was in progress. Out of the eighty-plus cars that had come to participate, only forty-five of them were eligible to run in this heat, and Kameron had started out eleventh. They had a hundred laps to run, and by lap fifty he was in the lead, and stayed that way. They were down to the white flag, and Kali held her breath as the cars entered turn one.

"Breathe," Kent yelled and grinned at the women who listened to him, but it didn't last long. Another car, who had been on Kameron's ass all weekend suddenly came out of nowhere, and was at his back fender. From where she stood it looked like that car took the lead going into turn three, but suddenly Kurtis actually screamed from beside her.

"FUCK YEAH!" He picked her up, twirled her around and kissed her. *"HE WON!"* Then, he kissed her again, and Kali saw everyone else in the booth cheering. She looked at the infield and saw Matt, who gave her two thumbs up, and then ran over to wait for the top five cars to come into the infield to be weighed, then Kameron would go to the winner's circle.

"Come on," Kurtis said as he grabbed her hand, and headed toward one of several golf carts parked behind their box. Everyone grinned and headed toward them, and Kyle rode with Kali and Kurtis, talking excitedly all the way.

Because cars were still coming off the track, they were able to shoot through them and come onto the track the way the cars had entered, and by the time the whole family was at the winner's circle in front of the stands, Kameron was just getting out of his car.

The track announcer was there with the mic to ask him questions, but he looked around frantically, ignoring him, and as soon as he saw Kali, he ran several feet to her and as she reached him he picked her up, twirled her around, and kissed her right in front of everyone. The crowd must have liked what they saw, because they started cheering, whistling and whooping for joy. Then, the announcer was there, and asked Kameron how he felt, then who he would like to thank.

"First, I'd like to thank my parents for supporting me all these years. I'd like to give a huge shout out to Dillard Auto Parts for sponsoring me and my brothers, and my other sponsors." And he began to name them off. As he did that, they crowded around them and were shuffled, and then the announcer held his mic out and asked one last question, and it was Kurtis who laughed.

"Not me, him." And he pointed to Kameron, who was leaning up against his car and had an arm around Kali.

"Aren't you Kameron Kilbourne?" The announcer frowned at him.

"Nope." Kurtis grinned. "I'm Kurtis, his twin."

"I'll be." The announcer grinned, then asked if he raced and what class. Finally, pictures were taken, and Kali ended up between Kameron and Kurtis, holding the checkered flag. After the pictures were taken, the announcer came back to them holding a bucket, asking Kameron to pull the winning 50/50 raffle. “Folks, Kameron Kilbourne’s about to pull the winning 50/50 ticket. If you’ll get your tickets out, please. Tonight’s pot the lucky winner will be taking home six thousand three hundred and sixty-six dollars.” He shook the gallon jug in front of Kameron, who reached in, swirled the tickets around and pulled one out. He read off the number, and only seconds later there was a scream of, ‘That’s me!’ from the stands.

“Go ahead and make your way to the announcer’s booth. Now who here would like to know how much the winning purse for the race is?” The announcer grinned when the stands were in an uproar. He held up his hands and looked at Kameron, and grinned.

“This weekend’s winner takes home three hundred seventy-nine thousand, four hundred eighty-one dollars and fifty cents.” He grinned when Kameron actually stumbled when he was presented with the huge check. “How does that make you feel?”

“Stunned,” Kameron said, and his fans in the stands went wild.

“I have to say, it seems like you’ve brought the most fans with you, but I have to tell you, before tonight I’d never heard of you. Could you tell us where you race?”

“My home track is Dusty Hill. I also race at State, McKay, Port Royal, Dog Hollow, and Eriez. I’m primarily out of southwestern New York and Northern Pennsylvania. And I’m going to put it out there to all my fans and fellow drivers. I’ll see you in Charlotte!” Then, he turned and hugged and kissed Kali one more time, before climbing into his car and he waited until everyone was in the golf carts, before they all drove off the track amidst cheers from the crowd.

Kurtis and Kali drove directly to the pits, and the rest of the family went back to the pit box and gathered their things. Kameron parked his car, climbed out and Kali stood off to the side while the brothers hugged, then Kameron took congratulations from his fellow drivers. By the time his family joined him, he was scowling and looking around.

"What's wrong?" Kyle asked as he jumped out of a golf cart. "You just won and you look pissed off."

"Where's Kali?"

"There." Kyle pointed, and Kali watched as Kameron whipped around and actually stalked her. When she realized what he was going to do, she gawked at him, then tried to turn and run, but she didn't get far. He grabbed her around the waist, picked her up and suddenly she was moving down the roadway. By the time she was turned around, she saw that Kurtis was driving a golf cart, while Kameron hugged her and started kissing the side of her neck. It wasn't long before they were at Kameron's RV.

Not letting her feet hit the ground. Kameron carried Kali into the RV, and grinned when Kurtis joined them, and locked the door after them. He was so pumped, and he saw from his brother's expression that he was going to take a step back this first round, and let Kameron have her all by himself. He grinned when he set Kali on her feet, and Kurtis held onto her shoulders. "I'll get her warmed up for you." He grinned and took Kali's face in his hands, and kissed her. Behind them, Kameron quickly stripped and took the shortest shower in the history of showers, and when he came out of the bathroom, he saw that Kurtis had Kali already half-naked and laid out on the bed.

He walked up to them completely naked, and after Kurtis unsnapped and unzipped her jeans, Kameron reached up, took her sneakers off and gripped the hem of her jeans and jerked them off, taking her panties with them.

"What the..." Kali asked. Startled she jerked her head away from Kurt's mouth, and looked at the foot of the bed and froze. Kameron stood there with a look in his eyes that she had never seen before, but it made her wet, wetter than normal. She also saw that his cock was hard and standing up, almost to his belly button, and the head was purple. She licked her lips and before she could say anything, he gripped her ankles and pulled her to the end of the bed. She watched as he took his cock in his hand, rubbed it through her wetness, then giggled when he swore when a condom wrapper landed on her lower belly. He glared at his brother, but grabbed the wrapper, tore it open and quickly slipped it on.

Gruffly he said, "This is going to be quick, let me know now if you're not ready."

"I'm ready." And before she had completed that statement, he slammed into her, causing them both to call out.

As soon as Kameron was fully seated, he fell forward onto his forearms and stared into her eyes, before he started pounding into her. Because it felt right, he began kissing her and when she wrapped her arms and legs around him, he sighed in relief and continued going fast. When she came, he released her mouth and watched her, but he didn't slow down to let her enjoy it.

"One more, baby," he said, and moved the hair from her face, then to help her along, he reached between them and played with her clit, and when she came again, he reared up, slammed into her one last time, and came along with her, filling the condom. He fell forward and wrapped his arms around her and held her tight to him. When both their breathing was under control. He reached between them, held onto the condom, and slowly slipped from her. He went into the bathroom and cleaned up. When he came back out he saw that Kurtis had covered her with the blankets, and was rubbing her hair.

Kameron went to the other side, and gently lifted her chin. "Are you okay?" he asked gently, and kissed the tip of her nose.

"Yeah, I'm fine."

She gave him a sluggish grin, and he kissed her gently on the lips, and whispered, "Sleep. It's early yet, and I thank you for letting me have you like that."

"Hey, no complaints here." She grinned again. "But, if you don't mind, I'm going to take a short nap."

"Don't mind at all." He grinned and kissed her again. "Do you want company?"

"Not really. No offense."

"None taken," Kameron said, and made sure she was tucked in, and quickly dressed and watched as Kurtis kissed her forehead, and together they went outside and began making up a bonfire. Shortly after it started, his family started arriving, along with Kali's, Kameron didn't even feel embarrassed, when Keith asked where Kali was.

"She's taking a short nap." He grinned, then Keith and the rest of them only shook their heads, and it wasn't long before a grill was going, and food was brought out.

"I have to say, Kameron," Lyle said. "For a minute there I didn't think you had a chance of winning, especially when that double zero car hit you from behind."

"And when you started eleventh and dropped back to twentieth." Chuck, Kali's brother-in-law shook his head in fascination. "Didn't think you'd ever get to the front."

Kameron grinned and pointed across the fire. "Thank Larry for that."

"What's that mean?" Lyle asked.

"I don't know how many times you've seen me race, but my car is tuned so that my best laps are in the last half of the race. Ever see the cars that start out in the lead and they're in that position most of the race, but then halfway through, or almost to the end of the race they run into problems or slow down?"

"Yes?"

"Any problems I have would be in the first half of the race. The last half it's like the car's settled in and ready to go. As the beginners begin to slow or have problems, I move forward."

"Damn," Lyle said, and shook his head. They spent until the early morning hours sitting around the fire and eating. Kameron made up a plate of everything, not knowing if Kali would wake, and took it into his RV, then covered it, and put it in his refrigerator. He went to the bedroom and looked in on her, and sighed when she was still sleeping. He also looked up when Kurtis joined him.

"Everyone's turning in. It's going on three. Do we wake her?"

"Naw, let's just crawl in beside her. She's already in the middle." Kameron grinned and began to undress. They both stripped down to nothing, and crawled in beside the woman of their dreams, and it wasn't long before they joined her in sleep.

*****

Several hours later, Kameron reached over to pull Kali to him, and frowned when his hand was punched.

"Not the right person," came the gruff reply from his brother. They both quickly lifted their heads and stared at each other.

"Where's Kali?" they asked at the same time, and thought they heard a giggle from the other room. They quickly donned their boxers and went out to investigate. They paused when they saw Kali sitting at the dining table with the plate of food Kameron had put in the refrigerator earlier. He yawned and rubbed his chest, and glanced at the clock and saw it was only eight in the morning.

"What are you doing up so early?"

"Early? Hell, it's late." She grinned and picked up a forkful of baked beans and held them out. "Want some?"

"Not really." Kameron scowled at her and turned to the kitchen, and grinned when he saw the coffee pot was full. He poured two cups, and took one to Kurt who had joined Kali at the table.

"So, what's on the agenda for today?" Kali asked when they were settled across from her.

"We go home. Larry packed up the car last night, and all he has to do is hook this RV up to the trailer, then he's good to go. The others have to pack up and they're heading home today. As for us, we just have to clean up the RV, then drive you back to your hotel and get your things, then we'll be ready to hit the road, unless you have other plans?"

"I only have to meet with Bloom at ten, after that I'm good to go. So, if you want I can take your truck over to the hotel, pack my things, check out, and check in with Matt to see if he needs anything. I can meet you back here, I can meet with Bloom, then we can leave afterward."

"Works for me," Kameron said, and handed her his truck keys. "Then we can pack up the RV, so that when we get home, we only have to grab our dirty laundry."

"And we can help Dad and Keith close up their campers and the other RVs. I personally want to check out mine, because Kyle's been staying in it with the other kids."

"Oh lord," Kali said, then grinned. As she finished eating, they discussed the race from last night, and when she was done, they kissed her, and she left to head back to the hotel. She was back at the track with plenty of time to spare, and they were headed home shortly after noon. They were all lost in their own thoughts as they started for home, but all of them felt relaxed in the silence.

CHAPTER TWENTY-EIGHT

Kali sighed as she looked up from her work, and was startled by how close Matt was standing next to her. "What the hell, Matt?"

"So you're back with us?"

"Excuse me?"

"You were zoned out. I've been calling you for the last ten minutes."

Kali frowned, but waved it away, by saying, "Just thinking of a different angle to what I'm going to be doing next weekend. Have you decided when you're going down?"

"The races are what?"

"Thursday, Friday, and Saturday. It's the last race of the season, it's for the World Short Track Championship."

"Are you going down with Kam and Kurt?"

"No, they're already there."

"Why?"

"Because, this weekend is the Championship for crate, next weekend is for super-late. The Kilbournes went down to Charlotte three days ago, and won't be back until after Kam's race next weekend."

"Aren't you going to be down there for Kurt?"

"We discussed it extensively before they left. You know we had an agreement that they don't interfere with my work, and I don't do the same with theirs."

"Yes."

"Well, I have meetings with Bloom, George Martin, Max Dillard, and Dad. I'll be leaving here next Tuesday, taking my time to drive down. I'll be there by Wednesday and spend the weekend with them."

"So, this isn't a working weekend for you?"

"Not in North Carolina, but here yes. That's why I'm not leaving for another week. What about you?"

"If you'll be okay here, I was thinking of heading out tomorrow. I'd like to get some pictures of Kurtis' race."

"Go ahead. And, of course, I'll be okay here. Why wouldn't I?"

"No reason," Matt said quickly, when he saw she was getting upset. He made a mental note to talk to her family and the twins before she came down next week. They continued discussing what he'd been working on. They were able to clear everything before Matt left for the day. "So, you're sure you'll be okay on your own?"

"Matt, if you ask me that one more time I'm going to fire you."

"Okay, okay." He held up his hands and grinned. "I'm going to just run upstairs and grab some of my equipment."

"That's fine," she said, and waved him away. When he came back down she was standing at her 'board' wall, and was moving items around, then stepped back and looked at it, then moved some more things around. Matt snapped his fingers, ran back upstairs, and grinned as he approached her.

"Hey, sorry, but I forgot to give you these." He grinned as he handed over some pictures and she scowled, but when she saw them she grinned.

"Thanks, Matt. I knew I was missing something." She turned back to the board, then added a couple of pictures he had given her, and Matt left feeling better that she was focused on her work.

A week later, Kali left her meeting on cloud nine, and looked over at her father when he joined her. "When are you leaving for North Carolina?" Keith asked her as they entered the parking lot.

"As soon as I get in my SUV and head south. You?"

"I was hoping to catch a ride with you. I've got your mother's car, Kelsey and Lyle took your mother and the kids in my truck, and Chuck drove Karen's minivan, and Karen drove Kelsey's car. No sense having an extra vehicle, so I stayed for this meeting, and was hoping to catch a ride with you."

"Sure, do you need to do anything before we leave, and are you okay if we stop every couple of hours?"

"I'm okay with it, and I'm even okay if you want to stop and get a room for the night. I won't ask if you want to share the driving."

"Thanks for that. So, why don't I follow you home, and you can put Mom's car in the garage and grab your bag?"

"My bag is here." He grinned and opened the trunk, and put it in the back of her SUV beside her things. They grinned, then Kali followed him home, and they were only forty-five minutes before they headed out. They didn't talk until they were on the expressway and heading south.

"So, what did you think of the meeting?" Kali asked.

"It was good. I learned a lot, both from George and Bloom. Personally, I think Bloom's learned a lot too. I can't wait for the spring to open again."

"I've been thinking of that."

"Oh?" Keith grinned when she didn't continue. "Come on, Kal, I can see you have something cooking, let's hear it."

"Will you be open to some suggestions?"

"Of course. Tomorrow is November 1st, so that means we have practically five full months to work out the details."

"Okay, here goes. Depending on the weather, how do you feel about coordinating with George and have a Season Kick-off."

"What's that mean?"

"You've been to State and McKay for their three-day events, and you've been to Ohio, now we're going to Charlotte, North Carolina for the end of season Championship races. Right?"

"Yes."

"What if you were to contact the daughter of the man who started your race track, and see if she had a list of all drivers who had ever raced there. We could have races Thursday, Friday and Saturday, like the other tracks do, but invite all the old timers who used to race there, and if she has any memorabilia that she'd like to donate, that would be great. I can come up with some great ads for it." She looked at her father with a grin, then sighed heavily. "However, if she doesn't want to donate them, then maybe she'd let us borrow whatever she might have for that weekend."

"And even though the past drivers might not be driving any longer, maybe we can get stories from them, or any old pictures." Keith began to wrap his head around what his daughter was talking about.

"Exactly. And are you really going to rename Dusty Hill Family Raceway, The Hill?"

"I'm not quite sure. Everyone I talk to always says they're going up the hill to the race. I thought it was fitting."

"How about this?" Kali grinned at him. "Why don't we interview the old timers and see what they call it? And I've been thinking of maybe when we come to an agreement on the date for this, we can send invitations in the mail, with something along the lines, if they show that letter, they can get into the pits for free, but would have to pay the entrance fee, or half price."

"That and maybe a five-dollar-off coupon on the entrance fee, but we'd have to talk about that. Maybe when I get back from North Carolina I can contact Becky, that's the original owner's daughter. I can talk to her and see if she has anything about the former drivers. I'd love to talk to them over the winter and come up with plans."

"Sounds good," Kali said, and they settled in and talked different ideas as she drove. They both had figured that it was a twelve-hour drive, and after only seven hours, Kali looked at her father, and sighed. "Do you mind if we find some place to pull over and grab some sleep?"

"Sure. Let's find someplace that has a restaurant nearby. I don't know about you, but I'm hungry."

Kali laughed when her stomach rumbled. She found what they were looking for twenty miles down the road. She gave a token protest when her father paid for the bill an hour later, and knew he wouldn't let her pay. They drove to the other end of the parking lot to a motel, and went in and each paid for their own room.

They ended up being side by side, and before they unlocked them, Kali asked, "If I get up early, want me to wake you, and we can hit the road early?"

"Sure, we're only halfway there, and if we get on the road early, we can get there faster. And, don't worry if it's two or three in the morning, that will be fine."

"Thanks, Dad." Kali kissed his cheek and went into the room, and realized that it was pretty clean, but she took a quick shower and was in bed shortly after. It didn't take long for her to fall into a deep sleep.

*****

At 3 a.m. she woke refreshed, and took another quick shower, then smiled as she made two cups of coffee, and grinned harder when she saw they had lids for the cups. She decided to wait to take her packed suitcase out to her truck, and opened the door and gave a small screech, then laughed. "Dad. What are you doing?"

"Same thing you appear to be doing." He grinned as he held up two cups of coffee.

Kali laughed when she saw that his hair was wet, and shook her head. "So, when did you wake?"

"When I heard your shower turn on." He sipped his coffee and set them on the hood of her car. "If you give me your keys, I'll put our bags in the truck." She handed them over, and made sure she had everything, and by the time they were on the road again, it was shortly before four in the morning.

They drove for about three hours, and pulled off to get gas and some breakfast, but didn't linger. By the time they arrived at the track, it was slow going, because there was a long line of campers, and RVs.

"So, where are we parked?"

"Pit parking." Keith grinned and reached into the back seat, and pulled his briefcase toward him. After it was on his lap, he opened it and pulled the paperwork they needed. He looked around and told her to follow the trucks pulling in that had cars on trailers, or car haulers. Kali automatically went toward them, and pulled into line. When they arrived at the head of the line, they were stopped, and Kali handed the attendant the paperwork her father had handed her.

"Okay, follow the cars, but when they go right, you go left, the pit camping is up there. I'm assuming you already have a camper there?"

"We do," Kali said, not bothering telling him that she was staying with Kurt and Kam. "Do we drive right up to our camper?"

"Actually, no. You'll see cars and trucks parked on the opposite side of the campers, so park there, then you'll have to walk to your site, and if you have them, make sure you have your wrist bands on."

"Thanks," Kali said, and put the SUV in gear and slowly followed the trucks, and when they went right, she went left. She found the parked vehicles, and was able to park at the end of one row. Luckily, they both only had a small suitcase, and with her purse over one shoulder, she pulled her suitcase behind her, and looked at her father. "Does Mom have our wrist bands?"

"I hope so." He grinned, then frowned. He paused and started looking around, and kept wrinkling his nose.

"What's wrong?"

"Do you smell that?"

"Is it a skunk?"

"Maybe," he said, and then chuckled. He leaned in and whispered, even though no one was around them. "It almost smells as if Kyle's been experimenting with his brothers' aftershave again." He grinned and they started forward, and the scent became stronger.

"Campers must be this way." Kali grinned and pointed toward the smell. They slowed their pace, and it was Keith that pointed out their campers. They stopped and watched the scene unfold before them. Standing with their arms crossed over their impressive chests that she personally had kissed every inch of them, were Kam and Kurt on one side, and Kyle on the other, standing the same way. Off to the side were the rest of the Kilbournes and the Kilpatricks. It looked like they were at a standstill. If it was a hundred years ago, she swore they would be wearing six shooters on their hips.

Kent caught sight of the newcomers, and only grinned, not letting on to the others that they were there.

"Kyle," Kent said firmly, and Kali saw that it took everything he had not to laugh, or grin. "Your brothers asked you a question."

"I know," he said, and continued to stare at them. "But I forgot what it was." He sighed, but didn't back down. Kali saw that Kam wiped the smirk off his face when he looked at Kurt, who did the same thing, but they didn't say anything.

"They asked you why you stink," Little Charlie said, and grinned when Kyle glared at him.

"I don't stink, I smell like a man. Unlike them." He pointed to his brothers. "And I smell this way, because my girlfriend's going to be here today."

"She's not your girlfriend," Kameron said.

"No, but she's my friend and she's a girl, and she's my girl friend."

"So, why don't you do her a favor and go take a shower again, and wash at least half that shit off? And you better hope like hell you didn't do your mixing in my RV," Kameron said. "You need to find a woman your own age."

"Why would I want to do that? I told you girls were yucky."

"But, Kali's a girl."

"No she's not. She's my friend."

Kali looked at him in shock. She must have made a noise, because everyone turned to look at her, and she saw Kameron and Kurtis grin when Kyle actually paled.

"What's up guys?" She decided to play it cool and see what was going on, even though she could see and smell it.

"Nothing," Kyle said, and started toward her, but when she sneezed he stopped and frowned. He took a step closer and she sneezed again, this time more than once. "What's wrong?"

"I'm allergic to pine."

"Oh shit," he said, and ran away. When they heard a door close in the distance, Kelsey, her brother frowned at her.

"Since when have you been allergic to pine?"

"I'm not. And I sneezed, because his scent was strong. I notice none of you were standing too close, and I didn't want to hurt his feelings and tell him he reeked." She grinned, then turned to her men.

"Hi."

"Hi," they said, and went right up to her, and first Kurtis, then Kameron kissed her. When they were done, they kept her between them when she greeted everyone else, and this time it was Ken who put the band on her wrist.

"So, how did you do?" she asked Kurtis, after they settled around the small campfire.

"I won." He grinned.

"Congratulations." She grinned, and actually sat on his lap and kissed him. "Sorry I wasn't here to congratulate you when you won."

"Me too, but we can make up for lost time. So, do you have to work this weekend?"

"Nope. I'm here as a fan."

"Good," he said, and hugged her. They settled around and talked, and it was a relaxing afternoon and early evening.

CHAPTER TWENTY-NINE

On Friday afternoon, Kali came out of Kameron's RV, and winced as she realized how sore she was. The men had showed her how much they had missed her, and she had decided to take a nap before that night's race. She saw that everyone was sitting around the fire, and as she approached she frowned, when she heard Kameron's deep voice.

"It's crippling. You don't want to be in a relationship when you don't know the woman."

"Yeah, and if she makes you run from the room and throw up, that's wrong," Kurtis said.

Kali stopped in her tracks, and sighed in frustration when a car further down in the pits started up, and she missed everything that was being said.

"Take it from someone who's been there," Kameron said. "Don't be in a relationship, or even start one if you feel unsure. Take Kali for instance." Kali sighed again when another car started up, and she missed what was being said. She knew it was wrong to eavesdrop, but she couldn't help it.

"Yeah, get out before you have too much invested," Kurtis said. "That's what Kameron and I do."

"And are going to do," Kameron said.

Kali couldn't listen to anymore, and while practically hyperventilating, she ran back to the RV and made it just in time to reach the bathroom, before she lost the contents of her stomach. She jerked when there was a knock on the door.

"Hey." Kam called out. "We're heading to the track, do you want us to wait for you?"

"No, I just got up, I'm going to take a shower and come over."

"Okay. Everyone else is already there, come over when you're ready."

"I will. And good luck tonight." She couldn't believe that they were having this conversation through the door, but one look at her expression in the mirror, and she was grateful for that small favor.

"Thanks. It's only five fifteen, but I have the drivers' meeting at five thirty. I probably won't see you before I take to the track. Can I at least get a good luck kiss?"

"Sure," Kali said, and quickly whipped off her shirt and bra, and held a towel to her chest. Thankfully, she'd already brushed her teeth after getting sick, and slowly opened the door. It didn't take Kam long to pull her to him and kiss her, but at the last minute she reached one hand up, and slowed the kiss down.

Afterward, Kam frowned at her, but only shook his head, and said, "You look tired. Sorry Kurt and I kept you up most of the day and night."

"Don't worry about it." Kali waved that off, then gave him a quick kiss, and sighed in relief when he turned to leave, but he turned back and winked at her.

"I'll see you in the winner's circle."

Kali laughed and pushed him away. "You will. Now go before you miss that drivers' meeting, then you won't be able to race."

"Fine," he said, and leaned in and kissed her quickly, then left. She stared after him, and Kurtis just looked in the RV and grinned.

"I'll see you when you get over there. We're in the box, come over when you're ready."

"I will, now get, I have to shower."

"Need any help?"

Kali laughed. "You know there's not enough room for one in here, let alone two, now get going, or Kam's going to be late for the drivers' meeting."

"Shit," Kurt said, and kissed his hand and blew on it toward her, laughing as he tripped down the stairs toward his brother. Kali waited for ten minutes, then quickly redressed and hurried out to the bedroom, and packed her suitcase. There was no way she was going to stay in a relationship with the two of them, or anyone for that matter, if they felt the way they did about her, and then to talk about how bad she was to be with among other people. Unacceptable. She was quickly packed, and as she went to leave the RV, she pulled open the drawers in the kitchen, and sighed in relief.

It took less than three minutes to write a quick note, and made sure it was secure on the counter, then on either side of it, she left a sealed envelope each with Kam and Kurt's name on them. She drew in a deep breath as she slowly exited the RV, and didn't release it until she reached her own SUV. She didn't breathe easier, until she was away from the track and on the main road, heading home.

Kali had a twelve-hour drive ahead of her, and she tried to keep her mind clear as she drove north, but it was hard. She ran into snow halfway through Pennsylvania, and decided not to fight it, and pulled over into a local hotel for the rest of the night. She showered, and after lying in bed she stared at the wall, thinking back to all the good times she'd had with both men. She knew it had been too good to be true, so she cleared her mind as best she could, and was finally able to get some sleep.

*****

Kurtis looked at his fathers and grinned, then high fived when Kameron crossed the finish line first. He turned to grab Kali and kiss her, but didn't see her, but he shrugged, and it was Kyle who grabbed his arm, and dragged him over to the golf carts. They made it to the winner's circle, and as soon as Kameron exited his car, he looked around and frowned when he didn't see Kali come running up to him. Instead, he grabbed his twin and hugged him.

"Where's Kali?"

"I don't know." Then, they were separated by the announcer and their family. Lost in the celebration, Kurtis continued to look around for Kali, and realized that she must have gone back to sleep back in the RV. Planning on how he and Kam were going to wake her, he rejoined his brother, and posed for the pictures and congratulations. It was almost two hours before they made it back to their family, and sighed in relief as they fell into a chair around the fire.

"Thanks." Kameron grinned as his mother handed him a plate of food, which he wolfed down. Halfway through his meal, he frowned when Kyle asked him a question.

"Hey, you get your note?"

"What note?"

"When I went into your RV, I saw a couple envelopes with your names on them. There was a note too, but I didn't look at that."

The twins frowned, but then jumped up and hurried into the RV, and stopped short when they saw what Kyle had been talking about. Kameron didn't realize he was scared, until he saw his hand shake as he reached out, and took the folded note that had both their names written on it. He drew in a deep breath and flipped it open, then sighed.

"Said she was called back with a problem at work. She wished me luck in the race and said she'd see us later." He passed the note to Kurtis, and they both breathed easier when they reached for the envelopes, and flipped them open.

"What the fuck?" they said at the same time as they both pulled out the exact same thing. Each envelope held one red and one black card. Attached to them were small notes that they realized were in Kali's handwriting. The note on the red card said that she had to stop the relationship, and that was all. The note on the black card said that the duration of the card was forever, and a message to never call her again, that she was done with the relationship.

Both men immediately pulled their cell phones, and called her. "Voicemail," they said and hung up. They stood there staring at the contents of the envelopes, then grabbed them and after clenching them in their fists, they went outside.

Kameron went right up to Matt, and demanded, "What the hell is going on?"

"What's that supposed to mean?"

"Kali left us," he said, and held out the two cards in his clenched fist, and he heard his family suck in their breath when they saw the cards.

"How long?" Kyle whispered into the silence. His expression showing shock and fear.

"Forever," Kurtis said, and handed his cards to his youngest brother.

"Holy shit, a red one and a black one. What the hell did you two do to piss her off so much to break up with you?"

"No clue," Kameron said, and sank into his chair. He ran his hand through his hair and sighed several times. "What the hell happened?" He looked at his brother and saw his confused look. He finally looked at Matt, and asked, "So, who else is working with you?"

"What do you mean?"

"Kali left a note saying she was called back to work. Was just wondering who would call her."

"Nobody that I know of. It's still just the two of us working at the office." He frowned, and it was Karen that asked him what was wrong. "It might be nothing, but she's been pretty foggy lately, but not all the time." He sighed. "Never mind, it's probably just my imagination."

"Talk to me, Matt," Karen said in her best mother voice, and looked over at her brother and parents. "Tell me exactly what Kali's doing."

"You all know I worked with her for six years at The Wright Group. I'm only saying this, because when she was working on an ad for a client, she'd stare at the story board she'd put together, and she would zone out a little. And by that, I mean her eyes were constantly moving over that board. It was like she could see the video in her head, just looking at that board.

"The day before I left to come down here, she was different. Yes, she was staring at the board, but there was nothing there." He waved his hand in front of his own face. "In the past, I'd watch the emotions cross her face, and could see them in her eyes. I'd take one step and she'd look at me and grin, but last week there was nothing there." Again, he waved his hand in front of his own face. "It took me ten minutes to get a response from her, and I don't know how long she was like that before I found her. I had been working upstairs.

"I came down to discuss something with her, and she was sitting at her desk staring into space. At first, I thought it was the normal Kali plotting stare, but I actually dropped my coffee cup and it shattered on the floor. Nothing, she didn't jump, didn't blink. I cleaned up the mess and went over, and waved my hand and snapped my fingers in front of her face. Nothing. Her eyes were like nobody was home."

"How did you get her out of it?"

"I kept talking to her and touching her shoulder, and giving her gentle shakes. When she came back, it was like nothing had happened."

"Next time that happens," Karen said firmly. "I want you to call me or Kelsey immediately."

"No, you're to call me," Keith said firmly.

"No, Dad. It's time. Kali can't continue like this, she needs to remember."

"But, her doctors said..."

"No, Dad." Kelsey spoke up then. "*You* say. Her doctors always encouraged us to tell her what happened. It's been you that was protecting her, which has been fine, but are you going to be there all the time? Since she moved out, how many episodes has she had? What if she has one when she's with Kam and Kurt. What are they going to do? Call you to come into their bedroom to deal with it. No, this time Karen and I are going to talk her out of her episode, and I asked the doctor what would happen if she remembered, and you know what he said?"

"No, what?" Keith frowned.

"That once she remembers and can come to terms with what happened, then there's a ninety-eight-percent chance she'll never have another one, then we won't have to walk on tenterhooks around her."

"No, absolutely not," Keith said, and jumped to his feet and paced behind their chairs, running his fingers through his hair in frustration. "I won't allow it."

"But, I will," Kathy said firmly, and looked at her husband. "Kelsey and Karen are right Keith, and you know it. It's time. And maybe it's better if she hears it from them. Don't get me wrong, you've been wonderful with her over the years, but what's going to happen if you're not available? What then? Will she be found on the street, and someone calls the cops, thinking she's a mental patient off her meds? No, it's time, well past time."

"Is she dangerous when she goes into one of her episodes?" Kameron asked. "I'm only asking, because she told Kurt and me once that she'd zone out at times, and had no idea why. I was just wondering if she would do something to cause herself or others harm."

"No," all the Kilpatricks said at once.

"When Kali has an episode, it's like she zones out," Karen said, and stood. "Kelsey."

"She'll be standing one minute, talking to you, then she'll look off into space." He pointed and everyone watched as Karen did just that. "Then, if she isn't sitting already she sits, and eventually draws her legs up to her chest, and wraps her arms around them, then she just sits like that and stares into space." He nodded to Karen as she got into the position. "In the past, Dad could always talk her back to us, and afterward it was like nothing happened. She never remembered anything." Kelsey sighed and looked up at his father. "But, not anymore. It's time, Dad."

"I agree," Kathy said again. She was the one that turned to Matt, and said, "If anything happens like that again, and you can't get her to come around in fifteen minutes, then you call Karen and Kelsey. You understand. Call Keith after you call them."

"Then, call us," Kameron said. He held up the cards still crushed in his hand, and said, "I don't give a rat's ass about these. We want to know. And we want to be there to help."

"Let me see if I have all of your numbers," Matt said, and he entered the ones he didn't have in his phone, and for a long time afterward everyone sat around the fire, lost in their own thoughts.

CHAPTER THIRTY

Matt frowned at the images on his computer, and rolled his chair back and studied them as he put them on what he jokingly told Kali was the big screen, but it was only a wall in his studio. He didn't like the way one of the pictures looked, and sighed. He yelled out. "Hey, Kali! Can you come up here a minute?" Not thinking anything of it, he went over the next set of pictures, and frowned when he realized it had been fifteen minutes, and Kali hadn't answered or arrived. Sighing deeply, he jumped to his feet and went down to her office. She wasn't there, but the side door stood wide open.

It was late March, and even though there was still snow at the edges of the yard and driveway, it was sunny and in the upper fifties. He went out the door and headed up to the house. Maybe she was getting herself a cup of coffee. He grinned, because he could use one. He went around the back of the house, and stopped dead in his tracks.

"KALI!" he yelled, and ran over to where she was on her hands and knees with her hands over her head. He dropped to the ground beside her and gently shook her. When she didn't respond, he felt all over for blood, and didn't find any injuries. Suddenly, he remembered the conversation he'd had with her family months ago. He swore as he reached for his phone, and realized it was still in his office. He ran and after he grabbed it, he ended up calling Keith, only to get voicemail, then the same thing happened when he called Kameron, then Kurtis.

"Son of a fucking bitch," he actually screamed, and then saw two numbers and sighed in relief as he hit one of those buttons.

"Hello."

"Karen?"

"Yes, who's this?"

"It's Matt, it's Kali."

"Shit, how long? Where are you, talk to me Matt."

"I don't know how long, I called her up to my office, but she never came up, so I went looking for her. I found her in the backyard on her hands and knees, and her hands are covering her head. She's not bleeding, but she's making these funny noises in her throat."

"Okay. I'm home, I'm only twelve miles away. I want you to run into her house, and get the thick, dark-green fleece blanket that's either on the back of the couch or the chair. Then, I want you to run out and flop it out, and let it settle on her like you do when you make a bed. Then, fold it down to uncover her head. You do that, and I'm going to call Kelsey."

"Okay, but you're on your way?"

"Yes, I'm already seven miles away." Karen hung up and called her brother. When he answered, she didn't bother to be polite. "Kelsey, Matt called, its Kali, and from what he said it's bad."

"How do you know?" Kelsey said, and ran to his home office, and started ripping open drawers. He saw Lyle stare at him in shock. "It's Kali."

"I'm driving," Lyle said, and reached into a different drawer, and grabbed a file. "Tell whoever that is we're on our way."

"We're on our way, Karen. Where are you?"

"Turning onto her street now. You?"

"Home, Mom and Dad have the kids, and are keeping them overnight, so we're only ten minutes away. So, Matt called? What did he say?" He pushed a button, and said, "You're on speaker and Lyle's driving."

"Good. He didn't say much. Only that he went looking for her, and found her in the backyard on her hands and knees with her hands over her head, and she's making funny noises in her throat."

"Fuck." It was Lyle who swore and tapped the file. "Is it the same position that's in the file?"

"I think so. I'm pulling into her driveway now. I had Matt get that green blanket from her living room. Do you want me to keep you on the phone?"

"It's up to you, we're turning onto her road now."

"Damn." Karen laughed. "I'll see you in a few." She hung up and ran around the back of her sister's house, and saw Matt on the ground beside Kali. "Kelsey's on his way. He'll be here in a few. So, you have no idea how long she's been like this?"

"None," Matt said, and walked away on his knees, but not too far away. "What do you need me to do? I've already called Keith, Kameron, and Kurtis, and I left messages. I have to admit I don't know what I said, but I think it's along the lines that something was wrong with Kali."

They looked up when two people came running around the corner, and Kelsey actually did a slide and ended up beside his sister. Together brother and sister put their hands on her back, and each drew a deep breath, but before anything could be said or done, Kameron and Kurtis came running around the corner. They took one look and dropped to their knees at her feet. "What do you need?" The asked the siblings, but reached out and each put a hand on one of her calves, making a connection to her.

"A couple towels, bottles of water, and a box of tissues," Kelsey said as he barked out the order. "Don't know if they'll be needed, but you never know, and we don't know how long she's been like this, or how long it's going to take her to come back to us. This is the worst we've ever seen her." He looked at his sister, ignored the others, and put his hand heavily on Kali's back, right between her shoulder blades.

"Hey, Kali, it's Kelsey."

"And Karen," Karen said, and put her hand beside her brother's. "We're here with you. Dad's on his way, but we're here now. You need to come back to us now."

"That's right, Kali. Come back to us. It's over, there's no more glass," he said, and reached up and covered her hands that were on top of her head. "It's all gone. It's been gone for twenty-three years. You're just doing this, having your episodes, because it's your memory coming back to you. Let it come, and come back to us with those memories intact. We can talk about everything then, but you need to come back to us first."

"Kelsey's right, Kali. It's time to bring those memories out, so we can all deal with them. But we can't deal with them without you."

"What's going on here?" came a booming voice, and it was the twins that jumped to their feet, and went to Keith's side. "You can't do this," he yelled at his two oldest children.

"Stow it, Da," Kelsey said angrily. "We've tried your way for twenty-two years and where has it gotten Kali? Nowhere. We're doing this our way, and when she comes back, we're telling her everything." Kelsey glared at his father. and saw him deflate right before his eyes.

He heard something, and leaned down so his ear was close to Kali. "What did you say?"

"I hurt. Make the hurt go away."

"It's gone, Kali. The hurt is all gone. All you have to do is come back to us, and you'll see it's gone."

Everyone watched as her hands began to flex on top of her head, and the siblings looked at each other and sighed in relief.

"That's it, Kali," Karen said. "See, your hands don't hurt anymore, you can move them. There's no more blood, and even the cut on the top of your head is healed."

Kameron and Kurtis looked at Keith in shock, and he only shook his head. "We'll explain," he bit out, and lowered down to be beside Karen.

"Come on, Baby Girl. Listen to Karen, she and Kelsey's right. We can't get rid of these episodes, until you come back to us and talk. See your hands are working, and there's no blood, and I bet if you try, you can actually talk. I want you to say something, so that we all know you're back with us. You're surrounded by everyone who loves you."

"The grass is wet," Kali said, and actually straightened her legs out and sighed deeply. She lowered her arms and opened her eyes, and looked at first her brother, then her sister and father. "So, you'll tell me what happened?"

"We will, but let's get you cleaned up first," Karen said, and suddenly Kameron and Kurtis were there helping her up. Kameron actually bent down and picked her up.

"Don't," he said firmly, when she looked like she was going to say something, then with Kurtis on his heels they went into the house.

Kurtis said over his shoulder, "We'll be out in twenty minutes. You might want to get some coffee on, it seems like it might be a long afternoon." He halted his brother, and went around and gently lifted Kali's face with a gentle finger on her chin. "Do you want everyone here? My parents? Kevin and Kyle?"

"Might as well tell everyone at once." She sighed and snuggled up against Kameron. The men exchanged relieved looks, and Kameron continued into the house, and they both sighed, hoping they could get to the bottom of why she'd left them almost five months ago.

Kurtis pulled his phone and called his father, and told him what was going on. After he hung up, he looked at Keith, and said, "Per Kali's permission, I just told my family to come over. Kameron's giving her a shower and helping her change her into warm clothes. Do you know if she'll slip into another episode?"

"Not with her talking." Keith sighed. "If your family's coming, I might as well call Kathy, and have her bring the kids over." He started opening cupboards and the refrigerator, and sighed. "Maybe we should order pizza or something."

"Son of a bitch," Kurtis said, and looked at Matt. "Want to go to the store with me?"

"Sure. I'll drive."

"Okay. Tell Kameron where I went, and don't start until everyone gets here. Karen, you might want to call Chuck."

"I did. He's going to go get the kids from school and come over. They're dismissed in half an hour."

"Works for me," he said, and he and Matt left, and for the first time was grateful the grocery store was closer to Kali than it was to his house. By the time they made it back to her house, his parents were just pulling in behind them, and everyone helped with the groceries. No one said a word about the number of bags there were, but then again, they were feeding twenty people. Matt went in and put the groceries on the counter and island, and went back out for more. By the time he came back in with the second load, the women had begun putting everything away.

"Coffee or tea for Kali?" Karen asked.

"Hot chocolate," Kurtis said. "If she was ever upset or in a bad mood, she always wanted hot chocolate, without marshmallows."

"Really?" Kathy asked in surprise, then actually wiped her tears. "She always had that when she was younger," she said, and everyone looked up when they saw first Kameron, then Kali walking slowly beside him.

"Kali, do you have a roaster?" Kerri asked over her shoulder, and grinned when it was Kameron who came over, and opened a cupboard and pulled it out. "Thanks." She grinned, and after rinsing it, she grabbed two huge roasts that Kurtis had bought, and put them in the pan and began rinsing and cutting up potatoes to put in the pan with them. Kathy had already cut up celery, carrots, and onions. Once everything was in the pan, they placed it in the oven and turned to help Karen, who was pouring coffee for everyone.

"That should take about three hours," Kerri said. "So we have plenty of time to discuss things. I know this isn't my house, but it started raining, if the kids can play someplace, then us adults can go into the living room and talk."

That's where Keith took over, and told Chuckie and Kyle that they were in charge of the younger kids, and took them to Kali's previous office, and showed them the board games that were stored on some shelves. When he joined the others in the living room, he saw that Kali was snuggled into the corner of the couch beneath the green blanket, with Kameron sitting on one side of her, and Kurtis had pulled up a folding chair and sat on her other side. He settled down beside his wife and looked at Kali.

"What do you remember?"

CHAPTER THIRTY-ONE

Kali looked around the room, and sighed. "I remember Mom going crazy to get Kelsey and Karen on the bus, and you were loading the truck. After they left for school, you and Mom took me to Grandma and Grandpa Kilpatricks. You and Mom left, I think it was for your work. I don't remember, I was too excited to spend the weekend with Grandma and Grandpa." She looked over at her siblings and grinned. "I got an extra day with them."

"You did." Kelsey laughed, then looked at the others. "Kali bragged that she was going to get to spend the whole day with Grandma while we were in school. As I'm sure you know, we are all three years apart. At the time Kali's talking about, she was three, Karen was six, and I was nine. Dad had an expo to go to for his business. Where was it?"

"Syracuse," Keith said. He nodded and looked back at his youngest child. "What else do you remember?"

"I remember making cookies with Grandma, they were chocolate chip. Then we were playing on the front porch." She looked to the others and sighed. "Grandma had a big front porch, and she had this huge swing. I loved that swing. Whenever I was over there I'd try to take my afternoon nap on that swing."

"Even in the winter." Kathy grinned. "Granted, it was an enclosed porch, but there was no heat out there."

"Continue," Keith said again.

"I remember the bus coming, and Kelsey and Karen got off it. Grandpa was still at work, and Grandma sat with us three kids on the porch, and listened to Kelsey and Karen talk about their day, then she went in to make us milk and cookies. Kelsey went in to use the bathroom, and I was swinging, and I heard Karen say she had to go to the bathroom. The next thing I remember is waking in the hospital, and my arms were bandaged from the tips of my fingers to my shoulders. That's all."

"First before I tell you what happened, I have to ask Kameron and Kurtis a question?" He turned his attention to them. "When you slept with Kali, how did she sleep?"

"Like the dead," Kameron said.

"Yeah, there were several times we had to put our hands on her to make sure she was still alive. Once she falls asleep, that's it. Hell, I don't think she even moves after she falls asleep."

"That's what I thought." Keith sighed and leaned forward with his forearms on his knees. "Kali's always slept like that, from the day she was born. When she came home she scared the hell out of us. We were forever putting a mirror up to her nose to see if she was breathing."

"Or, putting our hand over her back or chest." Kathy sighed. "What no one but Keith and I know is that between Kelsey and Karen, we had another child, and he died of SIDS. We feared that with Kali, because she slept so deeply."

"And that brings us to what happened that day. Yes, you fell asleep on the swing, you've done it numerous times before. It wasn't a big deal, and it was an enclosed porch. Mom was fixing milk and cookies for you, and Kelsey, then she sent one of you out to get Kali."

"It was me," Karen said. "I didn't want to go at first, because I wanted a cookie, and Grandma said it was all right to leave Kali sleeping for a few more minutes. After we all had our cookies and milk, because it was always hard to wake Kali, and that's not an excuse, but still, she'd just fallen asleep, so we knew we couldn't wake her for at least an hour."

"And no one is blaming anyone here," Keith said as he took his oldest daughter's hand in his. He kept ahold of it as he turned to Kali. "It was an hour after you fell asleep that Mom, Kels and Karen went to wake you, but Dad got home early and they played with him, so it was actually two hours from the time you fell asleep to when they went to wake you." He paused and Kali frowned.

"And?"

"You'd disappeared," Kelsey said bluntly. "It was Grandpa who was going to go tickle you awake, but you were gone. We didn't panic, but we searched the whole house and yard, and even went to all the neighbors and asked if they had seen you. They called the police, and because you were only three, they showed up immediately, and issued an AMBER Alert."

"What time of year was this?" Kameron frowned.

"Mid-September. Why?"

"Just wondering what she might have been wearing."

"Purple shorts, hot pink top, white sneakers with bright orange ankle socks." Karen grinned when everyone stared at Kali.

"What, I dressed myself that day. I liked bright colors."

"So what happened?" Kurtis asked.

"When the police came to my parents' house, getting information about Kali, the local police contacted the state police to come find me and Kathy at the expo. We had only checked into the hotel, but hadn't taken our bags to the room yet. We were at the convention center, and that's where the police found us, and told us that our daughter was missing. They actually gave us an escort all the way home. Oh, it wasn't lights and sirens, but two troopers rode with us, one in front and one in back.

"As we got closer to home, I went to take the exit I needed, but they pulled me over and said that they'd been talking to the police here, and we had to go to Buffalo Children's Hospital. We didn't have cell phones back then. We arrived and saw Mom and Dad and you two kids, and were told Kali was in surgery."

"So I was found. Where was I? What happened?" Kali asked, and unconsciously gripped both Kameron and Kurtis' hands.

"When the police were at Mom and Dad's." Kathy began. "Several other officers arrived on the same street. Do you remember Mrs. Baxter? She lived across the street from Grandma and Grandpa?"

Kali frowned and shook her head. "Wait, is she the one that always had all those kids at her house? I remember looking over there, and seeing them get off the bus, or playing in the yard."

"Yes, that's her. She was an emergent foster home. That means when there was an emergency situation where a child had to be placed, they went to Mrs. Baxter first."

"So, that's why they didn't stay there for long?"

"Yes." Keith took over again. "The police that showed up separately while others were talking to Mom and Dad were there, because at the other end of the street the owners reported a classic car stolen, while at the same time, Mrs. Baxter called and reported one of her kids missing."

"It was total confusion that afternoon," Kelsey said. "It seemed like every time we looked up, another cop car was arriving for some other part of the street, and all the neighbors were standing in their front yards, and people started coming home from work. It was a Friday."

"Then all of a sudden all the police officers jumped in their cars, and tore out of there like bats out of hell. They told Grandma and Grandpa they were looking into it, and we went inside, and because we didn't know what to do, Grandpa turned on the news, and it was all over the news."

"What was?" Kali asked.

"There was a huge accident. At least fifteen cars, and at the time we turned it on, the news was reporting at least one fatality."

"Meaning, someone was already dead?" Kyle asked from the doorway, and it was Kent who held out his arm, and his son ran to him and climbed on his lap. Then the other kids joined them, and the adults allowed them to listen to the rest of the story.

"Yes, that's what it means."

"Oh, continue," Kyle said, and kept quiet.

"The accident occurred, because a car was going the wrong way on the expressway during five o'clock traffic, on a Friday night. The police who were on the street with Mom and Dad, had already called in the theft of the car, and the disappearance of one of Mrs. Baxter's foster daughters. They responded to the accident. During this time we had just been notified, and were on the way home." Kathy rubbed her forehead as she retold the nightmare she'd lived years ago.

"After the fire and ambulance workers took care of the injured people, they began moving the cars. At one point a fireman crawled beneath two cars to hook up his tow strap, so one car could be pulled off of another one. He started screaming and yelling, and suddenly he was surrounded by everyone. He refused to come out, and asked to talk to one of the police officers that had called in the missing child report. The officer went to him and they talked, and suddenly all hell broke loose. With the fireman still under the car, they slowly pulled them apart, and when there was space he jumped up, and began issuing orders."

"Why?" Kali asked.

"This is what he found," Kelsey said, and opened a folder and passed her a picture from a newspaper clipping.

"What is it?" Kali frowned, not recognizing that the photo was of a child in the fetal position with their hands covering their head.

"You. Here, this is the crime scene photo." He passed a glossy eight by ten and watched as Kali frowned. "Can you give it to me all at once, then we can break it down?"

"Yes," Keith said, and moved so that he sat on the coffee table, then took her hands in his. "Mrs. Baxter had a foster child that had only been with her for a week. She came from the Albany area. She was an extremely troubled fifteen-year-old girl. She came onto the porch and took you. Just scooped you up and walked off the porch with you. She went down to the other end of the street, put you in the back of a car, then hotwired it, and drove off."

"She drove the wrong way on the expressway, and according to the witness statements, she never swerved or slowed down. She was finally stopped when she drove head first into a ten wheeler. Again, from reading the police reports and the witness statements, you went flying through the air, screaming. Crashes ensued, and the witnesses thought you'd been found.

"Barry, the firefighter who found you, covered you with a blanket, then put his fireman's jacket over you and they only put you on a backboard, and he kept his hand on you, between your shoulder blades, the entire way. They didn't want to straighten you out, they wanted the doctors at the hospital to do that."

"What happened to the girl who kidnapped Aunt Kali?" Charlie asked.

"She was killed when she hit the ten wheeler. It was later found out that the agency who brought her to Buffalo had failed to disclose all her medical problems. The case worker later said that Claire had been such a problem child that she was hard to place, and families would call and return her, so she didn't disclose her medical problems."

"What was wrong with her?"

"Bipolar and schizophrenia, and she was off her meds for at least a month. Mrs. Baxter didn't even know she was that sick."

"So what happened to me?"

"We don't know how you ended up like that." Keith pointed to the picture she was holding. "We might never know, but these are from different angles." He handed her pictures one by one, and after she studied them they were passed around so the others listening to the story could get a grasp on just what Kali had gone through.

"You had your hands over your head, and your forearms covered your face. Best the accident reenactors could tell was that you went flying through the windshield, hit either the truck, or the hood of the car. Somehow you automatically covered your head and face, but if you remember, you were tiny when you were little."

"So, what's wrong with her hands?" Kyle asked, but he pointed to the picture, not her actual hands.

"When they found her with her hands over her head." Keith got into that position, and it was Kathy who stood and went over to him.

"Your hands were so tiny, but there was a shard of glass that went through both of your hands and into your head, pinning your hands there. When you came flying through the windshield, you actually took the impact of your landing on your elbows, shattering both of them."

"So, my hands are this way because of glass?"

"Yes. The way the glass went in, it actually severed the nerve and tendon that move your ring and pinky fingers. The doctors were going to amputate, but your father and I vetoed that idea. We called the top orthopedic surgeon in the country to come in and reconstruct your elbows. We think you don't remember anything, because you were asleep when you were taken, and probably at the time of the crash. Then in the hospital, the doctors kept you in a medical-induced coma until the last surgery on your elbows, then they slowly brought you out of it."

"So, let me get this straight. I was kidnapped from Grandma's porch, put in a car, which my kidnapper stole, and caused an accident. She was killed, and I was permanently crippled."

"Stop," Kameron said. "You are not a cripple. You're just deformed, that's all."

"Same thing," Kali said, and jumped to her feet. She wrapped her arms around herself and gripped her elbows. No one said a word, until she could wrap her head around it.

CHAPTER THIRTY-TWO

It was almost twenty minutes later, when she turned to her parents. "What else? I feel like you haven't told me everything."

"At the hospital, when the doctors tried to intubate you, they saw that your vocal cords were swollen so badly that they couldn't get a tube down your throat, and had to go in through your neck."

"But, I don't have a scar."

"That's because once the swelling went down and they went through your throat, I rubbed vitamin E on it every day. I did the best I could with your arms, elbows and hands, but it didn't work as well."

"And the episodes? Where I zone out?"

"We believe when you get them while riding in the car, you might remember being awake when the crash happened. That's why you covered your head and face. But we don't know. At first, the doctors said it was best for you not to remember. That was while you were still in the hospital. I guess I took it one step further, and didn't want you to remember. As you can see from the pictures, it was horrific, and I didn't want you to have to live through that over, and over, and over again in nightmares."

"So, that's why you had me get my license at sixteen? How did you ever let me move out and buy my own house?"

"It was hard, but I had to let you go. And your brother and sister said you hadn't had an episode in years. The last one you had was the day you moved in here, but then last fall,

Matt had mentioned you had a small one before he went to North Carolina."

"So, Matt's been your spy with me all this time?"

"No, only since you came back from North Carolina," Karen said. "And that was under *my* direction. I told him if anything happened, then he had to call me and Kelsey first, before Dad. We told Dad it was time for you to know the truth."

Kali nodded, and with her hands still wrapped around herself, she turned to Kameron and Kurtis. "And what about you two? Why are you here?"

"Matt left a message on our phones that you were scaring the shit out of him," Kameron said. "And I see and hear you're spoiling for a fight. Bring it. Because I'm spoiling for one too, but I'm going first. Why the fuck did you black card Kurt and me?"

"What? Are you fucking nuts? Of course, I black carded you. You sit around the camp fire and tell whoever you were talking to that you were in a crippling relationship, and you." She rounded on Kurtis. "You tell them that you run from the room and have to throw up, because you're repulsed by looking at me? Of course I fucking black carded you." She fisted her hands and slammed them on her hips as she glared at the two of them. "Who the fuck wants to be in a relationship like that? I sure as hell didn't, so I black carded you and got the hell out of there!"

"Oh shit." This time it was Kevin who spoke. "That was all on me."

"No, I distinctively heard Kameron and Kurtis say those things, and my name was mentioned during that conversation."

"Yes and no," Kevin said, and actually stood and went to stand in front of her. He gently took her biceps in his hands, and didn't say anything until she looked directly at him. "You know Mom has two husbands. And you were in a relationship with both Kameron and Kurtis. I was wondering what it was like to be in a relationship like that, and I sure as hell wasn't going to horn in on Kam and Kurt's relationship with you. And I'm not going to wait ten years for Kyle to get up there in age. So a cousin of ours was talking about it. He's been dating someone, but I didn't really click with her.

"It was just the three of us at that fire the night you left. I was asking Kameron and Kurtis how they handled their relationship with Bridget."

"Who?"

"The girl we told you about when we decided to start this relationship," Kameron said. "Remember when we told you she'd go to Kurt and tell him lies about me? It came to the point that she would have a friend of hers hit her and leave bruises, then she'd go to Kurt and tell him I did that to her."

"That's why I left the room and went to get sick. I couldn't stomach the thought of my brother, my best friend, and my twin would treat the woman we loved like that."

"Or the woman we thought we loved. That relationship separated us for several months," Kam said. He sat forward and sighed, then looked at his twin. They both stood and looked at Kevin who stood back. The twins slowly went to her.

"If you would have stuck around, you would have heard a totally different story, when Kevin asked us what the difference between that relationship, and our relationship with you was."

"What?" Kali frowned and took a step back, when both of them dropped to a knee, and held up a blue velvet box. They flipped the lid and each took one of her hands.

"Kali, we fell in love with you before we even started our relationship. Would you make us the happiest men in the world and marry us?"

"Is that even possible?" Kali frowned, and then giggled when she saw their expressions. "Oh, you want an answer?"

"That would be nice." Kurtis said, and grinned. "And, yes, I want to marry you too."

"Yes," she said, and suddenly she had a ring slipped on her ring finger of her left hand, and then Kurtis was kissing her, and she was whipped around and being kissed by Kameron. Once she was steady on her feet, she was surrounded by her family and her future family.

When Kerri hugged her, she whispered in her ear, "We'll get together and talk sometime. Next time you hear them say something like that, confront them, or better yet, bash their heads together, like you do your siblings. I can't wait to see that happen."

Kali snorted a laugh, and grinned at her future mother-in-law, then she turned and was hugged by Kyle.

"So, does this mean you'll be joining Mom and me in the stands?"

"Nope."

"Why not? You'll be family."

"Because, I like my seat. You'll have to join me."

"We'll see," Kerri said, when Kyle looked at his mother.

"That usually means yes," Kyle said, then took one hand, then the other, and kissed the scar that was between her last two fingers on both hands. "I'm really sorry this happened to you, but it doesn't seem to have slowed you down. And if you don't remember any of it, I wouldn't worry about it if I was you. It's done, it's over, now you know what happened, you can not dwell on it."

"Thank you, Kyle," Kali said, and hugged him tightly, and shortly after that the kids went back to playing, then Kali walked up to her father and hugged him tightly.

"Thank you for trying to protect me all these years, and thank you for finally telling me the truth. I have to honestly say, I don't remember anything, and I may never, and I especially know I'm never going to remember the time I was in a coma, so don't feel bad if I have a nightmare. At least I'll know why, instead of feeling clueless, and I think with having Kam and Kurt know will be all the better."

"I know," Keith said, and hugged her to him. "So, how do you feel now?"

"The same. I mean, I didn't have an ah ha moment, but I think I'll be okay." She hugged him, and then giggled.

"What?"

"Now we have to come up with a way for everyone to sit, and how many plates I have."

"Got you covered." Kent grinned and he and Ken quickly left, and returned with a box full of dishes. "Kerri's been collecting things this summer at garage sales. They might not match what you already have."

"As long as they hold food and are clean, I don't really care." Kali grinned and watched as Matt directed some of the others inside with a couple of tables. When supper was finally ready, Kent was the one that made a toast.

"To a great addition to the Kilbourne family. Welcome Kali. Now you need to give us plenty of granddaughters. We had sons, and I want a little girl to spoil," he said, and reached over and actually plucked Missy from her father's arms, and planted her on his lap.

"And to two more sons to the Kilpatrick clan," Keith said, and everyone drank, then dug into the pot roast. During the meal they were making plans for the next weekend for the Spring Opening Season at The Hill. They discussed all the changes Keith had made over the winter, and Kerri grinned.

"As long as those damn bleacher seats are improved." Which caused everyone to laugh.

EPILOGUE

Two Years Later

"Ma'am, can I help you?" a fan at The Hill asked Kali as she stood and sighed. She was in her normal seat, and had to make her way over to the announcer's stand. She figured it would be easier to go across the top of the bleachers, rather than down thirty steps, over two sections, and back up.

"I need to go to the announcer's booth," she said, and put her hands on her lower back, and moaned as she rubbed the sore spot.

"If you don't mind, how far along are you?" the man asked, and indicated her very pregnant belly.

"Nine months. My due date was two days ago, and I'm carrying twins."

"Damn," he said, and another man joined them, and he went ahead and asked people to clear the area, and the first man helped her. Luckily, it was during intermission, and most of the fans were down at the concession stands. She paused to catch her breath and no one rushed her, and she glanced down and sighed in relief. She put her pinkies to her mouth and whistled, and grinned when Kyle and Kerri whipped around and looked. She waved and pointed to her belly, then to the announcer's stand.

By the time she arrived at the stand, Kerri and Kyle were there. "What's wrong?" Kerri asked.

"I think I'm in labor. Kyle can you go down and get the guys?"

"No," He grinned and opened the door, and yelled. "Keith, where the hell are you?"

"Here." He grinned, "What's up?"

"Where's your walkie?"

"Here."

He handed it over, and watched as Kyle grabbed it, and said, "Matt, this is the booth, Matt you there?"

"Matt here, who's this?"

"Kyle. I need you to do me a favor."

"What's that?"

"Go tell the ambulance driver to come over to the announcer's stand."

"Okay," he said, and the people watched him do just that, then Kyle grinned.

"With the ambulance." And they all laughed as the EMTs went back and jumped in. Kyle then grabbed the announcer's mic and grinned.

"If I could have everyone's attention please," he said into the mic. "Could the Kilbourne family please come to the announcer's stand? I repeat, could the Kilbourne family please come to the announcer's stand?" He grinned, then looked at the people in shock. "Oh, and the Kilpatrick family."

"Kyle, what's going on?" Keith asked, and reached for the mic.

Into it Kyle grinned, and said, so everyone could hear, "You're about to be a grandpa again. Kali's in labor." He put the mic down and watched for all of thirty seconds, then at least six golf carts came roaring out of the pits, onto the track and stopped beneath the flagman stand, and two men came through the small gate and up the steps like a bat out of hell.

"Kali!" they screamed and entered the room in a rush.

"Hey." She grinned at them.

"Hey," Kameron said as he kneeled down beside his wife, with Kurtis on the other side.

"Did your water break? Are you having contractions?"

"No, and I think so. My back is killing me, has been for the last two days."

"Why the hell didn't you tell us?" Kurtis scowled at her.

"Because, you were getting ready for the race. It was only a twinge here and there." They looked up as the EMTs came in, and they stopped and asked the same questions.

"Do you want to go to the hospital?" one of them asked.

"I probably should," she said, and the men helped her stand, and she screamed and gripped their arms. "Oh, shit."

"What?"

"My water just broke, and *OHMYGOD!*" she screamed, and actually doubled over, and ended up digging her nails into both their arms. The men helped her breathe through it, and it was Kerri that made the decision.

"I don't think she's going to make it to the hospital, or even down to the ambulance." She looked up and saw Karen enter.

"Kali, sweetie," Karen said from behind her. "We're going to lower you to the floor, then I'm going to check you. Chuck's on his way up." Her sister was a nurse, and her brother-in-law was a physician's assistant, and had helped deliver at least eight babies so far in his career. She had another contraction, and gripped Kam and Kurtis harder again.

"Easy," Chuck said as he entered, and took in the situation. "Sorry, but I ran to the car and got my bag." He opened it and passed his wife a pair of gloves, and then donned a pair for himself. He talked quietly with the EMTs, and it wasn't long before he looked up and grinned. "Okay, Kali, on your next contraction, I want you to push. The first head is crowning." She followed instructions, and after only three pushes she flopped back and sighed. She looked at her husbands' when she heard a baby's wail.

"It's a girl," Kerri said as she took the baby and cleaned it up, then handed her to the EMTs. Then, it was only minutes later when she delivered the second baby, causing Kali to slump back and sigh.

"Another girl," Kerri said.

It was Kyle that asked, "What are you going to name them?"

"We don't know yet."

"Can I make a suggestion?"

"What's that?" Kameron grinned as he took his firstborn daughter.

"No more fucking Ks."

"Language," everyone said, but then they laughed, when they realized what he'd said.

"Why not?" Kameron asked.

"Aren't we running out of K names?"

"I don't know." Kurtis grinned. "There's Kennedy, and Kira, or Katrina, or Katherine."

"I like the first two."

"But you're the uncle," Kameron said. "And the ultimate decision is up to Kali."

"I like the first two also." Kali grinned. "Kennedy and Kira," she said, and sighed as she was lifted onto the gurney, and she was handed the babies as her husbands, the EMTs and the grandfathers all helped her down to the ambulance, but both guys took a baby from her and held them up.

"It's a girl!" They yelled to the fans, and when they burst out in cheer, they handed the babies back and helped her down. When they climbed into the back of the ambulance, Kali frowned.

"What are you doing?"

"Going to the hospital with you."

"No you're not. You're going to get your ass out there and win your races."

"No, you're our wife and these are our babies, we're going with you." Kameron argued. Kali struggled to sit up, and the EMTs took the babies, and Kameron and Kurtis leaned down on either side of her and helped her to sit up. She reached up and put her hand on the outside of each of their heads, and actually banged them together. First time ever.

"What the hell, woman?" Kameron asked as he rubbed his head.

"Why type of example are you setting for your daughters, for not following through on your commitments by blowing off the race and coming to the hospital. We'll be fine, now get your ass out there and show the fans and your daughters how to win. After all, I just gave birth to the next generation of Kilbourne number eighteen drivers, you have to set an example for them."

"If you're sure?"

"I'm sure," she said, and kissed them quickly and when they backed away, she grinned. "That's good boys, now go win your race and then come see us."

"Yes ma'am." They grinned, then shut the door and watched as their family was driven away and then looked at each other. "We better go do as she says or she's going to kick our asses."

"I know." Kurtis grinned. Hours later they quietly opened the door to Kali's hospital room, and stared as she was breastfeeding one of their daughters. There hadn't been time to check them over before they were rushed away, and now that they had time, they picked up the one in her own bed, and actually stripped her down to her diaper. They counted her fingers and toes, and looked for birthmarks.

"What are you doing?" Kali laughed.

"Checking her out. I hate to sound stupid, but which one is this?"

"Kennedy. She has a tiny red raspberry on her left ribcage." She smiled as they checked it out, and then when she started burping Kira, Kameron took her, and when she did her duty he stripped her, and counted all her fingers and toes.

"Kira." Kali sighed as she put herself back together. "Red mark on the back of her neck." They inspected it and nodded. Once they were redressed, they sat down on either side of Kali, holding their daughters.

"Well?" Kali asked.

"We won." Kameron grinned. "Not only our races, but in finding, falling in love, and marrying the most wonderful woman in the world, and if I haven't told you yet, thank you for the most beautiful daughters a man could ask for."

"Ditto." Kurtis said, and reached down and kissed her, then Kam did the same thing. Kali smiled and settled back, and placed a hand on each of their thighs, and settled into sleep, knowing her daughters were safely in their Daddies' arms.

THE END

Thank you for taking the time to read this. If you enjoyed this book, please give it some love and leave a review at your preferred site.

You can contact me at:

E-mail: deannalrowley@yahoo.com

Facebook: https://www.facebook.com/Author-Deanna-L-Rowley-106623544172360

Website: https://deannarowley.com/

Newsletter: https://cheerful-artisan-8318.ck.page/

Goodreads: https://www.goodreads.com/search?q=Deanna+L.+Rowley&qid=1KYE0zxcp5

Book Bub: https://www.goodreads.com/search?q=Deanna+L.+Rowley&qid=1KYE0zxcp5

Again, thank you for taking the time to read this.

Please continue reading for other books available for sale and on pre-order.

Also by:

LOVE FOUND SERIES

Love Doesn't Exist

Love Is Fleeting

Love Conquers All

SPIES, LIES & RIDES

Aimee's Dilemma

Hank's Mission

Colt's Quest

George's Goal

Hogan's Handful

Witt's Warrior's

John's Journey

Gary's Turn

STORMVILLE – SUSPENSEFUL SEDUCTION WORLD

Samantha A. Cole

Bourbon Blaze

Neil's Wish

Ginny's Slow Sizzle

CAPE Investigations Series

Claiming Mia

Re-Claiming Mia

Protecting Claire

Challenging Claire

Taming Sue Ellen

Forgiving Heather

Defending Melody

Saving Kate

Susan Stoker's Universe

Saving Veronica

Lorna's Savior

Keeping Tymberly

Protecting Silver

Elle James' Brotherhood Protection World

Morgan

Ava

Joyce

Astrid

Not Her Series:

Not Her Dom

Not Her Choice

Not Her Rebound

Not Her Problem #1

Not Her Problem #2

Not Her His Fault

Not Her Doing

Stand-alones:

Double Trouble for Kali

Ruby's Destiny

Molly's Return

ABOUT THE AUTHOR

Deanna has loved to read all her life. She was in the third grade when she fell in love with books while working in the school library. She turned that love of reading into writing. Now Deanna can be found in her writing cave, sharing her keyboard with her furbaby, reading, or making quilts.

Don't miss out!

Visit the website below and you can sign up to receive emails whenever Deanna L. Rowley publishes a new book. There's no charge and no obligation.

https://books2read.com/r/B-A-WBNL-LVXXB

BOOKS 2 READ

Connecting independent readers to independent writers.

CPSIA information can be obtained
at www.ICGtesting.com
Printed in the USA
JSHW032120200622
27186JS00005B/157

9 798201 511937